Marcus Jastrow

Israelitish Prayer Book

Marcus Jastrow

Israelitish Prayer Book

ISBN/EAN: 9783744650496

Printed in Europe, USA, Canada, Australia, Japan

Cover: Foto ©Lupo / pixelio.de

More available books at **www.hansebooks.com**

עֲבוֹדַת יִשְׂרָאֵל

ISRAELITISH PRAYER BOOK,

FOR ALL THE

PUBLIC SERVICES OF THE YEAR.

Originally arranged by *Rev. Dr. Benjamin Szold*, of Baltimore.
Second Edition (Hebrew and German) revised by
Rev. Drs. M. Jastrow, of Philadelphia, and
H. Hochheimer, of Baltimore.

HEBREW AND ENGLISH EDITION,

In Text and Typographical arrangement fully corresponding
with the revised Hebrew-German Edition,

BY M. JASTROW,

RABBI OF THE CONGREGATION RODEF-SHALOM.

PHILADELPHIA:
PUBLISHED BY THE EDITOR.
1885.

Entered according to Act of Congress, in the year 1873, by
M. JASTROW,
in the Office of the Librarian of Congress, at Washington.

PREFACE.

As indicated by the title-page, the English edition of this Prayer and Hymn Book corresponds with the German edition by Rev. Dr. B. Szold both in arrangement and in text, so that either of them may be used in Divine Service while the prayers are read, or the hymns sung, in Hebrew, English or German.

As in the German, so in this edition, the method of a literal translation of the Hebrew prayers has been disregarded, and in lieu thereof a paraphrase chosen which renders the spirit of each prayer without burdening it with Oriental phraseology. By so doing, the Editor thinks, he has furnished an available Prayer Book for those who are not familiar with the Hebrew language.

The poetical pieces in this Book being, however, monuments of Hebrew poetry, have been rendered in verse, in imitation of the style of each poem either in meter or without, so as to give the reader an approximate idea of the Hebrew poetry of the Middle Ages.

In the thorough revision of the prosaic parts contained in the Book, the Editor acknowledges the aid of other hands, so that there might be spared no painstaking to make the style easy and smooth.

The following valuable renditions of poetical writings have been contributed by a friend and colleague: "O God whose grace," pp. 343, 421, and 465; "Lord, thy people," p. 425; "From thee my praise," p. 467; "O God, to thee," p. 491; and the Hoshaanoth, p. 581 to p. 585.

Preface.

for which contributions, the Editor avails himself of this opportunity to express his sincerest thanks.

The metrical translations of the Psalms in the Prayer Book (pp. 2, 15, and 50 to 56) are, with some alterations, taken from *The Psalms of David by Abner Jones*.

As to the Songs for Divine Services hereto attached, No. 17 is from Addison with some modifications, and No. 138 written by a friend. With a few exceptions the songs agree in meter with those of the German edition, so that the same melodies are adaptable for both.

For the remainder of the Psalms and Hymns, both in the Hymn and the Prayer Book, and for the translations of the Hebrew poems, the Editor, though with timidity, takes the responsibility upon himself alone, looking forward for a kind reception by the public for whom the book is intended. M. J.

PHILADELPHIA, Adar 12th 5633.
(March 10th 1873.)

FIRST PART.

PRAYERS

FOR

Sabbaths and Festivals.

CONTENTS OF THE FIRST PART.

PRAYERS FOR SABBATHS AND FESTIVALS.

	PAGE
Introductory Prayer	1
Service for the Eve	2
Service for the Morning	44
Hallel	86
Reading of the Torah	92
Additional Service	100
Afternoon Service	122

CONTENTS.

I. Prayers for Sabbaths and Festivals.

	PAGE
Introductory Prayer	1
Service for the Eve	2
Service for the Morning	44
Hallel	86
Reading of the Torah	92
Additional Service	100
Afternoon Service	122

II. Prayers for the New Year.

Introductory Prayer	127
Service for the Eve	128
Morning Service	156
Reading of the Torah	194
The Sounding of the Shofar	205
Additional Service	208
Afternoon Service	238

III. Prayers for the Day of Atonement.

Introductory Prayer	243
Service for the Eve	244
Morning Service	292
Reading of the Torah	368
Memorial Service for the Dead	379
Additional Service	396
Afternoon Service	450
Closing Service	488

IV. PRAYERS FOR WEEK DAYS.

	PAGE
Introductory Prayer	529
Morning Service	530
Prayer for the New Moon	560
Afternoon Service	565
Evening Service	567
Prayer for the Deceased in the house of Mourning	576

APPENDIX.

I. Hoshanoth	581
II. For Chanuckah	584
III. For Purim	585
IV. For the Ninth of Ab	587
V. Scriptural Portions for the Cycle of three Years	591
VI. The Annual Cycle arranged for three Years	593

GENERAL INFORMATION.

All Divine Services commence with the *Introductory Prayer*, which is to be found on the first page of each of the four parts of the Prayer Book. English Hymns may be inserted: In the Service for Sabbath Eve, in place of "*Lechah Dodi*;" in the Service for the Eve of Festivals, after the *Introduction of Prayers*, and before the *Concluding Prayer*; In the Morning Services, before and after the Sermon, before the *Additional Prayer* (Mussaf) and before the *Concluding Prayer*.

Introductory Prayer.

(THE CONGREGATION RISE.)

How beautiful are thy tents, O Jacob, thy dwelling places, O Israel! Through thy abundant goodness and mercy have I entered thy house, therefore will I reverently worship thee in thy holy sanctuary. O Lord! I love thy abiding place, even the spot where thy glory dwelleth. Here, then, will I worship, bend the knee, and lowly bow before the Lord, my Maker.

מַה־טֹּבוּ אֹהָלֶיךָ יַעֲקֹב מִשְׁכְּנֹתֶיךָ יִשְׂרָאֵל: וַאֲנִי בְּרֹב חַסְדְּךָ אָבֹא בֵיתֶךָ אֶשְׁתַּחֲוֶה אֶל־הֵיכַל קָדְשְׁךָ בְּיִרְאָתֶךָ: יְיָ אָהַבְתִּי מְעוֹן בֵּיתֶךָ וּמְקוֹם מִשְׁכַּן כְּבוֹדֶךָ: וַאֲנִי אֶשְׁתַּחֲוֶה וְאֶכְרָעָה אֶבְרְכָה לִפְנֵי־יְיָ עֹשִׂי:

CHOIR AND CONGREGATION.

Here we will worship,
Bend our knees
And lowly bow
Before the Lord, our Maker.

CHOIR AND CONGREGATION.

וַאֲנַחְנוּ נִשְׁתַּחֲוֶה.
וְנִכְרָעָה.
נְבָרְכָה.
לִפְנֵי יְיָ עֹשֵׂנוּ:

READER.

Here will I give forth my supplication unto thee, O Lord. Render this hour an acceptable one, O God, and in thy abundant mercy, answer me and grant me thy assistance. **Amen.**

READER.

וַאֲנִי תְפִלָּתִי לְךָ יְיָ עֵת רָצוֹן אֱלֹהִים בְּרָב־חַסְדֶּךָ עֲנֵנִי בֶּאֱמֶת יִשְׁעֶךָ:

(THE CONGREGATION ARE SEATED.)

תפלת ערבית לשבת ולרגלים

תפלת ערבית
לשבת ולרגלים

(תהלים כ״ט)

1. הָבוּ לַיְיָ בְּנֵי אֵלִים הָבוּ לַיְיָ כָּבוֹד וָעֹז: הָבוּ לַיְיָ כְּבוֹד שְׁמוֹ הִשְׁתַּחֲווּ לַיְיָ בְּהַדְרַת־קֹדֶשׁ: קוֹל יְיָ עַל־הַמָּיִם אֵל־הַכָּבוֹד הִרְעִים יְיָ עַל־מַיִם רַבִּים: קוֹל־יְיָ בַּכֹּחַ קוֹל יְיָ בֶּהָדָר: קוֹל יְיָ שֹׁבֵר אֲרָזִים וַיְשַׁבֵּר יְיָ אֶת־אַרְזֵי הַלְּבָנוֹן: וַיַּרְקִידֵם כְּמוֹ־עֵגֶל לְבָנוֹן וְשִׂרְיֹן כְּמוֹ בֶן־רְאֵמִים: קוֹל־יְיָ חֹצֵב לַהֲבוֹת אֵשׁ: קוֹל יְיָ יָחִיל מִדְבָּר יָחִיל יְיָ מִדְבַּר קָדֵשׁ: קוֹל יְיָ יְחוֹלֵל אַיָּלוֹת וַיֶּחֱשֹׂף יְעָרוֹת וּבְהֵיכָלוֹ כֻּלּוֹ אֹמֵר כָּבוֹד: יְיָ לַמַּבּוּל יָשָׁב וַיֵּשֶׁב יְיָ מֶלֶךְ לְעוֹלָם: יְיָ עֹז לְעַמּוֹ יִתֵּן יְיָ יְבָרֵךְ אֶת־עַמּוֹ בַשָּׁלוֹם:

(After the recitation of the above psalm, one of the following English prayers is said by the Rabbi. — On Sabbath, the service then continues with Nos. 2 and 3. — On Festivals not occurring on Sabbath, a hymn is sung after the English prayer, and then the service continues with No. 4.)

SERVICE FOR THE EVE OF SABBATHS AND FESTIVALS.

(*Psalm* 29.)

1. YE mighty, to the Lord assign || Dominion, glory, power divine; || Due praises to his name address, || Exalt him in his holiness. || His voice is high above the flood, || And loud proclaims the powerful God ; || His voice is heard from pole to pole, || When o'er the deep his thunders roll. || His voice the towering cedar breaks, || And Lebanon's high summit shakes; || His voice makes Sirion's forests bound || Like calves and unicorns around. || His voice with lightning hews the earth, || And Kadesh shakes, brings hinds to birth ; || His voice the mountain forest bares, || The earth, his temple, praise declares. || His throne was spread upon the flood, || And he shall reign the King and God; || His people's strength will he increase, || And bless them evermore with peace.

(After the recitation of the above psalm, one of the following English prayers is said by the Rabbi.—On Sabbath, the service then continues with Nos. 2 and 3.—On Festivals not occurring on Sabbath, a hymn is sung after the English prayer, and then the service continues with No. 4.)

INTRODUCTION OF PRAYERS.

ON SABBATHS.

Merciful Father! full of reverence for thee and trust in thy infinite love, we have entered this sanctuary consecrated to the glory of thy name, here to elevate and ennoble our feelings and thoughts.

Here we are removed from the bustle and strife of the world, freed from the cares of life, and enabled to think of thee and thy holy Sabbath. Thou hast been pleased to give us this day as a means of purifying our souls, so that we may gain in strength for the performance of our duties as men, and our mission as Israelites. To thee and thy service will we devote all those high powers with which thou hast endowed us, that we might testify on earth thy existence and glory.

By the solemn exercises with which we sanctify this day of rest before thee, our Lord and Father, we will purify our *minds*, so as to rise to a clearer understanding of thy perfections; we will concentrate our *hearts*, so as to increase in love for thee; we will draw closer the ties of *family affection*, so as to feel happy in the belief of that eternal kingdom of which the day of rest is to be the image;—yea, we will joyfully devote our *lives* to thee and thy service.

O bountiful Father! we thank thee for thy precious gift of the Sabbath, the observance of which surrounds our lives with such manifold blessings.

ON SPECIAL SABBATHS.

[And on this day, O Lord and Father, are our feelings of thankfulness, our emotions of love increased, as we are reminded

(*On the Sabbath during the Festival of Passover.*)

of those memorable days when thou didst deliver thy people Israel from servitude, that liberty should prepare them to become a nation of priests, and the bearers of thy light and truth.

(*On the Sabbath during the Festival of Tabernacles.*)

of the tabernacle of thy protection which thou didst extend over thy people Israel when they journeyed in the wilderness, the memory of which should fill our hearts with unshaken trust in both thy merciful and superintending providence, which leadeth forth nations and individuals to happiness and salvation.

(*On Sabbath Chanuckah.*)

of the glorious contest of the Jews under the heaven-inspired Hasmoneans against the Syrian enemies, who endeavored to exterminate Israel's holy faith from off the face of the earth.]

O Eternal Being, who art nigh unto those who call upon thee in truth, listen to our supplications and hearken unto the praises we render unto thee. Amen.

ON PASSOVER.

1. With emotions of joy do we appear before thee, O Lord, to celebrate the great festival of freedom. Thou didst redeem our ancestors from slavery and oppression, and vouchsafe unto them liberty and happiness. Thou didst remove the iron yoke of servitude from off their necks, and burst the chains which fettered their minds, so that they might arise from despondency to the zealous performance of the divine will.

Thou hast chosen thy people Israel as the standard-bearers of the truth that man was created free, and endowed with inalienable rights.

In order to spread this truth, thou hast seen fit to scatter us over the face of the earth, enduring trials and persecutions, because we have battled for the service of thy holy name. But even then, O Lord, has thy mercy never forsaken us; for as thou wast the deliverer of our fathers from Egypt, so hast thou been our protector and redeemer in all ages. Thou hast been with us in our wanderings, never permitting the waters of oppression to engulf us. Yea, thou hast been as a shield and protector to us in the hour of bitter trial, not permitting the glowing sun of human hatred to consume us, but ever preserving us in thy abundant mercy.

Again hast thou wrought deliverance for us, O Lord, and redeemed us from the yoke of religious persecution and hatred under which our fathers sighed, and in freedom are we able to lift up our eyes unto thee and bring our tribute of thanksgiving and praise unto thee, who art the redeemer of mankind, and the saviour of Israel.

Praise ye the Lord, for he is good; because to eternity endureth his kindness! Amen.

2. Again do we appear in thy presence, O Lord, as the Festival of Redemption is approaching its close, with praises and thanksgivings for thy wonderful care and protection. When our ancestors were at the shores of the Red Sea, and all hope of escape from their enemies seemed banished, thou didst send enlargement and deliverance. At thy divine command the waters were divided, and a path prepared for Israel, so that they might pass on dry land from peril to security. And up to this day do we daily experience thy government, wondrous and just.

Violence and haughtiness cannot endure; they vanish at thy rebuke, "Thus far shalt thou come, and no farther,"—while virtue goeth forth out of battle to triumph. And who more than thy people Israel has experienced the protection of thy powerful arm?

If it had not been thou who wast with us, when mankind, misled by fierce passions, rose up against us, they would have swallowed us up alive; the raging billows of human wrath would have overwhelmed us, but for thee, who interposed and saved us.

Praised be thou, O Lord, ruler of the destinies of men, who hast ever been our deliverer, the leader of truth to victory over falsehood and light over darkness.

And with this knowledge of thy will, grant, O Lord, that we may ever foster truth. Grant that the surging billows of passion may never overwhelm our good inclinations, but that our hearts may ever be directed to serve thee in truth and sincerity.

Vouchsafe unto us these blessings as we celebrate the festival which commemorates thy omnipotence and justice. Amen!

Service for the Eve of Sabbaths and Festivals.

ON SHABUOTH.

Eternal God! our Father and our King! elevated by sublime reminiscences, filled with holy awe, do we now welcome in thy sanctuary the beginning of the Festival of Pentecost. In thy infinite love hast thou chosen Israel from all nations as the earthly repositories of thy thoughts. Thou didst reveal unto us thy commands and statutes, the faithful performance of which will lead mankind to the highest perfection, and up to this day do we continue to disseminate over the earth new world-redeeming ideas which have been raised in the garden of thy law, and up to this day are we a race of teachers inspired with the principles which pervade our holy writings and traditions.

We are far removed from undue pride and haughty exultation over our fellow-men, by reason of our selection. We will ever remember that thou hast, in thy wisdom, assigned to every nation a mission to perform; that, amid the vast domains of intellectual culture and development, thou hast allotted a share of duty to all people; and therefore should we gratefully gather the flowers of knowledge which have been planted and tended by other hands than Israel. But, O Lord, our hearts rejoice over the inestimable privilege of having been chosen to spread the pure knowledge of thee, O God, and the love of man, over the whole face of the earth; and we pray thee to accept these joyful emotions as our offering of thanks, now and evermore.

May the possession of the *Torah* fill us with gladness, that we may bear in mind it is our life, the source of our continued existence as a religious community; and, therefore, be ever anxious to devote to it our brightest hours on earth, even the hours of retirement from worldly pursuits. But do thou, O God, never withdraw from us thy love, that we may ever be worthy of our sublime mission; and we will praise thee, the Beneficent, now and for ever. Amen.

ON SUCCOTH.

A brief interval has passed, O Lord, since our last solemn gathering in this sanctuary, and we again appear before thee, in order to commemorate thy wonderful care of Israel during the forty years of wandering in the wilderness, when our nation, in the youthful period of its existence, trustfully followed after thee, whom they had chosen, on soil that was not sown. It is that period which illustrates the truth that thou art the Leader and Educator of mankind. As were our fathers, so are we the witnesses of thy providence, the heralds of thy bountiful government on earth. Like them have we passed safely through many an inhospitable wilderness, through many a desert and waste, yet with the blazing pillar of thy law illumining our paths in the dark night of sorrow and distress, and with the cloud-pillar of thy mercy sheltering us by day from the scorching rays of trouble and danger.

Yea, thy people Israel are the witnesses of thy overshadowing providence! Thousands of years have rolled over our heads, and yet are we neither destroyed nor withered, but, like the fir-tree, ever renewing its green foliage, and preserving the fruit of religion unimpaired and unfading. Thus with all the vigor of youth can we participate in the endeavors of the human race for intellectual progress; even in its joys and sorrows, in its longings and desires for moral perfection, in its achievements for liberty, in its works for culture and refinement.

We are thy witnesses, ever preserved and sustained by thee. Thou didst not suffer us to perish, for the sake of thy great name and thy holy law.

Therefore is the Festival of Booths to us a feast of *joy* for thy protecting care; a feast of *thanksgiving* for thy merciful blessings and paternal protection unto all thy creatures; a feast of *admonition*, ever to work for the glorification of thy Holy Name; a feast of *trust*, that as in the past thou hast not abandoned nor forsaken us, so in the future shall we be sheltered by thy tent of protection.

Therefore will we sing thy mercies for ever, and make known thy faithfulness to all generations. Amen.

ON SH'MINI ATZERETH.

O Lord our God! we have assembled this evening to inaugurate the closing festival, appointed to us at this season, in order that we may review the holy convocations and festive gatherings of this month, the sublime lessons which they have taught us, the sacred emotions which they have aroused, the thoughts of repentance which they have invoked, the tidings of forgiveness which they have proclaimed, the joyous and grateful recollections which they have awakened, the fervent prayers which they have inspired;—that we may once more, before the expiration of this festive month, collect our thoughts in thy presence, and seriously examine the results of our frequent convocations for divine worship in thy house.

Thou didst call to us, on the first day of this month, that we should be reminded by the Shofar's sound that thou art the Sovereign of the universe, the Dispenser of life and death, riches and poverty,—judging in righteousness, rewarding with faithfulness, and punishing in love and mercy;—that we should humble ourselves before thee, and realize our feebleness and our insignificance before thy august throne.

As we stood before thee on the great day of Atonement, thou didst look mercifully on our fasting and penitence, and send to us thy greeting of pardon and forgiveness, so that we might be able, with renewed courage, to repair our wrongs, retrieve our shortcomings, and, in imitation of thy love toward us, be full of love for all mankind.

With the sacred melodies of the day of Atonement reverberating in our hearts, we heralded the Feast of Booths, which served to remind us of thy protecting care of Israel at all times, and the bounteous gifts with which the earth teems. Thou didst appoint that the sacred days of contemplation and repentance should be followed by days of thanksgiving and rejoicing, in order that we might feel the happiness with which the consciousness of purity always inspires the soul; and also, that we might consecrate to thy service the earthly goods with which thou hast blessed us.

Although the festival which we are now about to celebrate is not distinguished by any historical commemoration, nor marked by any particular symbols, yet is it full of deep significance. We recognize it, O

Service for the Eve of Sabbaths and Festivals.

Lord, as a feast of ideas, in order that we may take to heart that, although characterized by no special festivity to lead our thoughts to thee, yet should we be ever mindful of thy government on earth, and of the solemn admonitions of thy holy law; that thy Spirit should ever animate us, and so direct our feelings; that, at all times and in all places, we may be cognizant that it is thou who guidest us through the paths of life, that thou dost guard and support us; that we should submit to all thy dispensations in calmness and in trust, and remember our duties toward thee, whether partaking of joy or sorrow.

Let not the lessons of our sacred days of observance pass by unheeded. Let the ennoblement of our hearts and the purification of our souls be our harvest, —the fruits we gather in thy house to be taken to our own homes. Bless thou the work of our hands; grant full and ample success to all our undertakings for the welfare of our dear ones, and of humanity at large.

Let a joyous and yet a contented spirit prevail in our family circles, and keep far removed from them trials and misfortunes, grief and affliction.

And throughout all the days of our life will we render praise unto thee, who hast appointed thy festivals to consecrate and sanctify our existence. Amen!

ON SIMCHATH-TORAH.

O Lord and Father! with emotions of gratitude pervading our hearts do we welcome this festival appointed for the rejoicing of the Law. We recognize in the code which thou hast given us the faithful guide of our lives. O that this festival may prove a blessing unto us! Grant, O Lord, that we may ever rejoice in thy revealed word, that our hearts may be open to understand its sublime ideas, and our eyes unveiled to realize in it our never-failing fount of life!

May the commands of the Thorah be with us, whether enjoying happiness and prosperity, or partaking of sorrow and distress. Cause us, O Lord, to feel the celestial gladness which thy word inspires in the souls of all those who study and conceive it. And as thou didst bestow thy love upon us in choosing us as the repositories of thy will, as the bearers of true knowledge, so may thy love everlastingly rest upon us, that we may be instrumental in approximating the blissful future, when the whole world shall be brought to that knowledge which will gather all thy creatures in unity and concord, that thou art ONE, and thy name ONE. Amen!

GENERAL FESTIVE PRAYER.

Eternal God! with thankful hearts do we appear in thy presence, to celebrate the festive days which thou hast given us in kindness and in love.

Grant that we may realize the lofty import of all such occasions, and that by their sacred means we may purify our hearts and ennoble our souls, so as to fulfill our duties to thee.

Inspire us with the desire to labor for all works of holiness, and for the happiness of mankind.

May our festivals reaffirm within us the belief in thy bountiful providence, and cause us to devote our lives more and more to thy service. Amen!

תפלת ערבית לשבת ולרגלים

לְכָה דוֹדִי לִקְרַאת כַּלָּה. פְּנֵי שַׁבָּת נְקַבְּלָה:

לִקְרַאת שַׁבָּת לְכוּ וְנֵלְכָה. כִּי הִיא מְקוֹר הַבְּרָכָה. מֵרֹאשׁ מִקֶּדֶם נְסוּכָה. סוֹף מַעֲשֶׂה בְּמַחֲשָׁבָה תְּחִלָּה:

לְכָה דוֹדִי לִקְרַאת כַּלָּה. פְּנֵי שַׁבָּת נְקַבְּלָה:

הִתְעוֹרְרִי הִתְעוֹרְרִי. כִּי בָא אוֹרֵךְ קוּמִי אוֹרִי. עוּרִי עוּרִי שִׁיר דַּבֵּרִי. כְּבוֹד יְיָ עָלַיִךְ נִגְלָה:

לְכָה דוֹדִי לִקְרַאת כַּלָּה. פְּנֵי שַׁבָּת נְקַבְּלָה:

בּוֹאִי בְשָׁלוֹם עֲטֶרֶת בַּעְלָהּ. גַּם בְּשִׂמְחָה וּבְצָהֳלָה. תּוֹךְ אֱמוּנֵי עַם סְגֻלָּה. בּוֹאִי כַלָּה. בּוֹאִי כַלָּה:

לְכָה דוֹדִי לִקְרַאת כַּלָּה. פְּנֵי שַׁבָּת נְקַבְּלָה:

(תהלים צ״ב צ״ג)

מִזְמוֹר שִׁיר לְיוֹם הַשַּׁבָּת:

טוֹב לְהֹדוֹת לַיְיָ וּלְזַמֵּר לְשִׁמְךָ עֶלְיוֹן: לְהַגִּיד בַּבֹּקֶר חַסְדֶּךָ וֶאֱמוּנָתְךָ בַּלֵּילוֹת: עֲלֵי עָשׂוֹר וַעֲלֵי נָבֶל עֲלֵי הִגָּיוֹן בְּכִנּוֹר: כִּי שִׂמַּחְתַּנִי יְיָ בְּפָעֳלֶךָ בְּמַעֲשֵׂי יָדֶיךָ אֲרַנֵּן:

2. The Sabbath is coming, the heaven-allied;
Come, brethren, to meet the Sabbath, the Bride.

We meet thee, O Sabbath, with exulting hearts,
Thou fountain of bliss! All trouble departs.
Thou art creation's holiest thought;
What is first in plan, the last it is wrought.

The Sabbath is coming, the heaven-allied;
Come, brethren, to meet the Sabbath, the Bride.

Arouse thee, my soul, with all thy might—
The sun goes down, the Sabbath shines bright;
Arouse thee and sing a joyous lay,
Thy Lord appears with the Sabbath day.

The Sabbath is coming, the heaven-allied;
Come, brethren, to meet the Sabbath, the Bride.

Now come then, O Sabbath, thou crown of the Lord,
Bring joy in our dwellings and happy accord;
In the midst of the people who call thee their pride,
Be welcome, O Sabbath, be welcome, O Bride.

The Sabbath is coming, the heaven-allied;
Come, brethren, to meet the Sabbath, the Bride.

(*Psalms* 92, 93.)

3. *R'dr.*—Sing ye the song of the Sabbath day!

Ch. & Cong.—How good thy mercies to record
    In grateful songs, Almighty Lord;
    Thy watchful care by morning light,
    Thy never-failing truth by night;
    From decachord to sound acclaim,
    With lyre and harp to sing thy Name.
    For thou hast made thy works my joy,
    Thy doings shall my praise employ.

תפלת ערבית לשבת ולרגלים

מַה־גָּדְלוּ מַעֲשֶׂיךָ יְיָ מְאֹד עָמְקוּ מַחְשְׁבֹתֶיךָ: אִישׁ־בַּעַר לֹא יֵדָע וּכְסִיל לֹא־יָבִין אֶת־זֹאת: בִּפְרֹחַ רְשָׁעִים כְּמוֹ־עֵשֶׂב וַיָּצִיצוּ כָּל־פֹּעֲלֵי אָוֶן לְהִשָּׁמְדָם עֲדֵי־עַד:

וְאַתָּה מָרוֹם לְעֹלָם יְיָ:

כִּי הִנֵּה אֹיְבֶיךָ יְיָ כִּי־הִנֵּה אֹיְבֶיךָ יֹאבֵדוּ יִתְפָּרְדוּ כָּל־פֹּעֲלֵי אָוֶן: וַתָּרֶם כִּרְאֵים קַרְנִי בַּלֹּתִי בְּשֶׁמֶן רַעֲנָן: וַתַּבֵּט עֵינִי בְּשׁוּרָי בַּקָּמִים עָלַי מְרֵעִים תִּשְׁמַעְנָה אָזְנָי: צַדִּיק כַּתָּמָר יִפְרָח כְּאֶרֶז בַּלְּבָנוֹן יִשְׂגֶּה: שְׁתוּלִים בְּבֵית יְיָ בְּחַצְרוֹת אֱלֹהֵינוּ יַפְרִיחוּ: עוֹד יְנוּבוּן בְּשֵׂיבָה דְּשֵׁנִים וְרַעֲנַנִּים יִהְיוּ: לְהַגִּיד כִּי־יָשָׁר יְיָ צוּרִי וְלֹא־עַוְלָתָה בּוֹ:

יְיָ מָלָךְ גֵּאוּת לָבֵשׁ לָבֵשׁ יְיָ עֹז הִתְאַזָּר אַף־תִּכּוֹן תֵּבֵל בַּל־תִּמּוֹט: נָכוֹן כִּסְאֲךָ מֵאָז מֵעוֹלָם אָתָּה: נָשְׂאוּ נְהָרוֹת יְיָ נָשְׂאוּ נְהָרוֹת קוֹלָם יִשְׂאוּ נְהָרוֹת דָּכְיָם: מִקֹּלוֹת מַיִם רַבִּים אַדִּירִים מִשְׁבְּרֵי־יָם אַדִּיר בַּמָּרוֹם יְיָ: עֵדֹתֶיךָ נֶאֶמְנוּ מְאֹד לְבֵיתְךָ נַאֲוָה־קֹדֶשׁ יְיָ לְאֹרֶךְ יָמִים:

R'dr.—How great the wonders thou hast wrought!
  Thy counsels are a deep of thought,
  Which brutish men cannot discern,
  And fools will neither know nor learn.
  Though sinners thrive and prosper here,
  And wicked men in bloom appear,
  They only spring for death a prey,
  And lo! they flee and fade away;
  For they will not thy Name adore,

Ch. & Cong.—MOST HIGH AND BLESSED
        FOR EVERMORE.

R'dr.—Lord, in thy strength exalt my horn,
  And with fresh oil my head adorn;
  Then foes turned back mine eye shall cheer,
  Their ruin shall salute mine ear;
  For righteous men shall grow like palms:
  Like lofty cedars stretch their arms.
  Those planted in the courts of God
  Shall flourish in his blest abode;
  They shall in age with fruit abound,
  And ever blooming shall be found;
  To show that God, my rock of might,
  In all his dealings is upright.—
  Th' Eternal reigns enthron'd in light,
  Th' Eternal girds himself with might;
  The world is moveless fixed by thee:
  Thy throne is from eternity.
  The floods have raised their voice on high,
  The floods will raise their crashing cry;
  Than all the billows, when they roar,
  Thy majesty, O Lord, is more.

Ch. & Cong.—Thy word is firm and very sure,
  Thy statutes ever shall endure;
  And holiness shall long become
  Thy loved abode, our happy home.

תפלת ערבית לשבת ולרגלים

(The Congregation rise.)

READER.

בָּרְכוּ אֶת־יְיָ הַמְבֹרָךְ:

CHOIR AND CONGREGATION.

בָּרוּךְ יְיָ הַמְבֹרָךְ לְעוֹלָם וָעֶד:

(The Congregation are seated.)

י. בָּרוּךְ אַתָּה יְיָ אֱלֹהֵינוּ מֶלֶךְ הָעוֹלָם. אֲשֶׁר בִּדְבָרוֹ מַעֲרִיב עֲרָבִים. בְּחָכְמָה פּוֹתֵחַ שְׁעָרִים. וּבִתְבוּנָה מְשַׁנֶּה עִתִּים. וּמַחֲלִיף אֶת־הַזְּמַנִּים. וּמְסַדֵּר אֶת־הַכּוֹכָבִים בְּמִשְׁמְרוֹתֵיהֶם בָּרָקִיעַ כִּרְצוֹנוֹ. בּוֹרֵא יוֹם וָלָיְלָה. גּוֹלֵל אוֹר מִפְּנֵי־חֹשֶׁךְ וְחֹשֶׁךְ מִפְּנֵי־אוֹר. וּמַעֲבִיר יוֹם וּמֵבִיא לָיְלָה. וּמַבְדִּיל בֵּין יוֹם וּבֵין לָיְלָה. יְיָ צְבָאוֹת שְׁמוֹ. אֵל חַי וְקַיָּם תָּמִיד יִמְלוֹךְ עָלֵינוּ לְעוֹלָם וָעֶד. בָּרוּךְ אַתָּה יְיָ הַמַּעֲרִיב עֲרָבִים:

י. אַהֲבַת עוֹלָם בֵּית יִשְׂרָאֵל עַמְּךָ אָהָבְתָּ. תּוֹרָה וּמִצְוֹת חֻקִּים וּמִשְׁפָּטִים אוֹתָנוּ לִמַּדְתָּ. עַל־כֵּן יְיָ אֱלֹהֵינוּ בְּשָׁכְבֵנוּ וּבְקוּמֵנוּ נָשִׂיחַ בְּחֻקֶּיךָ. וְנִשְׂמַח בְּדִבְרֵי תוֹרָתֶךָ וּבְמִצְוֹתֶיךָ לְעוֹלָם וָעֶד. כִּי הֵם חַיֵּינוּ וְאֹרֶךְ יָמֵינוּ וּבָהֶם נֶהְגֶּה יוֹמָם וָלָיְלָה. וְאַהֲבָתְךָ אַל־תָּסִיר מִמֶּנּוּ לְעוֹלָמִים. בָּרוּךְ אַתָּה יְיָ אוֹהֵב עַמּוֹ יִשְׂרָאֵל:

(The Congregation rise.)

Reader.

Praise ye the Lord, unto whom all praise belongeth.

Choir and Congregation.

Praised be the Lord, unto whom all praise belongeth, now and for evermore.

(The Congregation are seated.)

4. Yea, praises unto thee, our God, Ruler of the universe, at whose command the shades of night are advancing, and from heaven's dark portals the shining stars appear and shed their glorious lustre. Thou hast assigned to them a station in the firmament, so that they may fulfill thy will, according to laws wise and unvaried. Thou biddest darkness vanish before light, and causest day and night to return with matchless regularity. When the toil of day has passed, thou usherest in the calm of evening, that it may invite us to praise thee, the Master of the heavenly hosts. Praised be thou, O Lord, who causest the evening to advance. Amen!

5. In like manner as the heavens make known thy glory, so is thy infinite love manifested through thy people Israel, unto whom thou didst impart the light of thy laws and statutes, even when the dark night of heathenism covered the earth. Therefore do we proclaim thy truth when we lie down and when we rise up. Yea, we rejoice in the mission assigned to us, by means of thy law, to make known thy existence and thy unity. It is this which has sustained us, and preserved our existence among all nations, and day and night will we be mindful thereof. But O, never withhold from us thy love, and unto thee be praises, O Lord, who hast in affection chosen Israel to be thy people. Amen!

קריאת שמע

6.

(This verse is said by the Reader, and then the Choir and Congregation repeat it while standing.)

שְׁמַע יִשְׂרָאֵל יְהוָֹה אֱלֹהֵינוּ יְהוָֹה אֶחָד:

בָּרוּךְ שֵׁם כְּבוֹד מַלְכוּתוֹ לְעוֹלָם וָעֶד:

(The Cong. take their seats, and the Rabbi recites the following.)

(דברים ו' ד' י״א י״ג במדבר ט״ו ל״ז)

וְאָהַבְתָּ אֵת יְיָ אֱלֹהֶיךָ בְּכָל־לְבָבְךָ וּבְכָל־נַפְשְׁךָ וּבְכָל־מְאֹדֶךָ: וְהָיוּ הַדְּבָרִים הָאֵלֶּה אֲשֶׁר אָנֹכִי מְצַוְּךָ הַיּוֹם עַל־לְבָבֶךָ: וְשִׁנַּנְתָּם לְבָנֶיךָ וְדִבַּרְתָּ בָּם בְּשִׁבְתְּךָ בְּבֵיתֶךָ וּבְלֶכְתְּךָ בַדֶּרֶךְ וּבְשָׁכְבְּךָ וּבְקוּמֶךָ: וּקְשַׁרְתָּם לְאוֹת עַל־יָדֶךָ וְהָיוּ לְטֹטָפֹת בֵּין עֵינֶיךָ: וּכְתַבְתָּם עַל־מְזֻזוֹת בֵּיתֶךָ וּבִשְׁעָרֶיךָ:

וְהָיָה אִם־שָׁמֹעַ תִּשְׁמְעוּ אֶל־מִצְוֹתַי אֲשֶׁר אָנֹכִי מְצַוֶּה אֶתְכֶם הַיּוֹם לְאַהֲבָה אֶת־יְיָ אֱלֹהֵיכֶם וּלְעָבְדוֹ בְּכָל־לְבַבְכֶם וּבְכָל־נַפְשְׁכֶם: וְנָתַתִּי מְטַר־אַרְצְכֶם בְּעִתּוֹ יוֹרֶה וּמַלְקוֹשׁ וְאָסַפְתָּ דְגָנֶךָ וְתִירשְׁךָ וְיִצְהָרֶךָ: וְנָתַתִּי עֵשֶׂב בְּשָׂדְךָ לִבְהֶמְתֶּךָ וְאָכַלְתָּ וְשָׂבָעְתָּ: הִשָּׁמְרוּ לָכֶם פֶּן־יִפְתֶּה לְבַבְכֶם וְסַרְתֶּם וַעֲבַדְתֶּם אֱלֹהִים אֲחֵרִים וְהִשְׁתַּחֲוִיתֶם לָהֶם: וְחָרָה אַף־יְיָ בָּכֶם וְעָצַר אֶת־

Service for the Eve of Sabbaths and Festivals.

6. THE CONFESSION OF FAITH.

(This verse is said by the Reader, and then the Choir and Congregation repeat it while standing.)

Hear, O Israel! The Lord is our God; the Lord is One!

Blessed be the name of his glorious kingdom for evermore.

(The Congregation take their seats, and the Rabbi recites the following scriptural passages:)

(Deut. vi. 4–9, xi. 13–21; Numb. xv. 37–41.)

And thou shalt love the Lord thy God with all thy heart, and with all thy soul, and with all thy might. And these words, which I command thee this day, shall be in thy heart. And thou shalt teach them diligently unto thy children, and shalt speak of them when thou sittest in thy house, and when thou walkest by the way; when thou liest down, and when thou risest up. And thou shalt bind them for a sign upon thy hand, and they shall be as frontlets between thy eyes. And thou shalt write them upon the door-posts of thy house, and upon thy gates.

And it shall come to pass, that if ye will hearken diligently unto my commandments which I command you this day, to love the Lord your God, and to serve him with all your heart and all your soul, then will I send rain for your land in its due season, the first rain and the latter rain, that thou mayest gather in thy corn, thy wine, and thy oil. And I will give grass in thy field for thy cattle, and thou shalt eat and be satisfied. Take heed of yourselves, lest your heart be deceived, and ye turn aside, and serve other gods, and worship them. For then the Lord's wrath will be kindled

תפלת ערבית לשבת ולרגלים

הַשָּׁמַיִם וְלֹא-יִהְיֶה מָטָר וְהָאֲדָמָה לֹא תִתֵּן אֶת-יְבוּלָהּ וַאֲבַדְתֶּם מְהֵרָה מֵעַל הָאָרֶץ הַטֹּבָה אֲשֶׁר יְיָ נֹתֵן לָכֶם: וְשַׂמְתֶּם אֶת-דְּבָרַי אֵלֶּה עַל-לְבַבְכֶם וְעַל-נַפְשְׁכֶם וּקְשַׁרְתֶּם אֹתָם לְאוֹת עַל-יֶדְכֶם וְהָיוּ לְטוֹטָפֹת בֵּין עֵינֵיכֶם: וְלִמַּדְתֶּם אֹתָם אֶת-בְּנֵיכֶם לְדַבֵּר בָּם בְּשִׁבְתְּךָ בְּבֵיתֶךָ וּבְלֶכְתְּךָ בַדֶּרֶךְ וּבְשָׁכְבְּךָ וּבְקוּמֶךָ: וּכְתַבְתָּם עַל-מְזוּזוֹת בֵּיתֶךָ וּבִשְׁעָרֶיךָ: לְמַעַן יִרְבּוּ יְמֵיכֶם וִימֵי בְנֵיכֶם עַל הָאֲדָמָה אֲשֶׁר נִשְׁבַּע יְיָ לַאֲבֹתֵיכֶם לָתֵת לָהֶם כִּימֵי הַשָּׁמַיִם עַל-הָאָרֶץ:

וַיֹּאמֶר יְיָ אֶל-מֹשֶׁה לֵּאמֹר: דַּבֵּר אֶל-בְּנֵי יִשְׂרָאֵל וְאָמַרְתָּ אֲלֵהֶם וְעָשׂוּ לָהֶם צִיצִת עַל-כַּנְפֵי בִגְדֵיהֶם לְדֹרֹתָם וְנָתְנוּ עַל-צִיצִת הַכָּנָף פְּתִיל תְּכֵלֶת: וְהָיָה לָכֶם לְצִיצִת וּרְאִיתֶם אֹתוֹ וּזְכַרְתֶּם אֶת-כָּל-מִצְוֹת יְיָ וַעֲשִׂיתֶם אֹתָם וְלֹא תָתוּרוּ אַחֲרֵי לְבַבְכֶם וְאַחֲרֵי עֵינֵיכֶם אֲשֶׁר-אַתֶּם זֹנִים אַחֲרֵיהֶם: לְמַעַן תִּזְכְּרוּ וַעֲשִׂיתֶם אֶת-כָּל-מִצְוֹתָי וִהְיִיתֶם קְדֹשִׁים לֵאלֹהֵיכֶם: אֲנִי יְיָ אֱלֹהֵיכֶם אֲשֶׁר הוֹצֵאתִי אֶתְכֶם מֵאֶרֶץ מִצְרַיִם לִהְיוֹת לָכֶם לֵאלֹהִים אֲנִי יְיָ אֱלֹהֵיכֶם:

Choir.

יְיָ אֱלֹהֵיכֶם אֱמֶת:

against you, and he will shut up the heavens, that there be no rain, and the land will not yield her fruit, and ye shall perish quickly from off the goodly land which the Lord giveth you. Therefore shall ye lay up these my words in your heart and in your soul, and bind them for a sign upon your hand, and they shall be as frontlets between your eyes. And ye shall teach them to your children, speaking of them when thou sittest in thy house, and when thou walkest by the way; when thou liest down, and when thou risest up. And thou shalt write them upon the door-posts of thy house, and upon thy gates. That your days may be multiplied, and the days of your children, in the land which the Lord swore unto your fathers to give them, as the days of heaven over the earth.

And the Lord spoke unto Moses, saying, Speak unto the children of Israel, and bid them to make themselves fringes in the borders of their garments, throughout their generations, and that they put upon the fringes of the borders a thread of blue. And it shall be unto you for a fringe, that ye may look upon it, and remember all the commandments of the Lord, and do them; and that ye seek not after the inclinations of your own heart and the delight of your eyes, in pursuit of which ye have been led astray. That ye may remember, and do all my commandments, and be holy unto your God. I am the Lord your God, who brought you out of the land of Egypt, to be your God: I am the Lord your God.

Choir.

The Lord your God is ever true and faithful!

תפלת ערבית לשבת ולרגלים

י. אֱמֶת וֶאֱמוּנָה כָּל־זֹאת וְקַיָּם עָלֵינוּ. כִּי הוּא יְיָ אֱלֹהֵינוּ וְאֵין זוּלָתוֹ וַאֲנַחְנוּ יִשְׂרָאֵל עַמּוֹ: הַפּוֹדֵנוּ מִיַּד־מְלָכִים. מַלְכֵּנוּ הַגּוֹאֲלֵנוּ מִכַּף כָּל־הֶעָרִיצִים: הָעֹשֶׂה גְדוֹלוֹת עַד־אֵין חֵקֶר. וְנִפְלָאוֹת עַד־אֵין מִסְפָּר: הַשָּׂם נַפְשֵׁנוּ בַּחַיִּים. וְלֹא־נָתַן לַמּוֹט רַגְלֵנוּ: הָעֹשֶׂה־לָּנוּ נִסִּים בְּפַרְעֹה. אוֹתוֹת וּמוֹפְתִים בְּאַדְמַת בְּנֵי־חָם. וַיּוֹצֵא אֶת־עַמּוֹ יִשְׂרָאֵל מִתּוֹכָם לְחֵרוּת עוֹלָם: הַמַּעֲבִיר בָּנָיו בֵּין גִּזְרֵי יַם־סוּף. וְהֶרְאָה לָהֶם גְּבוּרָתוֹ: שִׁבְּחוּ וְהוֹדוּ לִשְׁמוֹ. וּמַלְכוּתוֹ בְּרָצוֹן קִבְּלוּ עֲלֵיהֶם: מֹשֶׁה וּבְנֵי יִשְׂרָאֵל לְךָ עָנוּ שִׁירָה בְּשִׂמְחָה רַבָּה וְאָמְרוּ כֻלָּם:

Choir and Congregation.

מִי־כָמֹכָה בָּאֵלִם יְיָ. מִי כָּמֹכָה נֶאְדָּר בַּקֹּדֶשׁ. נוֹרָא תְהִלֹּת. עֹשֵׂה פֶלֶא:

מַלְכוּתְךָ רָאוּ בָנֶיךָ. בּוֹקֵעַ יָם לִפְנֵי מֹשֶׁה. זֶה אֵלִי עָנוּ וְאָמְרוּ:

Choir and Congregation.

יְיָ ׀ יִמְלֹךְ לְעֹלָם וָעֶד:

וְנֶאֱמַר כִּי־פָדָה יְיָ אֶת־יַעֲקֹב. וּגְאָלוֹ מִיַּד חָזָק מִמֶּנּוּ. בָּרוּךְ אַתָּה יְיָ גָּאַל יִשְׂרָאֵל:

יא. הַשְׁכִּיבֵנוּ יְיָ אֱלֹהֵינוּ לְשָׁלוֹם. וְהַעֲמִידֵנוּ מַלְכֵּנוּ לְחַיִּים. וּפְרוֹשׂ עָלֵינוּ סֻכַּת שְׁלוֹמֶךָ. וְתַקְּנֵנוּ בְּעֵצָה טוֹבָה מִלְּפָנֶיךָ. וְהוֹשִׁיעֵנוּ לְמַעַן שְׁמֶךָ. וְהָגֵן בַּעֲדֵנוּ. וְהָסֵר

7. True and unfailing is it unto us, that thou art the Lord our God, and that there is none else besides thee, while we, the children of Israel, are thy people. Thou hast delivered us from many a tyrannical power, and hast redeemed us from the hand of oppression. Without number are thy wonderful deeds, beyond mortal knowledge the miracles thou hast wrought for our sake. When hope had fled from our hearts, thou didst instill new life within us; when on the brink of destruction, thou didst interpose and save us. Even thou didst perform signs and wonders on our behalf, both when leading us from Egyptian slavery to everlasting freedom, and when paving a road through the sea, so that thy children might pass. Thus was thy marvelous power made known to them; and in acknowledging thy majesty, Moses and the children of Israel with one accord chanted the anthem of praise:

Choir and Congregation.—WHO AMONG THE MIGHTY IS LIKE UNTO THEE, O LORD? WHO IS LIKE UNTO THEE, GLORIFIED IN HOLINESS, FEARFUL IN PRAISED DEEDS, PERFORMING WONDERS?

Thy children beheld thy omnipotence, when the foaming billows of the sea were divided for their rescue. "This is my God," did they shout; and closing their song, they exclaimed:

Ch. & Cong.—THE LORD REIGNETH FOREVER AND EVER.

And thus art thou proclaimed in the words of inspiration: "The Lord is the redeemer of Jacob, his deliverer from the hand too powerful for him." Praised be thou, O Lord, who redeemest Israel. Amen!

---

8. O Lord our God! vouchsafe unto us thy protection, that we may lie down this night in peace, and awake in the morning to refreshed existence. Spread over us thy pavilion of peace, guide us with good

מֵעָלֵינוּ אוֹיֵב דֶּבֶר וְחֶרֶב וְרָעָב וְיָגוֹן. וְהָסֵר שָׂטָן מִלְּפָנֵינוּ וּמֵאַחֲרֵינוּ. וּבְצֵל כְּנָפֶיךָ תַּסְתִּירֵנוּ. כִּי אֵל שׁוֹמְרֵנוּ וּמַצִּילֵנוּ אָתָּה. וּשְׁמוֹר צֵאתֵנוּ וּבוֹאֵנוּ לְחַיִּים וּלְשָׁלוֹם מֵעַתָּה וְעַד עוֹלָם. וּפְרוֹשׂ עָלֵינוּ סֻכַּת שְׁלוֹמֶךָ. בָּרוּךְ אַתָּה יְיָ הַפּוֹרֵשׂ סֻכַּת שָׁלוֹם עָלֵינוּ וְעַל כָּל־עַמּוֹ יִשְׂרָאֵל:

(On the Sabbath.)

(שמות ל"א ט"ז)

וְשָׁמְרוּ בְנֵי־יִשְׂרָאֵל אֶת־הַשַּׁבָּת לַעֲשׂוֹת אֶת־הַשַּׁבָּת לְדֹרֹתָם בְּרִית עוֹלָם: בֵּינִי וּבֵין בְּנֵי יִשְׂרָאֵל אוֹת הִיא לְעֹלָם. כִּי־שֵׁשֶׁת יָמִים עָשָׂה יְיָ אֶת־הַשָּׁמַיִם וְאֶת־הָאָרֶץ וּבַיּוֹם הַשְּׁבִיעִי שָׁבַת וַיִּנָּפַשׁ:

(On Festivals.)

(ויקרא כ"ג מ"ד)

וַיְדַבֵּר מֹשֶׁה אֶת־מֹעֲדֵי יְיָ אֶל־בְּנֵי יִשְׂרָאֵל:

יִ֯תְגַּדַּל וְיִתְקַדַּשׁ שְׁמֵהּ רַבָּא. בְּעָלְמָא דִּי־בְרָא כִרְעוּתֵהּ. וְיַמְלִיךְ מַלְכוּתֵהּ בְּחַיֵּיכוֹן וּבְיוֹמֵיכוֹן. וּבְחַיֵּי דְכָל בֵּית יִשְׂרָאֵל. בַּעֲגָלָא וּבִזְמַן קָרִיב. וְאִמְרוּ אָמֵן:

Choir and Congregation.

אָמֵן יְהֵא שְׁמֵהּ רַבָּא מְבָרַךְ לְעָלַם וּלְעָלְמֵי עָלְמַיָּא:

Reader.

יִתְבָּרַךְ וְיִשְׁתַּבַּח וְיִתְפָּאַר וְיִתְרוֹמַם וְיִתְנַשֵּׂא וְיִתְהַדָּר וְיִתְעַלֶּה וְיִתְהַלָּל שְׁמֵהּ דְּקֻדְשָׁא בְּרִיךְ הוּא. לְעֵלָּא מִן כָּל־בִּרְכָתָא וְשִׁירָתָא תֻּשְׁבְּחָתָא וְנֶחָמָתָא דַּאֲמִירָן בְּעָלְמָא. וְאִמְרוּ אָמֵן:

counsels, and send us assistance for the sake of thy Holy Name. Be thou, at all times, our shield and protector from harm, our guardian from danger, our savior from all manner of trouble and distress. Keep far from us anxiety and sorrow, and shelter us under the shadow of thy wing; for it is in thee only, O God, that we put our trust. Guard then our going out and our coming in, that we may lead a life of happiness and contentment, and be ever surrounded by the blessing of peace. Praised be thou, O Lord, who spreadest thy pavilion of divine peace over us and all Israel. Amen!

(Exodus xxxi. 16.)   (*On the Sabbath.*)

The children of Israel shall keep the Sabbath, to observe it throughout their generations as a perpetual covenant. Between me and the children of Israel it is a sign for ever, that in six days the Lord created heaven and earth, and appointed the seventh day for rest and spiritual reflection.

(Leviticus xxiii. 44.)   (*On Festivals.*)

Moses proclaimed the festivals of the Lord unto the children of Israel.

---

9. Let the great Name of the Eternal be exalted and sanctified throughout the whole universe, which he hath created according to his will. May his kingdom soon be established over the whole earth, and may ye and all Israel live to partake of the blessings of that happy period; unto which say ye, Amen!

Choir and Congregation.—Amen! May his great Name be praised for ever and unto all eternity.

Reader.—Yea, let us praise and worship, magnify and exalt the Name of the Most Holy (blessed be he) whose glory exceedeth all the praises and hymns that may be rendered unto him by human lips. And let us say, Amen!

ברכת שבע

(The Congregation rise for silent prayer.)

I. בָּרוּךְ אַתָּה יְיָ אֱלֹהֵינוּ וֵאלֹהֵי אֲבוֹתֵינוּ. אֱלֹהֵי אַבְרָהָם אֱלֹהֵי יִצְחָק וֵאלֹהֵי יַעֲקֹב. הָאֵל הַגָּדוֹל הַגִּבּוֹר וְהַנּוֹרָא. אֵל עֶלְיוֹן. גּוֹמֵל חֲסָדִים טוֹבִים. וְקֹנֵה הַכֹּל. וְזוֹכֵר חַסְדֵי אָבוֹת. וּמֵבִיא גְאֻלָּה לִבְנֵי בְנֵיהֶם לְמַעַן שְׁמוֹ בְּאַהֲבָה:

(During the Penitential Days.)

זָכְרֵנוּ לַחַיִּים. מֶלֶךְ חָפֵץ בַּחַיִּים. וְכָתְבֵנוּ בְּסֵפֶר הַחַיִּים. לְמַעַנְךָ אֱלֹהִים חַיִּים:

מֶלֶךְ עוֹזֵר וּמוֹשִׁיעַ וּמָגֵן. בָּרוּךְ אַתָּה יְיָ מָגֵן אַבְרָהָם:

II. אַתָּה גִבּוֹר לְעוֹלָם אֲדֹנָי מְחַיֵּה מֵתִים אַתָּה רַב לְהוֹשִׁיעַ. (מַשִּׁיב הָרוּחַ וּמוֹרִיד הַגֶּשֶׁם:)

מְכַלְכֵּל חַיִּים בְּחֶסֶד מְחַיֵּה מֵתִים בְּרַחֲמִים רַבִּים סוֹמֵךְ נוֹפְלִים וְרוֹפֵא חוֹלִים וּמַתִּיר אֲסוּרִים וּמְקַיֵּם אֱמוּנָתוֹ לִישֵׁנֵי עָפָר. מִי כָמוֹךָ בַּעַל גְּבוּרוֹת וּמִי דּוֹמֶה לָּךְ מֶלֶךְ מֵמִית וּמְחַיֶּה וּמַצְמִיחַ יְשׁוּעָה:

(During the Penitential Days.)

מִי כָמוֹךָ אַב הָרַחֲמִים. זוֹכֵר יְצוּרָיו לַחַיִּים בְּרַחֲמִים:

וְנֶאֱמָן אַתָּה לְהַחֲיוֹת מֵתִים. בָּרוּךְ אַתָּה יְיָ מְחַיֵּה הַמֵּתִים:

III. אַתָּה קָדוֹשׁ וְשִׁמְךָ קָדוֹשׁ וּקְדוֹשִׁים בְּכָל־יוֹם יְהַלְלוּךָ סֶּלָה. בָּרוּךְ אַתָּה יְיָ הָאֵל הַקָּדוֹשׁ:

10. THE SEVEN-FOLD BENEDICTION.

(The Congregation rise for silent prayer.)

I. We arise to praise thee, O Lord our God, and the God of our fathers—God of Abraham, Isaac, and Jacob. Great and mighty art thou, and wondrous are thy works, O Author of the universe. In the abundance of thy mercy thou causest the virtues of the fathers to bring salvation to their children's children.

(*During the Penitential Days.*)

(Remember us and grant us life, O Eternal, who delightest in dispensing the blessings of life. Write us in the book of life, in order that we may proclaim thy mercy, O God of life.)

O Heavenly King! our Supporter, Savior, and Shield! Praised be thou, O Lord, the shield of Abraham.

II. Thou art ever omnipotent, O Lord, leading us unto life eternal, in thy abundant salvation.

(Thou biddest the winds to blow and the rain to descend.)

Thou sustainest in beneficence all living, and thy infinite love will attend us in the regions of a blessed hereafter. As thou supportest the falling, healest the sick, and loosenest the bonds of the oppressed, so doth thy faithfulness not abandon those who sleep in the dust. Who is like unto thee, Master of mighty acts? Who can be compared unto thee, O King, who, whether dispensing death or life, will cause salvation to spring forth?

(*During the Penitential Days.*)

(Yea, who is like unto thee, merciful Father, who in mercy rememberest thy creatures to life?)

We faithfully believe that thou wilt restore us from death unto life. Praised be thou, O Lord, who restorest the dead to life.

III. Thou art holy, and thy Name is holy, and it is a mission of holiness to praise thee daily. Praised be thou, O Lord, the Holy God.

תפלת ערבית לשבת ולרגלים

(On the Sabbath.)

IV. אַתָּה קִדַּשְׁתָּ אֶת יוֹם הַשְּׁבִיעִי לִשְׁמֶךָ. תַּכְלִית מַעֲשֵׂה שָׁמַיִם וָאָרֶץ. וּבֵרַכְתּוֹ מִכָּל־הַיָּמִים וְקִדַּשְׁתּוֹ מִכָּל־הַזְּמַנִּים. וְכֵן כָּתוּב בְּתוֹרָתֶךָ:

וַיְכֻלּוּ הַשָּׁמַיִם וְהָאָרֶץ וְכָל־צְבָאָם: וַיְכַל אֱלֹהִים בַּיּוֹם הַשְּׁבִיעִי מְלַאכְתּוֹ אֲשֶׁר עָשָׂה וַיִּשְׁבֹּת בַּיּוֹם הַשְּׁבִיעִי מִכָּל־מְלַאכְתּוֹ אֲשֶׁר עָשָׂה: וַיְבָרֶךְ אֱלֹהִים אֶת־יוֹם הַשְּׁבִיעִי וַיְקַדֵּשׁ אֹתוֹ כִּי בוֹ שָׁבַת מִכָּל־מְלַאכְתּוֹ אֲשֶׁר־בָּרָא אֱלֹהִים לַעֲשׂוֹת:

(On Festivals.)

IV. אַתָּה בְחַרְתָּנוּ מִכָּל־הָעַמִּים. אָהַבְתָּ אוֹתָנוּ. וְרָצִיתָ בָּנוּ. וְקִדַּשְׁתָּנוּ בְּמִצְוֹתֶיךָ. וְקֵרַבְתָּנוּ מַלְכֵּנוּ לַעֲבוֹדָתֶךָ. וְשִׁמְךָ הַגָּדוֹל וְהַקָּדוֹשׁ עָלֵינוּ קָרָאתָ:

וַתִּתֶּן־לָנוּ יְיָ אֱלֹהֵינוּ בְּאַהֲבָה (שַׁבָּתוֹת לִמְנוּחָה וּ) מוֹעֲדִים לְשִׂמְחָה חַגִּים וּזְמַנִּים לְשָׂשׂוֹן. אֶת־יוֹם (הַשַּׁבָּת הַזֶּה וְאֶת־יוֹם)

(Atzereth)	(Succoth)	(Shabuoth)	(Passover)
חַג הָעֲצֶרֶת הַשְּׁמִינִי	חַג הַסֻּכּוֹת הַזֶּה.	חַג הַשָּׁבֻעוֹת הַזֶּה.	חַג הַמַּצּוֹת הַזֶּה.
זְמַן שִׂמְחָתֵנוּ	זְמַן שִׂמְחָתֵנוּ	זְמַן מַתַּן תּוֹרָתֵנוּ	זְמַן חֵרוּתֵנוּ
הַזֶּה.			

(בְּאַהֲבָה) מִקְרָא קֹדֶשׁ זֵכֶר לִיצִיאַת מִצְרָיִם:

---

*) The words in parenthesis are said if the feast occurs on Sabbath.

Service for the Eve of Sabbaths and Festivals.

וַיְ

(*On the Sabbath.*)

IV. Thou hast consecrated the seventh day for the worship of thy Name, it being the completion and crowning work of thy creation. Thou hast blessed it above all other days, and hast sanctified it with a mission above all other festivals, even as we read in thy law:

"The heaven and the earth and all their hosts were finished, for God had completed on the seventh day all the work which he had made, and rested on the seventh day from all his work which he had made. And God blessed the seventh day and sanctified it, since he rested on it from all his work which God created and made."

(*On Festivals.*)

Thou hast chosen us from among all nations, and in thy love hast assigned unto us the priestly mission of spreading the knowledge of thy Holy Name, so that we may not alone perform thy commandments, but consecrate ourselves to thy service.

And in the abundance of thy kindness hast thou given us *(Sabbaths for rest and) festive seasons for delight, even this *(Sabbath and this) day of the Feast of

Matzoth, the anniversary of our delivery from bondage,	*Shebuoth*, reminding us of the revelation at Mount Sinai,	*Succoth*, devoted to joy and thanks for thy merciful protection,	*Sh'mini Atzereth*, consecrated to a joyful conclusion of the festive season,

a holy convocation, reminding us of our mission from our going out from Egypt.

---

* The words in parenthesis are said if the feast occurs on Sabbath.

תפלת ערבית לשבת ולרגלים

(On the Sabbath.)

אֱלֹהֵינוּ וֵאלֹהֵי אֲבוֹתֵינוּ. רְצֵה בִמְנוּחָתֵנוּ. קַדְּשֵׁנוּ בְּמִצְוֹתֶיךָ. וְתֵן חֶלְקֵנוּ בְּתוֹרָתֶךָ. שַׂבְּעֵנוּ מִטּוּבֶךָ. וְשַׂמְּחֵנוּ בִישׁוּעָתֶךָ. וְטַהֵר לִבֵּנוּ לְעָבְדְּךָ בֶּאֱמֶת. וְהַנְחִילֵנוּ יְיָ אֱלֹהֵינוּ בְּאַהֲבָה וּבְרָצוֹן שַׁבַּת קָדְשֶׁךָ. וְיִשְׂמְחוּ בָךְ יִשְׂרָאֵל אֹהֲבֵי שְׁמֶךָ. בָּרוּךְ אַתָּה יְיָ מְקַדֵּשׁ הַשַּׁבָּת:

(On Festivals.)

אֱלֹהֵינוּ וֵאלֹהֵי אֲבוֹתֵינוּ. יַעֲלֶה וְיָבֹא זִכְרוֹנֵנוּ וְזִכְרוֹן אֲבוֹתֵינוּ. וְזִכְרוֹן כָּל עַמְּךָ בֵּית יִשְׂרָאֵל לְפָנֶיךָ. לְחֵן וּלְחֶסֶד וּלְרַחֲמִים לְחַיִּים וּלְשָׁלוֹם בְּיוֹם

(Passover) (Shabuoth) (Succoth) (Atzereth)

חַג הַמַּצּוֹת הַזֶּה. חַג הַשָּׁבֻעוֹת הַזֶּה. חַג הַסֻּכּוֹת הַזֶּה. הַשְּׁמִינִי חַג הָעֲצֶרֶת הַזֶּה.

זָכְרֵנוּ יְיָ אֱלֹהֵינוּ בּוֹ לְטוֹבָה. וּפָקְדֵנוּ בוֹ לִבְרָכָה. וְהוֹשִׁיעֵנוּ בוֹ לְחַיִּים. וּבִדְבַר יְשׁוּעָה וְרַחֲמִים. חוּס וְחָנֵּנוּ. וְרַחֵם עָלֵינוּ וְהוֹשִׁיעֵנוּ. כִּי אֵלֶיךָ עֵינֵינוּ. כִּי אֵל מֶלֶךְ חַנּוּן וְרַחוּם אָתָּה:

אֱלֹהֵינוּ וֵאלֹהֵי אֲבוֹתֵינוּ. (רְצֵה בִמְנוּחָתֵנוּ) קַדְּשֵׁנוּ בְּמִצְוֹתֶיךָ. וְתֵן חֶלְקֵנוּ בְּתוֹרָתֶךָ. שַׂבְּעֵנוּ מִטּוּבֶךָ. וְשַׂמְּחֵנוּ בִישׁוּעָתֶךָ. וְטַהֵר לִבֵּנוּ לְעָבְדְּךָ בֶּאֱמֶת. וְהַנְחִילֵנוּ יְיָ אֱלֹהֵינוּ (בְּאַהֲבָה וּבְרָצוֹן) בְּשִׂמְחָה וּבְשָׂשׂוֹן (שַׁבָּת וּ)מוֹעֲדֵי קָדְשֶׁךָ. וְיִשְׂמְחוּ בָךְ יִשְׂרָאֵל אוֹהֲבֵי שְׁמֶךָ. בָּרוּךְ אַתָּה יְיָ מְקַדֵּשׁ (הַשַּׁבָּת וְ)יִשְׂרָאֵל וְהַזְּמַנִּים:

(*On the Sabbath.*)

O our God, and the God of our fathers! grant that our Sabbath rest may render us worthy of thy grace. Sanctify our lives for the performance of thy commandments. Satisfy us with thy abundant goodness, and grant us joy through thy salvation. Purify our hearts to serve thee in truth, and permit us to enjoy thy holy Sabbath, in full love for thy Holy Name. Praised be thou, O Lord, who hast sanctified the Sabbath.

(*On Festivals.*)

O our God, and the God of our fathers! we beseech thee to permit our memorial, and the memorial of our ancestors, and even of all thy people Israel, to ascend and come before thee, so that we may obtain grace, favor, and blessing, mercy, life, and peace, on this day of

| the Feast of Matzoth. | the Feast of Pentecost. | the Feast of Booths. | the Feast of Conclusion |

Vouchsafe unto us thy blessing, and save us from the sorrows and trials of life. And as thy Holy Word is full of the assurance of salvation and benign compassion, so mayest thou save and compassionate us, whose eyes are directed to thee, our Heavenly King, who rulest all mankind in mercy and love.

O our God, and the God of our fathers! (grant that our Sabbath rest may render us worthy of thy grace.) Sanctify our lives for the performance of thy commandments. Satisfy us with thy abundant goodness, and grant us joy through thy salvation. Purify our hearts, to serve thee in truth, and permit us to enjoy thy holy (Sabbath and) Festivals, in full love for thy Holy Name. Praised be thou, O Lord, who hast sanctified (the Sabbath and) Israel and the Festivals.

תפלת ערבית לשבת ולרגלים

v. רְצֵה יְיָ אֱלֹהֵינוּ בְּעַמְּךָ יִשְׂרָאֵל. וְתִפְלָּתָם בְּאַהֲבָה תְקַבֵּל. וּתְהִי לְרָצוֹן תָּמִיד עֲבוֹדַת יִשְׂרָאֵל עַמֶּךָ.

(On the New Moon and in the Festival Week.)

(אֱלֹהֵינוּ וֵאלֹהֵי אֲבוֹתֵינוּ. יַעֲלֶה וְיָבֹא זִכְרֹנֵנוּ וְזִכְרוֹן אֲבוֹתֵינוּ. וְזִכְרוֹן כָּל עַמְּךָ בֵּית יִשְׂרָאֵל לְפָנֶיךָ. לְחֵן וּלְחֶסֶד וּלְרַחֲמִים לְחַיִּים וּלְשָׁלוֹם בְּיוֹם

(Succoth.) (Passover.) (New Moon.)

חַג הַסֻּכּוֹת הַזֶּה.   חַג הַמַּצּוֹת הַזֶּה.   רֹאשׁ הַחֹדֶשׁ הַזֶּה.

זָכְרֵנוּ יְיָ אֱלֹהֵינוּ בּוֹ לְטוֹבָה. וּפָקְדֵנוּ בוֹ לִבְרָכָה. וְהוֹשִׁיעֵנוּ בוֹ לְחַיִּים. וּבִדְבַר יְשׁוּעָה וְרַחֲמִים. חוּס וְחָנֵּנוּ. וְרַחֵם עָלֵינוּ וְהוֹשִׁיעֵנוּ. כִּי אֵלֶיךָ עֵינֵינוּ. כִּי אֵל מֶלֶךְ חַנּוּן וְרַחוּם אָתָּה:)

בָּרוּךְ אַתָּה יְיָ שֶׁאוֹתְךָ לְכַדְּךָ בְּיִרְאָה נַעֲבוֹד:

v. מוֹדִים אֲנַחְנוּ לָךְ. שָׁאַתָּה הוּא יְיָ אֱלֹהֵינוּ וֵאלֹהֵי אֲבוֹתֵינוּ לְעוֹלָם וָעֶד. צוּר חַיֵּינוּ. מָגֵן יִשְׁעֵנוּ. אַתָּה הוּא לְדוֹר וָדוֹר. נוֹדֶה לְּךָ וּנְסַפֵּר תְּהִלָּתֶךָ. עַל חַיֵּינוּ הַמְּסוּרִים בְּיָדֶךָ. וְעַל נִשְׁמוֹתֵינוּ הַפְּקוּדוֹת לָךְ. וְעַל נִסֶּיךָ שֶׁבְּכָל-יוֹם עִמָּנוּ. וְעַל נִפְלְאוֹתֶיךָ וְטוֹבוֹתֶיךָ שֶׁבְּכָל-עֵת. עֶרֶב וָבֹקֶר וְצָהֳרָיִם. הַטּוֹב כִּי לֹא-כָלוּ רַחֲמֶיךָ. וְהַמְרַחֵם כִּי לֹא-תַמּוּ חֲסָדֶיךָ. מֵעוֹלָם קִוִּינוּ לָךְ:*

Service for the Eve of Sabbaths and Festivals.

V. O Lord our God, bestow thy grace upon thy people Israel. Accept the prayers of those who approach thee in love, and let the worship of thy people Israel be ever pleasing unto thee.

(*On the New Moon and in the Festival Week.*)

(O our God, and the God of our fathers! especially do we beseech thee to permit our memorial and the memorial of our ancestors, and even the memorial of all thy people Israel, to ascend and come before thee, so that we may obtain grace, favor and mercy, life and peace on this day of the

(New Moon). (Feast of Matzoth). (Feast of Succoth).

Vouchsafe unto us thy blessing, and save us from the sorrows and trials of life. And as thy Holy Word is full of the assurance of salvation and benign compassion, so mayest thou save and compassionate us, whose eyes are directed to thee, our Heavenly King, who rulest all mankind in mercy and love.)

Praised be thou, O Lord, unto whom alone do we render reverence and adoration. Amen!

VI. We render our heartfelt thanks unto thee, our God and the God of our fathers, who art the firm stay of our existence, our shield of protection at all times. We, indeed, thank thee, and proclaim thy praise for our lives which are in thy hands, for our souls which are under thy guardianship, for the marks of thy providential care which we daily receive, and for the wonderful gifts which thou dost dispense unto us morning, noon, and night. Thou art good, for thy mercies never fail; and thy loving-kindness never ceaseth from thy people, for thou hast been their hope and trust from the distant past to the present moment of our lives.*

תפלת ערבית לשבת ולרגלים

וְעַל־כֻּלָּם יִתְבָּרַךְ וְיִתְרוֹמַם שִׁמְךָ מַלְכֵּנוּ תָּמִיד לְעוֹלָם וָעֶד:

(During the Penitential Days.)
וּכְתוֹב לְחַיִּים טוֹבִים כָּל־בְּנֵי בְרִיתֶךָ:

וְכֹל הַחַיִּים יוֹדוּךָ סֶּלָה. וִיהַלְלוּ אֶת־שִׁמְךָ בֶּאֱמֶת. הָאֵל יְשׁוּעָתֵנוּ וְעֶזְרָתֵנוּ סֶּלָה. בָּרוּךְ אַתָּה יְיָ הַטּוֹב שִׁמְךָ וּלְךָ נָאֶה לְהוֹדוֹת:

VII. שִׂים שָׁלוֹם טוֹבָה וּבְרָכָה חֵן וָחֶסֶד וְרַחֲמִים עָלֵינוּ וְעַל כָּל־יִשְׂרָאֵל עַמֶּךָ. בָּרְכֵנוּ אָבִינוּ כֻּלָּנוּ כְּאֶחָד בְּאוֹר פָּנֶיךָ. כִּי בְאוֹר פָּנֶיךָ נָתַתָּ לָּנוּ יְיָ אֱלֹהֵינוּ תּוֹרַת חַיִּים וְאַהֲבַת חֶסֶד וּצְדָקָה וּבְרָכָה וְרַחֲמִים וְחַיִּים וְשָׁלוֹם וְטוֹב בְּעֵינֶיךָ לְבָרֵךְ אֶת־עַמְּךָ יִשְׂרָאֵל בְּכָל־עֵת וּבְכָל־שָׁעָה בִּשְׁלוֹמֶךָ:

(On Chanuckah.)
יעל הַנִּסִּים. וְעַל הַפֻּרְקָן. וְעַל הַגְּבוּרוֹת. וְעַל הַתְּשׁוּעוֹת. וְעַל הַמִּלְחָמוֹת. שֶׁעָשִׂיתָ לַאֲבוֹתֵינוּ בַּיָּמִים הָהֵם בַּזְּמַן הַזֶּה: בִּימֵי מַתִּתְיָהוּ בֶּן־יוֹחָנָן הַכֹּהֵן. חַשְׁמוֹנַי וּבָנָיו. כְּשֶׁעָמְדָה מַלְכוּת יָוָן הָרְשָׁעָה עַל עַמְּךָ יִשְׂרָאֵל. לְהַשְׁכִּיחָם תּוֹרָתֶךָ. וּלְהַעֲבִירָם מֵחֻקֵּי רְצוֹנֶךָ. וְאַתָּה בְּרַחֲמֶיךָ הָרַבִּים. עָמַדְתָּ לָהֶם בְּעֵת צָרָתָם. רַבְתָּ אֶת־רִיבָם. דַּנְתָּ אֶת־דִּינָם. נָקַמְתָּ אֶת־נִקְמָתָם. מָסַרְתָּ גִבּוֹרִים בְּיַד חַלָּשִׁים. וְרַבִּים בְּיַד מְעַטִּים. וּטְמֵאִים בְּיַד טְהוֹרִים. וּרְשָׁעִים בְּיַד צַדִּיקִים. וְזֵדִים בְּיַד עוֹסְקֵי תוֹרָתֶךָ. וּלְךָ עָשִׂיתָ שֵׁם גָּדוֹל וְקָדוֹשׁ בְּעוֹלָמֶךָ. וּלְעַמְּךָ יִשְׂרָאֵל עָשִׂיתָ תְּשׁוּעָה גְדוֹלָה וּפֻרְקָן כְּהַיּוֹם הַזֶּה. וְאַחַר כֵּן בָּאוּ בָנֶיךָ לִדְבִיר בֵּיתֶךָ. וּפִנּוּ אֶת־הֵיכָלֶךָ. וְטִהֲרוּ אֶת־מִקְדָּשֶׁךָ. וְהִדְלִיקוּ נֵרוֹת בְּחַצְרוֹת קָדְשֶׁךָ. וְקָבְעוּ שְׁמוֹנַת יְמֵי חֲנֻכָּה אֵלּוּ. לְהוֹדוֹת וּלְהַלֵּל לְשִׁמְךָ הַגָּדוֹל: (ועל כלם)

Service for the Eve of Sabbaths and Festivals.

And for all these mercies will we praise thy Holy Name, our King, now and for evermore.
(*On the Penitential Days.*)
(Vouchsafe a blissful life unto all the children of thy covenant.)
O that all living would pay homage unto thee, and praise thy name in truth, O Lord, our help and assistance. Blessed be thou, O Lord, whose name is the All-bountiful, and unto whom the praises of man should be gratefully rendered. Amen!

VII. We now implore thee to grant us the precious gift of peace and to instill within us a contented spirit, benevolence and love. Bless all of us together with the light of thy countenance, so that we may learn to practice charity and righteousness, and to perform deeds of benevolence and love, whereby peace and happiness may be spread around us, in like manner as thou hast blessed thy people Israel, amid all the vicissitudes of life.

*(*On Chanuckah.*)*
Specially do we render thanks unto thee, O Lord, for our wonderful preservation from persecution and danger, and for the mighty deeds wrought on our behalf in ancient times at this particular season.

In the days of the Hasmonean priest Mattathias and his sons, when the wicked Grecian government, under Antiochus Epiphanes, sought to exterminate thy people Israel, to cast thy law into oblivion, and compel them to transgress thy statutes, thou didst protect them in thy abundant mercy. Thou didst defend their cause and restore their rights. Thou didst deliver the mighty into the hands of the weak; the many into the hands of the few; the wicked into the hands of the righteous; the defiled into the hands of the pure; and the arrogant into the hands of the followers of thy law. Thus didst thou make known thy power and thy Holy Name unto the nations of the earth, by means of thy wondrous redemption and salvation of thy people Israel, which remains a memorable event even unto this day.

After that, thy children entered thy sanctuary at Jerusalem, cleansed it from all the defilements of idolatry, reëstablished thy service, illuminated the courts of thy temple, and appointed these eight days of Chanuckah for the praise and glorification of thy great Name.

Service for the Eve of Sabbaths and Festivals. 38

(*On the Penitential Days.*)

בְּסֵפֶר חַיִּים בְּרָכָה וְשָׁלוֹם וּפַרְנָסָה טוֹבָה. נִזָּכֵר וְנִכָּתֵב לְפָנֶיךָ אֲנַחְנוּ וְכָל עַמְּךָ בֵּית יִשְׂרָאֵל לְחַיִּים טוֹבִים וּלְשָׁלוֹם.

בָּרוּךְ אַתָּה יְיָ עוֹשֵׂה הַשָּׁלוֹם:

אֱלֹהַי נְצוֹר לְשׁוֹנִי מֵרָע וּשְׂפָתַי מִדַּבֵּר מִרְמָה. וְלִמְקַלְלַי נַפְשִׁי תִדּוֹם. וְנַפְשִׁי כֶּעָפָר לַכֹּל תִּהְיֶה: פְּתַח לִבִּי בְּתוֹרָתֶךָ וּבְמִצְוֹתֶיךָ תִּרְדּוֹף נַפְשִׁי. וְכֹל הַחוֹשְׁבִים עָלַי רָעָה מְהֵרָה הָפֵר עֲצָתָם וְקַלְקֵל מַחֲשַׁבְתָּם: עֲשֵׂה לְמַעַן שְׁמֶךָ. עֲשֵׂה לְמַעַן יְמִינֶךָ. עֲשֵׂה לְמַעַן קְדֻשָּׁתֶךָ. עֲשֵׂה לְמַעַן תּוֹרָתֶךָ. לְמַעַן יֵחָלְצוּן יְדִידֶיךָ הוֹשִׁיעָה יְמִינְךָ וַעֲנֵנִי: יִהְיוּ לְרָצוֹן אִמְרֵי־פִי וְהֶגְיוֹן לִבִּי לְפָנֶיךָ יְיָ צוּרִי וְגוֹאֲלִי: עֹשֶׂה שָׁלוֹם בִּמְרוֹמָיו הוּא יַעֲשֶׂה שָׁלוֹם עָלֵינוּ וְעַל כָּל־יִשְׂרָאֵל. אָמֵן:

(*On the Penitential Days.*)

(And especially on these solemn days of penitence do we pray thee to remember and inscribe us, and all the people of the house of Israel, in the book of life, blessing, peace, and prosperity.)

Praised be thou, O Lord, the never-failing fount of peace. Amen!

O my God! guard my tongue from evil and my lips from uttering deceit. Grant me forbearance unto those who deal ill towards me, and a calm and meek disposition unto all my fellow-beings. Open my heart to receive thy sacred teachings, so that my conduct may evidence the fulfillment of thy commandments. Frustrate the plans and destroy the devices of all those who meditate evil against me, for the sake of thy Holy Name. May the words I have uttered and the meditations of my heart be acceptable before thee, O Lord, my Rock and my Redeemer; and mayest thou, who causest peace to reign on high, grant peace unto us and all Israel. Amen!

11. PRAYERS IN MEMORY OF THE DEAD.

Reader.

Every believer in God, whose unity it is the mission of Israel to proclaim, will partake of the everlasting life of futurity, as we read in the Holy Scriptures: "Thy people are all the righteous, and will inherit the eternal kingdom." Happy is he who adheres to the law and performs the will of his Creator; he will gain a good name while living, and will depart from earth with a good name. Of him it is said: "Better is the fragrance of a good name than the perfume of precious oil; even better is the day of death (to him) than the day of birth." In the paths of virtue there is life, and in its ways there is immortality.

Yea, there is a future where thy hope will not be cut off; for know that it is in the world to come that the righteous will find their complete reward.

כָּל־יִשְׂרָאֵל יֵשׁ לָהֶם חֵלֶק לְעוֹלָם הַבָּא. שֶׁנֶּאֱמַר וְעַמֵּךְ כֻּלָּם צַדִּיקִים. לְעוֹלָם יִירְשׁוּ אָרֶץ: אַשְׁרֵי מִי שֶׁעָמְלוּ בַתּוֹרָה. וְעָשָׂה רְצוֹן יוֹצְרוֹ. גָּדַל בְּשֵׁם טוֹב. וְנִפְטָר בְּשֵׁם טוֹב מִן הָעוֹלָם. וְעָלָיו נֶאֱמַר טוֹב שֵׁם מִשֶּׁמֶן טוֹב וְיוֹם הַמָּוֶת מִיּוֹם הִוָּלְדוֹ: בְּאֹרַח צְדָקָה חַיִּים וְדֶרֶךְ נְתִיבָה אַל־מָוֶת: כִּי אִם־יֵשׁ אַחֲרִית וְתִקְוָתְךָ לֹא תִכָּרֵת: וְדַע שֶׁמַּתַּן שְׂכָרָם שֶׁל צַדִּיקִים לֶעָתִיד לָבֹא:

(Mourners, and those observing the anniversary of a parent's death, will rise and say with the Reader, in a low voice, the *Kaddish* on the following page.)

תפלת ערבית לשבת ולרגלים

Reader and Mourners.

12. יִתְגַּדַּל וְיִתְקַדַּ"שׁ שְׁמֵהּ רַבָּא. בְּעָלְמָא דִּי־בְרָא כִרְעוּתֵהּ וְיַמְלִיךְ מַלְכוּתֵהּ בְּחַיֵּיכוֹן וּבְיוֹמֵיכוֹן וּבְחַיֵּי דְכָל בֵּית יִשְׂרָאֵל בַּעֲגָלָא וּבִזְמַן קָרִיב וְאִמְרוּ אָמֵן:

Congregation.

אָמֵן יְהֵא שְׁמֵהּ רַבָּא מְבָרַךְ לְעָלַם וּלְעָלְמֵי עָלְמַיָּא.

Reader and Mourners.

יִתְבָּרַךְ וְיִשְׁתַּבַּח וְיִתְפָּאַר וְיִתְרוֹמַם וְיִתְנַשֵּׂא וְיִתְהַדָּר וְיִתְעַלֶּה וְיִתְהַלָּל שְׁמֵהּ דְּקוּדְשָׁא בְּרִיךְ הוּא לְעֵלָּא מִן כָּל־בִּרְכָתָא וְשִׁירָתָא תֻּשְׁבְּחָתָא וְנֶחָמָתָא דַּאֲמִירָן בְּעָלְמָא וְאִמְרוּ אָמֵן:

Read. תִּתְקַבַּל צְלוֹתְהוֹן וּבָעוּתְהוֹן דְּכָל יִשְׂרָאֵל. קֳדָם אֲבוּהוֹן דִּי בִשְׁמַיָּא. וְאִמְרוּ אָמֵן:)

Reader and Mourners.

עַל יִשְׂרָאֵל וְעַל צַדִּיקַיָּא. וְעַל כָּל מָן דְּאִתְפְּטַר מִן עָלְמָא הָדֵין כִּרְעוּתֵהּ דֶּאֱלָהָא. יְהֵא לְהוֹן שְׁלָמָא רַבָּא. וְחוּלָקָא טָבָא לְחַיֵּי עָלְמָא דְאָתֵי. וְחִסְדָּא וְרַחֲמֵי כֵּן קֳדָם מָרֵא שְׁמַיָּא וְאַרְעָא. וְאִמְרוּ אָמֵן:

יְהֵא שְׁלָמָא רַבָּא מִן שְׁמַיָּא וְחַיִּים טוֹבִים עָלֵינוּ וְעַל־כָּל־יִשְׂרָאֵל. וְאִמְרוּ אָמֵן:

עֹשֶׂה שָׁלוֹם בִּמְרוֹמָיו. הוּא בְּרַחֲמָיו יַעֲשֶׂה שָׁלוֹם עָלֵינוּ. וְעַל כָּל־יִשְׂרָאֵל. וְאִמְרוּ אָמֵן:

Reader and Mourners.

12. Let the great Name of the Eternal be exalted and sanctified throughout the whole universe, which he hath created according to his will. May his kingdom soon be established in the whole earth, and may you and all Israel live to partake of the blessings of that happy period. Unto which say ye, Amen!

Congregation.

Amen! May his great Name be praised for ever and unto all eternity

Reader and Mourners.

Yea, let us praise and worship, magnify and exalt the Name of the Most Holy, (blessed be he,) whose glory exceedeth all the praises and hymns that may be rendered unto him by human lips. And let us say, Amen!

Reader.

May the prayer and supplications of the whole house of Israel be accepted in the presence of their Father in heaven. And say ye, Amen!

Reader and Mourners.

O that Israel and all the righteous who have departed from this world, and all those who bow with submission to God's inscrutable will, may enjoy the fullness of peace and happiness in the world to come. May they obtain mercy and forgiveness from the Lord of heaven and earth. And say ye, Amen!

And may the fullness of heavenly peace and a happy life on earth be granted unto us and all Israel. And say ye, Amen!

May he who causeth peace to reign on high, cause peace to prevail among us and all Israel. And say ye, Amen!

Service for the Eve of Sabbaths and Festivals. 42

CONCLUDING PRAYER.

It is a duty incumbent on us to praise the Sovereign Lord of the universe, to give honor unto him, who is the Creator of heaven and earth, who hath removed us from idolatry and superstition, and brought us to the knowledge of light and truth, which have become our happy portion in his service.

(Choir and Congregation rise.)

WE BEND THE KNEE, BOW DOWN, AND GIVE HOMAGE TO THE SUPREME KING, THE MOST HOLY. BLESSED BE HE.

(The Congregation take their seats.)

He hath stretched out the heavens and established the earth, and the residence of his glory is most exalted, even in the heavens above. He is God, and none besides.

Choir and Congregation.

HE IS GOD, AND NONE BESIDES.

Yea, it is an eternal truth that he is our King, and none besides him; for thus is it written in the law: "Know thou this day, and take to heart, that the Eternal is God in the heavens above and on the earth beneath, and there is none else."

We therefore trust speedily to behold thy triumphant glory, O Lord our God, when idolatry will be exterminated from the earth, and the clouds of doubt and error be entirely dispelled. Then will the whole universe recognize thy glorious kingdom, all mankind will acknowledge and call upon thy Name, and every sinner turn in penitence to thee. Yea, all will then know and understand, that before thee alone must every knee bend, to thee alone must every tongue swear fealty, all prostrating themselves and giving honor to thy most Holy Name. All will acknowledge thy dominion, and thou wilt be their Sovereign Ruler for evermore. For thine is the kingdom, and for ever wilt thou reign in glory, as it is written in thy law, "The Lord will reign for ever and ever;" and furthermore is it written, "The Everlasting will be King over all the earth; on that day will it be acknowledged that the Lord is ONE, and his name ONE."

Choir and Congregation.

ON THAT DAY THE LORD EVERLASTING
WILL BE ONE, AND HIS NAME ONE.

BENEDICTION.

May the blessing of Divine Providence rest upon you all, O congregation.

"The Lord bless and preserve thee. The Lord cause his countenance to shine upon thee, and be gracious unto thee. The Lord lift up his countenance unto thee, and grant thee peace."

"May peace abide within thy walls, prosperity within thy habitations."

May the Eternal bless the President of the United States and all the constituted authorities, the Governor and officers of this State and this city, that through them order may be preserved, and right and liberty be fostered.

May the Almighty God send unto you and your dear ones the blessings of his day of rest (the delight of his festivals), that the sacred observance of the Sabbath (of this festive day) may impress you with increased faith and fill your souls with heavenly peace. O Lord, give strength unto thy people, bless thy people with peace! Amen!

Choir and Congregation.

HIS PEOPLE'S STRENGTH WILL HE INCREASE,
AND BLESS THEM EVERMORE WITH PEACE! AMEN.

תפלת שחרית
לשבת ולרגלים

1. אֱלֹהַי נְשָׁמָה שֶׁנָּתַתָּ בִּי טְהוֹרָה הִיא. אַתָּה בְרָאתָהּ. אַתָּה יְצַרְתָּהּ. אַתָּה נְפַחְתָּהּ בִּי. וְאַתָּה מְשַׁמְּרָהּ בְּקִרְבִּי. וְאַתָּה עָתִיד לִטְּלָהּ מִמֶּנִּי. וּלְהַחֲזִירָהּ לֶעָתִיד לָבֹא: כָּל־זְמַן שֶׁהַנְּשָׁמָה בְקִרְבִּי מוֹדֶה אֲנִי לְפָנֶיךָ. יְיָ אֱלֹהַי וֵאלֹהֵי אֲבוֹתַי. בָּרוּךְ אַתָּה יְיָ רִבּוֹן כָּל־הַמַּעֲשִׂים אֲדוֹן כָּל־הַנְּשָׁמוֹת:

---

2. בָּרוּךְ אַתָּה יְיָ אֱלֹהֵינוּ מֶלֶךְ הָעוֹלָם. אֲשֶׁר נָתַן לַשֶּׂכְוִי בִינָה לְהַבְחִין בֵּין יוֹם וּבֵין לָיְלָה:

בָּרוּךְ אַתָּה יְיָ אֱלֹהֵינוּ מֶלֶךְ הָעוֹלָם. שֶׁעָשַׂנִי יִשְׂרָאֵל:

בָּרוּךְ אַתָּה יְיָ אֱלֹהֵינוּ מֶלֶךְ הָעוֹלָם. פּוֹקֵחַ עִוְרִים:

בָּרוּךְ אַתָּה יְיָ אֱלֹהֵינוּ מֶלֶךְ הָעוֹלָם. מַתִּיר אֲסוּרִים:

בָּרוּךְ אַתָּה יְיָ אֱלֹהֵינוּ מֶלֶךְ הָעוֹלָם. זוֹקֵף כְּפוּפִים:

בָּרוּךְ אַתָּה יְיָ אֱלֹהֵינוּ מֶלֶךְ הָעוֹלָם. אוֹזֵר יִשְׂרָאֵל בִּגְבוּרָה:

בָּרוּךְ אַתָּה יְיָ אֱלֹהֵינוּ מֶלֶךְ הָעוֹלָם. עוֹטֵר יִשְׂרָאֵל בְּתִפְאָרָה:

SERVICE FOR THE MORNING OF SABBATHS AND FESTIVALS.

1. My God, the soul which thou hast placed in my body is pure, for it is a portion of thy Holy Spirit, an emanation from thee, who art the fountain of purity. Thou hast created it and formed it. Thou hast breathed it into me, and dost carefully guard it within me. When thou seest fit, thou wilt take it from me, but wilt restore it in the eternal happiness of the future world. Whilst this soul shall continue within me will I adore thee, O Lord my God, and God of my fathers. Blessed be thou, O Lord, Author of all works, Source of all souls.

2. Blessed be thou, O Lord our God, Ruler of the universe, who hast given to man intelligence to distinguish between day and night.
Blessed be thou, O Lord our God, Ruler of the universe, who didst grant me the privilege of being born in the faith of Israel.
Blessed be thou, O Lord our God, Ruler of the universe, who removest the bonds of darkness from the eyes of the blind.
Blessed be thou, O Lord our God, Ruler of the universe, who loosenest the fetters of the oppressed.
Blessed be thou, O Lord our God, Ruler of the universe, who raisest up those who are cast down.
Blessed be thou, O Lord our God, Ruler of the universe, who girdest Israel with the strength of faith.
Blessed be thou, O Lord our God, Ruler of the universe, who crownest Israel with the diadem of their priestly mission.

תפלת שחרית לשבת ולרגלים

יְהִי רָצוֹן מִלְּפָנֶיךָ יְיָ אֱלֹהֵינוּ וֵאלֹהֵי אֲבוֹתֵינוּ. שֶׁתַּרְגִּילֵנוּ בְּתוֹרָתֶךָ. וְדַבְּקֵנוּ בְּמִצְוֹתֶיךָ. וְאַל תְּבִיאֵנוּ לֹא לִידֵי נִסָּיוֹן וְלֹא לִידֵי בִזָּיוֹן. וְהַרְחִיקֵנוּ מֵאָדָם רָע וּמֵחָבֵר רָע. וְדַבְּקֵנוּ בְּיֵצֶר הַטּוֹב וּבְמַעֲשִׂים טוֹבִים. וְכוֹף אֶת־יִצְרֵנוּ לְהִשְׁתַּעְבֶּד־לָךְ. וּתְנֵנוּ הַיּוֹם וּבְכָל־יוֹם לְחֵן וּלְחֶסֶד וּלְרַחֲמִים בְּעֵינֶיךָ וּבְעֵינֵי כָל־רוֹאֵנוּ. וְתִגְמְלֵנוּ חֲסָדִים טוֹבִים. בָּרוּךְ אַתָּה יְיָ גּוֹמֵל חֲסָדִים טוֹבִים:

---

3. בָּרוּךְ שֶׁאָמַר וְהָיָה הָעוֹלָם. בָּרוּךְ עוֹשֶׂה בְרֵאשִׁית. בָּרוּךְ אוֹמֵר וְעוֹשֶׂה. בָּרוּךְ גּוֹזֵר וּמְקַיֵּם. בָּרוּךְ מְרַחֵם עַל הָאָרֶץ. בָּרוּךְ כִּי רַחֵם עַל הַבְּרִיּוֹת. בָּרוּךְ מְשַׁלֵּם שָׂכָר טוֹב לִירֵאָיו. בָּרוּךְ חַי לָעַד וְקַיָּם לָנֶצַח. בָּרוּךְ פּוֹדֶה וּמַצִּיל. בָּרוּךְ הוּא וּבָרוּךְ שְׁמוֹ:

בָּרוּךְ אַתָּה יְיָ אֱלֹהֵינוּ מֶלֶךְ הָעוֹלָם. הָאֵל הָאָב הָרַחֲמָן הַמְהֻלָּל בְּפִי עַמּוֹ מְשֻׁבָּח וּמְפֹאָר בִּלְשׁוֹן חֲסִידָיו וַעֲבָדָיו. וּבְשִׁירֵי דָוִד עַבְדְּךָ נְהַלֶּלְךָ יְיָ אֱלֹהֵינוּ בִּשְׁבָחוֹת וּבִזְמִירוֹת נְגַדֶּלְךָ וּנְשַׁבֵּחֲךָ וּנְפָאֶרְךָ וְנַזְכִּיר שִׁמְךָ וְנַמְלִיכְךָ מַלְכֵּנוּ אֱלֹהֵינוּ יָחִיד חֵי הָעוֹלָמִים. מֶלֶךְ מְשֻׁבָּח וּמְפֹאָר עֲדֵי־עַד שְׁמוֹ הַגָּדוֹל. בָּרוּךְ אַתָּה יְיָ מֶלֶךְ מְהֻלָּל בַּתִּשְׁבָּחוֹת:

Service for the Morning of Sabbaths and Festivals.

Be pleased to assist us, O Lord! that we may be instrumental in furthering the glorious aims of Israel, by walking in thy law and firmly adhering to thy precepts. Suffer us not to fall into temptation or disgrace, but do thou animate our hearts with lofty impulses, and endue us with strength to subject our inclinations to thy divine will. Grant that our purity of life may obtain for us grace, favor, and benevolence in thy sight and in the sight of all mankind, and that we may enjoy the abundance of thy beneficence. Blessed be thou, O Lord! who bestowest bountifully goodness and beneficence. Amen.

---

8. Blessed be he, at whose word the world was called into existence. Blessed be he who fulfills what he promises, and establishes what he ordains. Blessed be he who provides the earth with marks of his mercy for all who dwell thereon. Blessed be he who bestows a good reward upon those who fear him. Blessed be the ever-living and all-powerful God, the deliverer and redeemer of all mankind. *Blessed be he, and blessed be his name!*

Blessed be thou, O Lord our God, Ruler of the universe, the almighty and all-merciful Father, who accordest unto thy people and those who fear thee the privilege of praising thy loving kindness. And with the psalms of David, thy faithful servant, will we extol thy great name; with songs and hymns will we render homage unto our King, the only God, the Source of all life! unto whom be praise and glory now and for evermore. Blessed be thou, O Lord and King, for the blissful privilege we enjoy of chanting thy praises and glory. Amen.

תפלת שחרית לשבת ולרגלים

ON SABBATHS.

(תהלים צ״ב צ״ג)

מִזְמוֹר שִׁיר לְיוֹם הַשַּׁבָּת:

Choir and Congregation.

טוֹב לְהֹדוֹת לַיְיָ וּלְזַמֵּר לְשִׁמְךָ עֶלְיוֹן: לְהַגִּיד בַּבֹּקֶר חַסְדֶּךָ וֶאֱמוּנָתְךָ בַּלֵּילוֹת: עֲלֵי עָשׂוֹר וַעֲלֵי־נָבֶל עֲלֵי הִגָּיוֹן בְּכִנּוֹר: כִּי שִׂמַּחְתַּנִי יְיָ בְּפָעֳלֶךָ בְּמַעֲשֵׂי יָדֶיךָ אֲרַנֵּן:

מַה־גָּדְלוּ מַעֲשֶׂיךָ יְיָ מְאֹד עָמְקוּ מַחְשְׁבֹתֶיךָ: אִישׁ בַּעַר לֹא יֵדָע וּכְסִיל לֹא־יָבִין אֶת־זֹאת: בִּפְרֹחַ רְשָׁעִים כְּמוֹ־עֵשֶׂב וַיָּצִיצוּ כָּל־פֹּעֲלֵי אָוֶן לְהִשָּׁמְדָם עֲדֵי־עַד:

Choir and Congregation.

וְאַתָּה מָרוֹם לְעֹלָם יְיָ:

כִּי הִנֵּה אֹיְבֶיךָ יְיָ כִּי־הִנֵּה אֹיְבֶיךָ יֹאבֵדוּ יִתְפָּרְדוּ כָּל־פֹּעֲלֵי אָוֶן: וַתָּרֶם כִּרְאֵים קַרְנִי בַּלֹּתִי בְּשֶׁמֶן רַעֲנָן: וַתַּבֵּט עֵינִי בְּשׁוּרָי בַּקָּמִים עָלַי מְרֵעִים תִּשְׁמַעְנָה אָזְנָי: צַדִּיק כַּתָּמָר יִפְרָח כְּאֶרֶז בַּלְּבָנוֹן יִשְׂגֶּה: שְׁתוּלִים בְּבֵית יְיָ בְּחַצְרוֹת אֱלֹהֵינוּ יַפְרִיחוּ: עוֹד יְנוּבוּן בְּשֵׂיבָה דְּשֵׁנִים וְרַעֲנַנִּים יִהְיוּ: לְהַגִּיד כִּי־יָשָׁר יְיָ צוּרִי וְלֹא־עַוְלָתָה בּוֹ:

Choir and Congregation.

לְהַגִּיד כִּי־יָשָׁר יְיָ צוּרִי וְלֹא־עַוְלָתָה בּוֹ:

ON SABBATHS.
(*Psalm* 92.)

4. *R'dr.*—Sing ye the song of the Sabbath day!

Ch. & Cong.—How good thy mercies to record
In grateful songs, Almighty Lord;
Thy watchful care by morning light,
Thy never-failing truth by night;
From decachord to sound acclaim,
With lyre and harp to sing thy Name!
For thou hast made thy works my joy,
Thy doings shall my praise employ.

R'dr.—How great the wonders thou hast wrought!
Thy counsels are a deep of thought,
Which brutish men cannot discern,
And fools will neither know nor learn.
Though sinners thrive and prosper here,
And wicked men in bloom appear,
They only spring for death a prey,
And lo! they flee and fade away;
For they will not thy Name adore,

Ch. & Cong.—MOST HIGH AND BLESSED
FOR EVERMORE.

R'dr.—Lord, in thy strength exalt my horn,
And with fresh oil my head adorn;
Then foes turned back mine eye shall cheer,
Their ruin shall salute mine ear;
For righteous men shall grow like palms,
Like lofty cedars stretch their arms.
Those planted in the courts of God
Shall flourish in his blest abode;
They shall in age with fruit abound,
And ever blooming shall be found;

Ch. & Cong.—TO SHOW THAT GOD, MY ROCK OF MIGHT,
IN ALL HIS DEALINGS IS UPRIGHT.

ON PASSOVER.

(תהלים ל״ד)

אֲבָרְכָה אֶת־יְיָ בְּכָל־עֵת תָּמִיד תְּהִלָּתוֹ בְּפִי: בַּיָי תִּתְהַלֵּל נַפְשִׁי יִשְׁמְעוּ עֲנָוִים וְיִשְׂמָחוּ: גַּדְּלוּ לַיָי אִתִּי וּנְרוֹמְמָה שְׁמוֹ יַחְדָּו: דָּרַשְׁתִּי אֶת־יְיָ וְעָנָנִי וּמִכָּל־מְגוּרוֹתַי הִצִּילָנִי: הִבִּיטוּ אֵלָיו וְנָהָרוּ וּפְנֵיהֶם אַל־יֶחְפָּרוּ: זֶה עָנִי קָרָא וַיְיָ שָׁמֵעַ וּמִכָּל־צָרוֹתָיו הוֹשִׁיעוֹ: חֹנֶה מַלְאַךְ יְיָ סָבִיב לִירֵאָיו וַיְחַלְּצֵם: טַעֲמוּ וּרְאוּ כִּי־טוֹב יְיָ אַשְׁרֵי הַגֶּבֶר יֶחֱסֶה־בּוֹ: יְראוּ אֶת־יְיָ קְדֹשָׁיו כִּי־אֵין מַחְסוֹר לִירֵאָיו: כְּפִירִים רָשׁוּ וְרָעֵבוּ וְדֹרְשֵׁי יְיָ לֹא־יַחְסְרוּ כָל־טוֹב: לְכוּ בָנִים שִׁמְעוּ־לִי יִרְאַת יְיָ אֲלַמֶּדְכֶם: מִי הָאִישׁ הֶחָפֵץ חַיִּים אֹהֵב יָמִים לִרְאוֹת טוֹב: נְצֹר לְשׁוֹנְךָ מֵרָע וּשְׂפָתֶיךָ מִדַּבֵּר מִרְמָה: סוּר מֵרָע וַעֲשֵׂה־טוֹב בַּקֵּשׁ שָׁלוֹם וְרָדְפֵהוּ: עֵינֵי יְיָ אֶל־צַדִּיקִים וְאָזְנָיו אֶל־שַׁוְעָתָם: פְּנֵי יְיָ בְּעֹשֵׂי רָע לְהַכְרִית מֵאֶרֶץ זִכְרָם: צָעֲקוּ וַיְיָ שָׁמֵעַ וּמִכָּל־צָרוֹתָם הִצִּילָם: קָרוֹב יְיָ לְנִשְׁבְּרֵי־לֵב וְאֶת־דַּכְּאֵי־רוּחַ יוֹשִׁיעַ: רַבּוֹת רָעוֹת צַדִּיק וּמִכֻּלָּם יַצִּילֶנּוּ יְיָ: שֹׁמֵר כָּל־עַצְמוֹתָיו אַחַת מֵהֵנָּה לֹא נִשְׁבָּרָה: תְּמוֹתֵת רָשָׁע רָעָה וְשֹׂנְאֵי צַדִּיק יֶאְשָׁמוּ: פֹּדֶה יְיָ נֶפֶשׁ עֲבָדָיו וְלֹא יֶאְשְׁמוּ כָּל־הַחֹסִים בּוֹ:

ON PASSOVER.

(Psalm 34.)

5. At all times I will bless the Lord, || His praise shall tune my voice. || He is my glory; hear the word, || Ye humble, and rejoice! || Come, help me laud || Our gracious God, || Exalt him as our choice. || The Lord relieved me from all fright || In answer to my prayers. || Men look to him, their eyes grow bright, || and no reproach is theirs. || This poor man's cry || Was heard on high, || And he was saved from cares. || His angels round his fearers move || To save them when distressed. || Come, taste and see how great his love! || Blest all who on him rest. || Young lions may || In vain seek prey; || Who seek the Lord are blest. || Come, children, hearken to my lays, || I'll teach his fear to you. || What man desires a length of days, || And would be prospered too? — || Thy lips restrain, || From guile refrain, || Do good, and peace pursue! — || His ears to all the just are bowed, || His eyes to them inclined. || His face is set against the proud, || To cast their name behind. || But he is near || The crushed to cheer, || The broken heart to bind. || Around the just lurk many woes, || From all saves God alone. || But sin the sinner overthrows; || In gloom the wicked moan. || The Lord sets clear || His servants here, || Redeems them for his own.

תפלת שחרית לשבת ולרגלים

ON SHABUOTH.
(תהלים י״ט)

6. הַשָּׁמַיִם מְסַפְּרִים כְּבוֹד־אֵל וּמַעֲשֵׂה יָדָיו מַגִּיד הָרָקִיעַ: יוֹם לְיוֹם יַבִּיעַ אֹמֶר וְלַיְלָה לְלַיְלָה יְחַוֶּה־דָּעַת: אֵין אֹמֶר וְאֵין דְּבָרִים בְּלִי נִשְׁמָע קוֹלָם: בְּכָל־הָאָרֶץ ׀ יָצָא קַוָּם וּבִקְצֵה תֵבֵל מִלֵּיהֶם לַשֶּׁמֶשׁ שָׂם אֹהֶל בָּהֶם: וְהוּא כְּחָתָן יֹצֵא מֵחֻפָּתוֹ יָשִׂישׂ כְּגִבּוֹר לָרוּץ אֹרַח: מִקְצֵה הַשָּׁמַיִם מוֹצָאוֹ וּתְקוּפָתוֹ עַל־קְצוֹתָם וְאֵין נִסְתָּר מֵחַמָּתוֹ:

תּוֹרַת יְיָ תְּמִימָה מְשִׁיבַת נָפֶשׁ
עֵדוּת יְיָ נֶאֱמָנָה מַחְכִּימַת פֶּתִי:

פִּקּוּדֵי יְיָ יְשָׁרִים מְשַׂמְּחֵי־לֵב
מִצְוַת יְיָ בָּרָה מְאִירַת עֵינָיִם:

יִרְאַת יְיָ ׀ טְהוֹרָה עוֹמֶדֶת לָעַד
מִשְׁפְּטֵי־יְיָ אֱמֶת צָדְקוּ יַחְדָּו:

הַנֶּחֱמָדִים מִזָּהָב וּמִפַּז רָב
וּמְתוּקִים מִדְּבַשׁ וְנֹפֶת צוּפִים:

גַּם־עַבְדְּךָ נִזְהָר בָּהֶם בְּשָׁמְרָם עֵקֶב רָב: שְׁגִיאוֹת מִי־יָבִין מִנִּסְתָּרוֹת נַקֵּנִי: גַּם מִזֵּדִים חֲשֹׂךְ עַבְדֶּךָ אַל־יִמְשְׁלוּ־בִי אָז אֵיתָם וְנִקֵּיתִי מִפֶּשַׁע רָב: יִהְיוּ לְרָצוֹן אִמְרֵי־פִי וְהֶגְיוֹן לִבִּי לְפָנֶיךָ יְיָ צוּרִי וְגֹאֲלִי:

ON SHABUOTH.
(Psalm 19.)

6. The heavens declare the praise of God, ‖ The skies show forth his work abroad, ‖ Day unto day shall utter speech, ‖ And night to night shall knowledge teach. ‖ No form of language strikes the ear, ‖ No vocal sound is there to hear. ‖ Their words through all the world are gone, ‖ Their line is round creation drawn. ‖ In them he gave the sun his place. ‖ Lo, he appears in bridal grace, ‖ When from his chamber forth he hies ‖ In giant strength to course the skies. ‖ He starts from where the heavens end, ‖ His circuits to their term extend. ‖ His rays light up the world complete, ‖ And nought is hidden from his heat.

> The law of God is pure in plan,
> And renovates the soul of man.
> His words of truth, without disguise,
> Have power to make the simple wise.
> His statutes are conceived in right,
> And yield the heart a sweet delight.
> The Lord's commands with clearness shine,
> Invest the eyes with light divine.
> The fear of God is clean and pure,
> It shall from age to age endure.
> His judgments strike the wondering view,
> Are altogether just and true.
> Their worth is priceless, is untold,
> Their value is above fine gold.
> Their sweetness, too, doth far excel
> The purest honey from the cell.

Their warning is to me a guard; ‖ In keeping them is great reward. ‖ But who can guard 'gainst sins unknown? ‖ Lord, thou wilt clear me, thou alone. ‖ Oh, hush the passions' storm within, ‖ That I be faultless, clear from sin. ‖ What my mouth speaks, what thinks my heart, ‖ Accept, O Lord! My rock thou art.

ON SUCCOTH AND SH'MINI ATZERETH.

(תהלים ל״ג)

רַנְּנוּ צַדִּיקִים בַּיְיָ לַיְשָׁרִים נָאוָה תְהִלָּה: הוֹדוּ לַיְיָ בְּכִנּוֹר בְּנֵבֶל עָשׂוֹר זַמְּרוּ־לוֹ: שִׁירוּ לוֹ שִׁיר חָדָשׁ הֵיטִיבוּ נַגֵּן בִּתְרוּעָה: כִּי־יָשָׁר דְּבַר־יְיָ וְכָל־מַעֲשֵׂהוּ בֶּאֱמוּנָה: אֹהֵב צְדָקָה וּמִשְׁפָּט חֶסֶד יְיָ מָלְאָה הָאָרֶץ: בִּדְבַר יְיָ שָׁמַיִם נַעֲשׂוּ וּבְרוּחַ פִּיו כָּל־צְבָאָם: כֹּנֵס כַּנֵּד מֵי הַיָּם נֹתֵן בְּאוֹצָרוֹת תְּהוֹמוֹת: יִירְאוּ מֵיְיָ כָּל־הָאָרֶץ מִמֶּנּוּ יָגוּרוּ כָּל־יֹשְׁבֵי תֵבֵל: כִּי הוּא אָמַר וַיֶּהִי הוּא צִוָּה וַיַּעֲמֹד: יְיָ הֵפִיר עֲצַת גּוֹיִם הֵנִיא מַחְשְׁבוֹת עַמִּים: עֲצַת יְיָ לְעוֹלָם תַּעֲמֹד מַחְשְׁבוֹת לִבּוֹ לְדֹר וָדֹר: אַשְׁרֵי הַגּוֹי אֲשֶׁר־יְיָ אֱלֹהָיו הָעָם בָּחַר לְנַחֲלָה לוֹ: מִשָּׁמַיִם הִבִּיט יְיָ רָאָה אֶת־כָּל־בְּנֵי הָאָדָם: מִמְּכוֹן־שִׁבְתּוֹ הִשְׁגִּיחַ אֶל כָּל־יֹשְׁבֵי הָאָרֶץ: הַיֹּצֵר יַחַד לִבָּם הַמֵּבִין אֶל־כָּל־מַעֲשֵׂיהֶם: אֵין הַמֶּלֶךְ נוֹשָׁע בְּרָב־חָיִל גִּבּוֹר לֹא־יִנָּצֵל בְּרָב־כֹּחַ: שֶׁקֶר הַסּוּס לִתְשׁוּעָה וּבְרֹב חֵילוֹ לֹא יְמַלֵּט: הִנֵּה עֵין יְיָ אֶל־יְרֵאָיו לַמְיַחֲלִים לְחַסְדּוֹ: לְהַצִּיל מִמָּוֶת נַפְשָׁם וּלְחַיּוֹתָם בָּרָעָב: נַפְשֵׁנוּ חִכְּתָה לַיְיָ עֶזְרֵנוּ וּמָגִנֵּנוּ הוּא: כִּי־בוֹ יִשְׂמַח לִבֵּנוּ כִּי בְשֵׁם קָדְשׁוֹ בָטָחְנוּ: יְהִי חַסְדְּךָ יְיָ עָלֵינוּ כַּאֲשֶׁר יִחַלְנוּ לָךְ:

ON SUCCOTH AND SH'MINI ATZERETH.
(*Psalm* 33.)

7. Exult, ye righteous, in the Lord, || His praise becometh you; || Wake up ten strings, the harp and chord, || With songs sublime and new. || His word is straight, and true his deeds, || In justice he delights. || His mercy o'er all earth proceeds, || A sun by days and nights. || His word the heaven's high arches reared, || His breath their hosts arrayed, || A storehouse for the sea prepared, || And deep on deep has laid. || Let all earth fear the Mighty God, || Her sons be filled with awe! || When he said "Be," lo, there it stood, || And all obeyed his law. || The Lord did quell the nations' rage, || The peoples' plans make vain. || His counsels stand from age to age, || And his designs remain. || O happy nation, truly blest, || Whose God the Eternal is, || A heritage by him possessed || And chosen to be his! || On all mankind his glances dart, || He sees them from his throne; || To him, the moulder of the heart, || The deeds of all are known. || The king no numerous armies save, || The valiant not his might; || Vain is the steed, though nerved and brave, || For victory or for flight. || He looks on those with kind esteem || Who on his grace rely, || And will their souls from death redeem, || In famine food supply. || He is our stay, our help and shield, || In him our souls confide. || To heartfelt joys our cares will yield, || For his name is our guide. || Thy grace to us may be revealed, || As we in thee abide!

(תהלים קמ״ה)

8. אֲרוֹמִמְךָ אֱלוֹהַי הַמֶּלֶךְ וַאֲבָרְכָה שִׁמְךָ לְעוֹלָם וָעֶד: בְּכָל־יוֹם אֲבָרְכֶךָּ וַאֲהַלְלָה שִׁמְךָ לְעוֹלָם וָעֶד: גָּדוֹל יְיָ וּמְהֻלָּל מְאֹד וְלִגְדֻלָּתוֹ אֵין חֵקֶר: דּוֹר לְדוֹר יְשַׁבַּח מַעֲשֶׂיךָ וּגְבוּרֹתֶיךָ יַגִּידוּ: הֲדַר כְּבוֹד הוֹדֶךָ וְדִבְרֵי נִפְלְאֹתֶיךָ אָשִׂיחָה: וֶעֱזוּז נוֹרְאֹתֶיךָ יֹאמֵרוּ וּגְדֻלָּתְךָ אֲסַפְּרֶנָּה: זֵכֶר רַב־טוּבְךָ יַבִּיעוּ וְצִדְקָתְךָ יְרַנֵּנוּ: חַנּוּן וְרַחוּם יְיָ אֶרֶךְ אַפַּיִם וּגְדָל־חָסֶד: טוֹב־יְיָ לַכֹּל וְרַחֲמָיו עַל־כָּל־מַעֲשָׂיו: יוֹדוּךָ יְיָ כָּל־מַעֲשֶׂיךָ וַחֲסִידֶיךָ יְבָרְכוּכָה: כְּבוֹד מַלְכוּתְךָ יֹאמֵרוּ וּגְבוּרָתְךָ יְדַבֵּרוּ: לְהוֹדִיעַ לִבְנֵי הָאָדָם גְּבוּרֹתָיו וּכְבוֹד הֲדַר מַלְכוּתוֹ: מַלְכוּתְךָ מַלְכוּת כָּל־עוֹלָמִים וּמֶמְשַׁלְתְּךָ בְּכָל־דּוֹר וָדֹר: סוֹמֵךְ יְיָ לְכָל־הַנֹּפְלִים וְזוֹקֵף לְכָל־הַכְּפוּפִים: עֵינֵי כֹל אֵלֶיךָ יְשַׂבֵּרוּ וְאַתָּה נוֹתֵן־לָהֶם אֶת־אָכְלָם בְּעִתּוֹ: פּוֹתֵחַ אֶת־יָדֶךָ וּמַשְׂבִּיעַ לְכָל־חַי רָצוֹן: צַדִּיק יְיָ בְּכָל־דְּרָכָיו וְחָסִיד בְּכָל־מַעֲשָׂיו: קָרוֹב יְיָ לְכָל־קֹרְאָיו לְכֹל אֲשֶׁר יִקְרָאֻהוּ בֶאֱמֶת: רְצוֹן־יְרֵאָיו יַעֲשֶׂה וְאֶת־שַׁוְעָתָם יִשְׁמַע וְיוֹשִׁיעֵם: שׁוֹמֵר יְיָ אֶת־כָּל־אֹהֲבָיו וְאֵת כָּל־הָרְשָׁעִים יַשְׁמִיד: תְּהִלַּת יְיָ יְדַבֶּר פִּי וִיבָרֵךְ כָּל־בָּשָׂר שֵׁם קָדְשׁוֹ לְעוֹלָם וָעֶד: וַאֲנַחְנוּ ׀ נְבָרֵךְ יָהּ מֵעַתָּה וְעַד־עוֹלָם הַלְלוּיָהּ:

(*Psalm* 145.)

8. I'll praise thee, Lord, my God and King, || And ever bless thy name, || Day after day untiring sing || and loud extol thy fame. || "Great is the Lord, no search can reach || His might, no word his praise." || Past ages of thy doings preach || And sound thy grand displays. || Like them, thy glorious majesty, || Thy wonders tune *my* song; || And as *they* tell thy victory, || So claims thy might my tongue. || Their memory proclaims thy grace, || And of thy deeds they sing. || "The Lord is gracious to each race, || Kind and long-suffering. || The Lord is good to all abroad, || Lets shine on all his rays." || Oh, may all creatures praise thee, God, || As thy true servants praise! || Let them proclaim thy glorious reign, || To men thy deeds commend. || Thy Kingdom ever shall remain, || Thy rule shall never end. || God lifts the feeble when they fall, || And makes the helpless stand; || He sends supplies of food to all || Who wait upon his hand. || He sends content to all that live, || His treasure ne'er decays; || His works abundant mercy give, || And righteous are his ways. || To answer prayer he's ever nigh || For all who seek aright; || He sends redemption when they cry || Who in his truth delight. || He safely keeps his servants all, || Destroys all wickedness; || His praise, therefore, my lips shall call; || His Name all flesh may bless!

But as to us, we will adore
His Holy Name for evermore. Hallelujah.

תפלת שחרית לשבת ולרגלים

נִשְׁמַת כָּל־חַי תְּבָרֵךְ אֶת־שִׁמְךָ יְיָ אֱלֹהֵינוּ. וְרוּחַ כָּל־בָּשָׂר תְּפָאֵר וּתְרוֹמֵם זִכְרְךָ מַלְכֵּנוּ תָּמִיד. מִן־הָעוֹלָם וְעַד־הָעוֹלָם אַתָּה אֵל. וּמִבַּלְעָדֶיךָ אֵין לָנוּ מֶלֶךְ גּוֹאֵל וּמוֹשִׁיעַ. פּוֹדֶה וּמַצִּיל. וּמְפַרְנֵס וּמְרַחֵם. בְּכָל־עֵת צָרָה וְצוּקָה. אֵין לָנוּ מֶלֶךְ אֶלָּא אָתָּה: אֱלֹהֵי הָרִאשׁוֹנִים וְהָאַחֲרוֹנִים. הַמְנַהֵג עוֹלָמוֹ בְּחֶסֶד וּבְרִיּוֹתָיו בְּרַחֲמִים. לְךָ לְבַדְּךָ אֲנַחְנוּ מוֹדִים: אִלּוּ פִינוּ מָלֵא שִׁירָה כַּיָּם. וּלְשׁוֹנֵנוּ רִנָּה כַּהֲמוֹן גַּלָּיו. וְשִׂפְתוֹתֵינוּ שֶׁבַח כְּמֶרְחֲבֵי רָקִיעַ. אֵין אֲנַחְנוּ מַסְפִּיקִים לְהוֹדוֹת לְךָ יְיָ אֱלֹהֵינוּ וֵאלֹהֵי אֲבוֹתֵינוּ. עַל־כָּל הַטּוֹבוֹת שֶׁעָשִׂיתָ עִם־אֲבוֹתֵינוּ וְעִמָּנוּ: מִמִּצְרַיִם גְּאַלְתָּנוּ יְיָ אֱלֹהֵינוּ. וּמִבֵּית עֲבָדִים פְּדִיתָנוּ. בְּרָעָב זַנְתָּנוּ. וּבְשָׂבָע כִּלְכַּלְתָּנוּ. מֵחֶרֶב הִצַּלְתָּנוּ. וּמִדֶּבֶר מִלַּטְתָּנוּ. וּמֵחֳלָיִם רָעִים וְנֶאֱמָנִים דִּלִּיתָנוּ: עַד־הֵנָּה עֲזָרוּנוּ רַחֲמֶיךָ. וְלֹא־עֲזָבוּנוּ חֲסָדֶיךָ. וְאַל־תִּטְּשֵׁנוּ יְיָ אֱלֹהֵינוּ לָנֶצַח: עַל־כֵּן אֵבָרִים שֶׁפִּלַּגְתָּ בָּנוּ. וְרוּחַ וּנְשָׁמָה שֶׁנָּפַחְתָּ בְּאַפֵּינוּ. וְלָשׁוֹן אֲשֶׁר שַׂמְתָּ בְּפִינוּ. הֵן הֵם יוֹדוּ וִיבָרְכוּ. וִישַׁבְּחוּ וִימַלִּיכוּ אֶת־שִׁמְךָ מַלְכֵּנוּ. כִּי כָל־פֶּה לְךָ יוֹדֶה. וְכָל־לָשׁוֹן לְךָ תִשָּׁבַע. וְכָל־בֶּרֶךְ לְךָ תִכְרַע. וְכָל־קוֹמָה לְפָנֶיךָ תִשְׁתַּחֲוֶה. וְכָל־לְבָבוֹת יִירָאוּךָ. וְכָל־קֶרֶב וּכְלָיוֹת

59   Service for the Morning of Sabbaths and Festivals.

9. The breath of all living shall praise thy Name, O Lord our God, and the spirit of all creatures ever proclaim thy glory. From everlasting unto everlasting is thy existence as the one true God, besides whom we acknowledge no ruler, redeemer, or savior. When visited by trouble and distress, thou didst deliver and rescue us, thou didst sustain us in thy great mercy, because thy providential care is as unending as thyself. From the remotest times hast thou been our shield; yea, unto the latest generations wilt thou be our protector. Thou rulest the whole universe with kindness and fillest thy creatures with love, O Eternal Being, unto whom alone our praises are due. We know that how replete soever human lips may be with praises, or how eloquent the tongue of man, yet could we never adequately express the manifold thanks due unto thee for all the mercies which thou hast bestowed on our ancestors and ourselves. Thou didst deliver us from Egyptian thralldom, and redeem us from the house of bondage. When famine threatened to consume us, thou didst provide food, and didst with plenty sustain us. When the sword was uplifted against us, thou didst protect us. When pestilence visited the earth, and the fierce passions of mankind sought to make us answerable for thy dispensations, thou didst furnish us with a means of escape. Oh! from what numerous evils and long-continued afflictions didst thou protect us! Yea, hitherto have thy tender mercies supported us, and thy kindness hath not forsaken us, neither wilt thou ever abandon us. Therefore shall all our mental and physical energies, all the vital powers with which thou hast endowed us, unite in rendering thanks and praise, homage and adoration unto thy Name, our King and Ruler. Yea, every mouth should thank thee, every tongue adore thee, every knee bend unto thee, and even the most exalted bow down before thee. Every heart

תפלת שחרית לשבת ולרגלים

יְזַמְּרוּ לְשִׁמְךָ. הָאֵל הַגָּדוֹל הַגִּבּוֹר וְהַנּוֹרָא. אֵל עֶלְיוֹן. קֹנֵה שָׁמַיִם וָאָרֶץ:

הַמֶּלֶךְ הַיּוֹשֵׁב עַל כִּסֵּא רָם וְנִשָּׂא:

שׁוֹכֵן עַד מָרוֹם וְקָדוֹשׁ שְׁמוֹ. וְכָתוּב רַנְּנוּ צַדִּיקִים בַּיְיָ לַיְשָׁרִים נָאוָה תְהִלָּה: בְּפִי יְשָׁרִים תִּתְהַלָּל. וּבְדִבְרֵי צַדִּיקִים תִּתְבָּרַךְ. וּבִלְשׁוֹן חֲסִידִים תִּתְרוֹמָם. וּבְקֶרֶב קְדוֹשִׁים תִּתְקַדָּשׁ:

(The Congregation rise.)

בָּרוּךְ אַתָּה יְיָ. אֵל מֶלֶךְ גָּדוֹל בַּתִּשְׁבָּחוֹת. אֵל הַהוֹדָאוֹת. אֲדוֹן הַנִּפְלָאוֹת. הַבּוֹחֵר בְּשִׁירֵי זִמְרָה. מֶלֶךְ אֵל חֵי הָעוֹלָמִים:

---

10. יִתְגַּדַּל וְיִתְקַדַּשׁ שְׁמֵהּ רַבָּא. בְּעָלְמָא דִי־בְרָא כִרְעוּתֵהּ. וְיַמְלִיךְ מַלְכוּתֵהּ בְּחַיֵּיכוֹן וּבְיוֹמֵיכוֹן. וּבְחַיֵּי דְכָל בֵּית יִשְׂרָאֵל. בַּעֲגָלָא וּבִזְמַן קָרִיב. וְאִמְרוּ אָמֵן:

Choir and Congregation.

אָמֵן יְהֵא שְׁמֵהּ רַבָּא מְבָרַךְ לְעָלַם וּלְעָלְמֵי עָלְמַיָּא:

Reader.

יִתְבָּרַךְ וְיִשְׁתַּבַּח וְיִתְפָּאַר וְיִתְרוֹמַם וְיִתְנַשֵּׂא וְיִתְהַדָּר וְיִתְעַלֶּה וְיִתְהַלָּל שְׁמֵהּ דְּקֻדְשָׁא בְּרִיךְ הוּא. לְעֵלָּא מִן כָּל־בִּרְכָתָא וְשִׁירָתָא תֻּשְׁבְּחָתָא וְנֶחָמָתָא דַּאֲמִירָן בְּעָלְמָא. וְאִמְרוּ אָמֵן:

should worship thee, and all our faculties join in chanting thy praise, O great and Omnipotent God, Owner of heaven and earth.

O King! enthroned in Majesty on High! Thou abidest in infinity; wondrous and holy are thy attributes, unsearchable are thy ways. And yet the Holy Scriptures say: "Exult in the Lord, O ye righteous, for his praise becometh the upright." Therefore do the lips of the upright praise thee, and with the utterances of the righteous art thou blessed. The tongues of the pious extol thee, and from the midst of the saints is holiness ascribed unto thee.

(The Congregation rise.)

Blessèd be thou, O Lord, Almighty King! magnified in hymns of praise and thanksgiving. Thy wondrous deeds are unspeakable, and yet art thou pleased to accept the songs and chants of psalmody with which we approach thy throne, O ever-living King of the universe.

---

10. Let the great Name of the Eternal be exalted and sanctified throughout the whole universe, which he hath created according to his will. May his kingdom soon be established over the whole earth, and may ye and all Israel live to partake of the blessings of that happy period. Unto which say ye, Amen.

Choir and Congregation.

Amen! May his great Name be praised for ever and unto all eternity.

Reader.

Yea, let us praise and worship, magnify and exalt the Name of the Most Holy, (blessed be he,) whose glory exceedeth all the praises and hymns that may be rendered unto him by human lips. And let us say, Amen!

תפלת שחרית לשבת ולרגלים

Reader.

בָּרְכוּ אֶת־יְיָ הַמְבֹרָךְ:

Choir and Congregation.

בָּרוּךְ יְיָ הַמְבֹרָךְ לְעוֹלָם וָעֶד:

(The Congregation are seated.)

---

11. בָּרוּךְ אַתָּה יְיָ אֱלֹהֵינוּ מֶלֶךְ הָעוֹלָם יוֹצֵר אוֹר וּבוֹרֵא חֹשֶׁךְ עֹשֶׂה שָׁלוֹם וּבוֹרֵא אֶת־הַכֹּל:

(On Sabbaths, or Festivals occurring on the Sabbath.)

(הַכֹּל יוֹדוּךָ וְהַכֹּל יְשַׁבְּחוּךָ. וְהַכֹּל יֹאמְרוּ אֵין קָדוֹשׁ כַּיְיָ: הַכֹּל יְרוֹמְמוּךָ סֶּלָה יוֹצֵר הַכֹּל. הָאֵל הַמֵּאִיר לְעוֹלָם כֻּלּוֹ וּלְיוֹשְׁבָיו:)

*

הַמֵּאִיר לָאָרֶץ וְלַדָּרִים עָלֶיהָ בְּרַחֲמִים. וּבְטוּבוֹ מְחַדֵּשׁ בְּכָל־יוֹם תָּמִיד מַעֲשֵׂה־בְרֵאשִׁית: מָה רַבּוּ מַעֲשֶׂיךָ יְיָ. כֻּלָּם בְּחָכְמָה עָשִׂיתָ. מָלְאָה הָאָרֶץ קִנְיָנֶךָ: הַמֶּלֶךְ הַמְרוֹמָם לְבַדּוֹ מֵאָז. הַמְשֻׁבָּח וְהַמְפֹאָר וְהַמִּתְנַשֵּׂא מִימוֹת עוֹלָם: אֱלֹהֵי עוֹלָם בְּרַחֲמֶיךָ הָרַבִּים רַחֵם עָלֵינוּ. אֲדוֹן עֻזֵּנוּ צוּר מִשְׂגַּבֵּנוּ. מָגֵן יִשְׁעֵנוּ מִשְׂגָּב בַּעֲדֵנוּ:

(On Sabbaths, or Festivals occurring on the Sabbath.)

(אֵל אֲשֶׁר שָׁבַת מִכָּל־הַמַּעֲשִׂים. בַּיּוֹם הַשְּׁבִיעִי הִתְעַלָּה וְיָשַׁב עַל־כִּסֵּא כְבוֹדוֹ: תִּפְאֶרֶת עָטָה לְיוֹם הַמְּנוּחָה. עֹנֶג קָרָא לְיוֹם הַשַּׁבָּת: זֶה שֶׁבַח שֶׁל יוֹם הַשְּׁבִיעִי. שֶׁבּוֹ שָׁבַת אֵל מִכָּל־מְלַאכְתּוֹ: וְיוֹם הַשְּׁבִיעִי מְשַׁבֵּחַ וְאוֹמֵר.

63 Service for the Morning of Sabbaths and Festivals.

Reader.
Praise ye the Lord, unto whom all praise belongeth.
Choir and Congregation.
Praised be the Lord, unto whom all praise belongeth, now and for evermore.
(The Congregation are seated.)

11. Yea, we praise thee, O Lord our God, Ruler of the Universe, who causest light and darkness to alternate, and promotest the peace and harmony of all creation.
(On Sabbaths, or Festivals occurring on the Sabbath.)
(All give thanks unto thee, and all utter thy praises! All proclaim: None is holy like the Eternal! All extol thee, Former of all, who givest light to the whole world and the inhabitants thereof.)

* * *

Thou givest light unto the earth, gladdening those who dwell thereon, greeting us day after day with thy kindness and renewing the wonders of thy creation. "How great are thy works, O Lord! in wisdom hast thou made them all; the earth is full of thy treasures." Thou art exalted, O King! and to thee alone is reverential praise and glory due; for the beginning of all things manifesteth thy greatness. O Lord Eternal, in thy infinite mercy have compassion on us, like as from old thou hast been our defence and our fortress, our shield and our refuge.
(On Sabbaths, or Festivals occurring on the Sabbath.)
(Nature's Master ceased from work on the seventh day, establishing thereon his throne of everlasting Majesty. Yea, with glory hath he crowned the day of rest, appointing the Sabbath for a day of spiritual delight. This is the sublime distinction of the seventh day, that it proclaimeth the perfection of God's crea-

מִזְמוֹר שִׁיר לְיוֹם הַשַּׁבָּת טוֹב לְהוֹדוֹת לַיְיָ: לְפִיכָךְ יְפָאֲרוּ וִיבָרְכוּ לָאֵל כָּל־יְצוּרָיו. שֶׁבַח יְקָר וּגְדֻלָּה יִתְּנוּ לָאֵל מֶלֶךְ יוֹצֵר כֹּל: הַמַּנְחִיל מְנוּחָה לְעַמּוֹ יִשְׂרָאֵל בִּקְדֻשָּׁתוֹ. בְּיוֹם שַׁבַּת קֹדֶשׁ: שִׁמְךָ יְיָ אֱלֹהֵינוּ יִתְקַדַּשׁ וְזִכְרְךָ מַלְכֵּנוּ יִתְפָּאַר. בַּשָּׁמַיִם מִמַּעַל וְעַל הָאָרֶץ מִתָּחַת:)

. . .

תִּתְבָּרַךְ יְיָ אֱלֹהֵינוּ עַל־שֶׁבַח מַעֲשֵׂה יָדֶיךָ. וְעַל־מְאוֹרֵי־אוֹר שֶׁעָשִׂיתָ יְפָאֲרוּךָ סֶּלָה. בָּרוּךְ אַתָּה יְיָ יוֹצֵר הַמְּאוֹרוֹת:

---

12. אַהֲבָה רַבָּה אֲהַבְתָּנוּ יְיָ אֱלֹהֵינוּ. חֶמְלָה גְדוֹלָה וִיתֵרָה חָמַלְתָּ עָלֵינוּ. אָבִינוּ מַלְכֵּנוּ. בַּעֲבוּר אֲבוֹתֵינוּ שֶׁבָּטְחוּ בָךְ. וַתְּלַמְּדֵם חֻקֵּי חַיִּים. כֵּן תְּחָנֵּנוּ וּתְלַמְּדֵנוּ: אָבִינוּ הָאָב הָרַחֲמָן. רַחֵם עָלֵינוּ. וְתֵן בְּלִבֵּנוּ לְהָבִין וּלְהַשְׂכִּיל. לִשְׁמֹעַ לִלְמֹד וּלְלַמֵּד. לִשְׁמֹר וְלַעֲשׂוֹת. וּלְקַיֵּם אֶת־כָּל־דִּבְרֵי תַלְמוּד תּוֹרָתֶךָ בְּאַהֲבָה: וְהָאֵר עֵינֵינוּ בְּתוֹרָתֶךָ. וְדַבֵּק לִבֵּנוּ בְּמִצְוֹתֶיךָ. וְיַחֵד לְבָבֵנוּ לְאַהֲבָה וּלְיִרְאָה שְׁמֶךָ. וְלֹא־נֵבוֹשׁ לְעוֹלָם וָעֶד. כִּי בְשֵׁם קָדְשְׁךָ הַגָּדוֹל וְהַנּוֹרָא בָּטָחְנוּ. נָגִילָה וְנִשְׂמְחָה בִּישׁוּעָתֶךָ: כִּי אֵל פּוֹעֵל יְשׁוּעוֹת אָתָּה. וּבָנוּ בָחַרְתָּ מִכָּל־עַם וְלָשׁוֹן. וְקֵרַבְתָּנוּ לְשִׁמְךָ הַגָּדוֹל סֶלָה בֶּאֱמֶת. לְהוֹדוֹת לְךָ וּלְיַחֶדְךָ בְּאַהֲבָה. בָּרוּךְ אַתָּה יְיָ הַבּוֹחֵר בְּעַמּוֹ יִשְׂרָאֵל בְּאַהֲבָה:

tion, and is the herald of the Lord, proclaiming the song of the Sabbath-day: "How good is it to praise the Eternal!" Therefore should all his creatures bless and glorify him, and render homage and adoration to the Great Author of Nature, the Holy One, who vouchsafed unto his people the gracious boon of the Sabbath's sacred repose. Thy Name be sanctified, O Lord God! and thy Majesty exalted, as in the heavens above, so on the earth beneath.)

* * *

O that we could exceed in uttering thy praise, beyond all that thy handiwork declares; yea, more than the heavenly luminaries unceasingly announce. Blessed be thou, O Lord, Author of refulgent light. Amen!

---

12. In thy inexhaustible love, O Lord our God! didst thou give us spiritual light, causing it to shine upon us through thy benignity and grace. Our Father and King, as thou didst give thy law as a tree of life to our ancestors who trusted in thee, so be gracious unto us also, and incline our hearts to its sacred teachings, and instill within us the desire for knowledge and understanding, that we may perceive and comprehend all its inculcations, and be enabled to learn and teach, to observe and practise them in devoted love. O! illumine our eyes with thy Torah! Cause us to love thy precepts, and let us so act in the love and fear of thy Name, that we may never be put to shame for our deeds. Unwavering is our trust in thy holy Name, that thou wilt gladden us through thy salvation. For thou, O God! seekest the salvation of all mankind, and hast selected us from all nations and tongues to perform thy service, by proclaiming thy unity in truth and love. Blessed be thou, O Lord, who hast chosen thy people Israel for a mission of love. Amen.

קְרִיאַת שְׁמַע

(This verse is said by the Reader, and then the Choir and Congregation repeat it while standing.)

שְׁמַע יִשְׂרָאֵל יְהֹוָה אֱלֹהֵינוּ יְהֹוָה אֶחָד:

בָּרוּךְ שֵׁם כְּבוֹד מַלְכוּתוֹ לְעוֹלָם וָעֶד:

(The Cong. take their seats, and the Rabbi recites the following.)

(דברים ו׳ ד׳ י״א י״ג במדבר ט״ו ל״ז)

וְאָהַבְתָּ אֵת יְיָ אֱלֹהֶיךָ בְּכָל־לְבָבְךָ וּבְכָל־נַפְשְׁךָ וּבְכָל־מְאֹדֶךָ: וְהָיוּ הַדְּבָרִים הָאֵלֶּה אֲשֶׁר אָנֹכִי מְצַוְּךָ הַיּוֹם עַל־לְבָבֶךָ: וְשִׁנַּנְתָּם לְבָנֶיךָ וְדִבַּרְתָּ בָּם בְּשִׁבְתְּךָ בְּבֵיתֶךָ וּבְלֶכְתְּךָ בַדֶּרֶךְ וּבְשָׁכְבְּךָ וּבְקוּמֶךָ: וּקְשַׁרְתָּם לְאוֹת עַל־יָדֶךָ וְהָיוּ לְטֹטָפֹת בֵּין עֵינֶיךָ: וּכְתַבְתָּם עַל־מְזֻזוֹת בֵּיתֶךָ וּבִשְׁעָרֶיךָ:

וְהָיָה אִם־שָׁמֹעַ תִּשְׁמְעוּ אֶל־מִצְוֹתַי אֲשֶׁר אָנֹכִי מְצַוֶּה אֶתְכֶם הַיּוֹם לְאַהֲבָה אֶת־יְיָ אֱלֹהֵיכֶם וּלְעָבְדוֹ בְּכָל־לְבַבְכֶם וּבְכָל־נַפְשְׁכֶם: וְנָתַתִּי מְטַר־אַרְצְכֶם בְּעִתּוֹ יוֹרֶה וּמַלְקוֹשׁ וְאָסַפְתָּ דְגָנֶךָ וְתִירֹשְׁךָ וְיִצְהָרֶךָ: וְנָתַתִּי עֵשֶׂב בְּשָׂדְךָ לִבְהֶמְתֶּךָ וְאָכַלְתָּ וְשָׂבָעְתָּ: הִשָּׁמְרוּ לָכֶם פֶּן־יִפְתֶּה לְבַבְכֶם וְסַרְתֶּם וַעֲבַדְתֶּם אֱלֹהִים אֲחֵרִים וְהִשְׁתַּחֲוִיתֶם לָהֶם: וְחָרָה אַף־יְיָ בָּכֶם וְעָצַר אֶת־

13. THE CONFESSION OF FAITH.

(This verse is said by the Reader, and then the Choir and Congregation repeat it while standing.)

Hear, O Israel! The Lord is our God; the Lord is One!

Blessed be the name of his glorious kingdom for evermore.

(The Congregation take their seats, and the Rabbi recites the following scriptural passages:)

(Deut. vi. 4–9, xi. 13–21; Numb. xv. 37–41.)

And thou shalt love the Lord thy God with all thy heart, and with all thy soul, and with all thy might. And these words, which I command thee this day, shall be in thy heart. And thou shalt teach them diligently unto thy children, and shalt speak of them when thou sittest in thy house, and when thou walkest by the way; when thou liest down, and when thou risest up. And thou shalt bind them for a sign upon thy hand, and they shall be as frontlets between thy eyes. And thou shalt write them upon the door-posts of thy house, and upon thy gates.

And it shall come to pass, that if ye will hearken diligently unto my commandments which I command you this day, to love the Lord your God, and to serve him with all your heart and all your soul, then will I send rain for your land in its due season, the first rain and the latter rain, that thou mayest gather in thy corn, thy wine, and thy oil. And I will give grass in thy field for thy cattle, and thou shalt eat and be satisfied. Take heed of yourselves, lest your heart be deceived, and ye turn aside, and serve other gods, and worship them. For then the Lord's wrath will be kindled

תפלת שחרית לשבת ולרגלים

הַשָּׁמַיִם וְלֹא־יִהְיֶה מָטָר וְהָאֲדָמָה לֹא תִתֵּן אֶת־יְבוּלָהּ וַאֲבַדְתֶּם מְהֵרָה מֵעַל הָאָרֶץ הַטֹּבָה אֲשֶׁר יְיָ נֹתֵן לָכֶם: וְשַׂמְתֶּם אֶת־דְּבָרַי אֵלֶּה עַל־לְבַבְכֶם וְעַל־נַפְשְׁכֶם וּקְשַׁרְתֶּם אֹתָם לְאוֹת עַל־יֶדְכֶם וְהָיוּ לְטוֹטָפֹת בֵּין עֵינֵיכֶם: וְלִמַּדְתֶּם אֹתָם אֶת־בְּנֵיכֶם לְדַבֵּר בָּם בְּשִׁבְתְּךָ בְּבֵיתֶךָ וּבְלֶכְתְּךָ בַדֶּרֶךְ וּבְשָׁכְבְּךָ וּבְקוּמֶךָ: וּכְתַבְתָּם עַל־מְזוּזוֹת בֵּיתֶךָ וּבִשְׁעָרֶיךָ: לְמַעַן יִרְבּוּ יְמֵיכֶם וִימֵי בְנֵיכֶם עַל הָאֲדָמָה אֲשֶׁר נִשְׁבַּע יְיָ לַאֲבֹתֵיכֶם לָתֵת לָהֶם כִּימֵי הַשָּׁמַיִם עַל־הָאָרֶץ:

וַיֹּאמֶר יְיָ אֶל־מֹשֶׁה לֵּאמֹר: דַּבֵּר אֶל־בְּנֵי יִשְׂרָאֵל וְאָמַרְתָּ אֲלֵהֶם וְעָשׂוּ לָהֶם צִיצִת עַל־כַּנְפֵי בִגְדֵיהֶם לְדֹרֹתָם וְנָתְנוּ עַל־צִיצִת הַכָּנָף פְּתִיל תְּכֵלֶת: וְהָיָה לָכֶם לְצִיצִת וּרְאִיתֶם אֹתוֹ וּזְכַרְתֶּם אֶת־כָּל־מִצְוֹת יְיָ וַעֲשִׂיתֶם אֹתָם וְלֹא תָתוּרוּ אַחֲרֵי לְבַבְכֶם וְאַחֲרֵי עֵינֵיכֶם אֲשֶׁר אַתֶּם זֹנִים אַחֲרֵיהֶם: לְמַעַן תִּזְכְּרוּ וַעֲשִׂיתֶם אֶת־כָּל־מִצְוֹתָי וִהְיִיתֶם קְדֹשִׁים לֵאלֹהֵיכֶם: אֲנִי יְיָ אֱלֹהֵיכֶם אֲשֶׁר הוֹצֵאתִי אֶתְכֶם מֵאֶרֶץ מִצְרַיִם לִהְיוֹת לָכֶם לֵאלֹהִים אֲנִי יְיָ אֱלֹהֵיכֶם:

Choir.

יְיָ אֱלֹהֵיכֶם אֱמֶת:

against you, and he will shut up the heavens, that there be no rain, and the land will not yield her fruit, and ye shall perish quickly from off the goodly land which the Lord giveth you. Therefore shall ye lay up these my words in your heart and in your soul, and bind them for a sign upon your hand, and they shall be as frontlets between your eyes. And ye shall teach them to your children, speaking of them when thou sittest in thy house, and when thou walkest by the way; when thou liest down, and when thou risest up. And thou shalt write them upon the door-posts of thy house, and upon thy gates. That your days may be multiplied, and the days of your children, in the land which the Lord swore unto your fathers to give them, as the days of heaven over the earth.

And the Lord spoke unto Moses, saying, Speak unto the children of Israel, and bid them to make themselves fringes in the borders of their garments, throughout their generations, and that they put upon the fringes of the borders a thread of blue. And it shall be unto you for a fringe, that ye may look upon it, and remember all the commandments of the Lord, and do them; and that ye seek not after the inclinations of your own heart and the delight of your eyes, in pursuit of which ye have been led astray. That ye may remember, and do all my commandments, and be holy unto your God. I am the Lord your God, who brought you out of the land of Egypt, to be your God: I am the Lord your God.

Choir.

The Lord your God is ever true and faithful!

תפלת שחרית לשבת ולרגלים

14. אֱמֶת וְיַצִּיב וְנָכוֹן וְקַיָּם. הַדָּבָר הַזֶּה עָלֵינוּ לְעוֹלָם וָעֶד. אֱמֶת וֶאֱמוּנָה חֹק וְלֹא יַעֲבוֹר:

אֱמֶת שָׁאַתָּה הוּא יְיָ אֱלֹהֵינוּ וֵאלֹהֵי אֲבוֹתֵינוּ. מַלְכֵּנוּ מֶלֶךְ אֲבוֹתֵינוּ. גּוֹאֲלֵנוּ גּוֹאֵל אֲבוֹתֵינוּ. יוֹצְרֵנוּ צוּר יְשׁוּעָתֵנוּ. פּוֹדֵנוּ וּמַצִּילֵנוּ מֵעוֹלָם שְׁמֶךָ. אֵין אֱלֹהִים זוּלָתֶךָ:

אֱמֶת אַתָּה הוּא רִאשׁוֹן וְאַתָּה הוּא אַחֲרוֹן. וּמִבַּלְעָדֶיךָ אֵין לָנוּ מֶלֶךְ גּוֹאֵל וּמוֹשִׁיעַ. מִמִּצְרַיִם גְּאַלְתָּנוּ יְיָ אֱלֹהֵינוּ. וּמִבֵּית עֲבָדִים פְּדִיתָנוּ. וְיַם־סוּף בָּקַעְתָּ. וִידִידִים הֶעֱבַרְתָּ בְּתוֹכוֹ לַחֲרָבָה:

עַל־זֹאת שִׁבְּחוּ אֲהוּבִים וְרוֹמְמוּ אֵל. וְנָתְנוּ יְדִידִים זְמִירוֹת שִׁירוֹת וְתִשְׁבָּחוֹת. בְּרָכוֹת וְהוֹדָאוֹת לְמֶלֶךְ אֵל חַי וְקַיָּם. רָם וְנִשָּׂא. גָּדוֹל וְנוֹרָא. מַשְׁפִּיל גֵּאִים. וּמַגְבִּיהַּ שְׁפָלִים. מוֹצִיא אֲסִירִים. וּפוֹדֶה עֲנָוִים. וְעוֹזֵר דַּלִּים. וְעוֹנֶה לְעַמּוֹ בְּעֵת שַׁוְּעָם אֵלָיו:

תְּהִלּוֹת לְאֵל עֶלְיוֹן. בָּרוּךְ הוּא וּמְבוֹרָךְ. מֹשֶׁה וּבְנֵי יִשְׂרָאֵל לְךָ עָנוּ שִׁירָה. בְּשִׂמְחָה רַבָּה. וְאָמְרוּ כֻלָּם:

Choir and Congregation.

מִי־כָמֹכָה בָּאֵלִם יְיָ מִי כָּמֹכָה נֶאְדָּר בַּקֹּדֶשׁ נוֹרָא תְהִלֹּת עֹשֵׂה פֶלֶא:

14. True, firm, unshaken, and stable is this word unto us for ever and ever! yea, a truth unchangeable, a statute unalterable!

The past lays before us the truth, and makes us confident that what thou hast been to our fathers, thou wilt be to us, even a guide, protector, and redeemer, the Rock of our salvation, our Savior and Deliverer. From old such is thy name, and there is no almighty power save thine.

It is a truth that thou art the first and the last, and without thee we have neither King, Redeemer, nor Savior. Thou didst give evidence of this in redeeming us from Egypt, and bringing us out of the house of bondage; and wonderful was thy salvation at the Red Sea, when thou didst lead thy chosen ones safely through its foaming billows.

The hearts of our ancestors were filled with emotions of gratitude for all this, and gave forth songs and chants, benedictions and thanksgivings unto thee, Fountain of life, Ever-existing God! They witnessed thy lofty and sublime acts, thy great and awe-inspiring deeds! They beheld that thou didst overthrow the haughty and raise up the lowly, that thou didst free the enslaved and redeem the depressed, O Helper of the needy and Hearer of the supplications of thy people whenever their petitions come before thee.

Therefore did they utter praises to the God on High, blessed be he, yea, ever blessed. Even Moses and the children of Israel, in accents of joy, chanted the song of praise in unison, shouting:

Choir and Congregation.

WHO AMONG THE MIGHTY IS LIKE UNTO THEE, O LORD! WHO IS LIKE UNTO THEE, GLORIFIED IN HOLINESS, FEARFUL IN PRAISED DEEDS, PERFORMING WONDERS!

תפלת שחרית לשבת ולרגלים

שִׁירָה חֲדָשָׁה שִׁבְּחוּ גְאוּלִים לְשִׁמְךָ עַל־שְׂפַת הַיָּם יַחַד כֻּלָּם הוֹדוּ וְהִמְלִיכוּ וְאָמְרוּ:

Choir and Congregation.

יְיָ יִמְלֹךְ לְעֹלָם וָעֶד:

וְנֶאֱמַר גֹּאֲלֵנוּ יְיָ צְבָאוֹת שְׁמוֹ קְדוֹשׁ יִשְׂרָאֵל. בָּרוּךְ אַתָּה יְיָ גָּאַל יִשְׂרָאֵל:

16. ברכת שבע

(The Congregation rise and pray with the Reader in a low voice.)

I. בָּרוּךְ אַתָּה יְיָ אֱלֹהֵינוּ וֵאלֹהֵי אֲבוֹתֵינוּ. אֱלֹהֵי אַבְרָהָם אֱלֹהֵי יִצְחָק וֵאלֹהֵי יַעֲקֹב. הָאֵל הַגָּדוֹל הַגִּבּוֹר וְהַנּוֹרָא. אֵל עֶלְיוֹן. גּוֹמֵל חֲסָדִים טוֹבִים. וְקֹנֵה הַכֹּל. וְזוֹכֵר חַסְדֵי אָבוֹת. וּמֵבִיא גְאֻלָּה לִבְנֵי בְנֵיהֶם לְמַעַן שְׁמוֹ בְּאַהֲבָה:

(During the Penitential Days.)

זָכְרֵנוּ לַחַיִּים. מֶלֶךְ חָפֵץ בַּחַיִּים.
וְכָתְבֵנוּ בְּסֵפֶר הַחַיִּים. לְמַעַנְךָ אֱלֹהִים חַיִּים:

מֶלֶךְ עוֹזֵר וּמוֹשִׁיעַ וּמָגֵן. בָּרוּךְ אַתָּה יְיָ מָגֵן אַבְרָהָם:

II. אַתָּה גִּבּוֹר לְעוֹלָם אֲדֹנָי מְחַיֵּה מֵתִים אַתָּה רַב לְהוֹשִׁיעַ. (מַשִּׁיב הָרוּחַ וּמוֹרִיד הַגֶּשֶׁם:)

מְכַלְכֵּל חַיִּים בְּחֶסֶד מְחַיֵּה מֵתִים בְּרַחֲמִים רַבִּים סוֹמֵךְ נוֹפְלִים וְרוֹפֵא חוֹלִים וּמַתִּיר אֲסוּרִים וּמְקַיֵּם אֱמוּנָתוֹ לִישֵׁנֵי עָפָר. מִי כָמוֹךָ בַּעַל גְּבוּרוֹת וּמִי דוֹמֶה לָּךְ מֶלֶךְ מֵמִית וּמְחַיֶּה וּמַצְמִיחַ יְשׁוּעָה:

Service for the Morning of Sabbaths and Festivals.

Yea, the redeemed ones chanted a new song at the seashore when recognizing thy providence, and in united chorus did they acknowledge thy sovereignty, exclaiming:

Choir and Congregation.
THE LORD WILL REIGN FOR EVER AND EVER

And thus it is recorded in the Holy Scriptures, "Our Redeemer, the Lord of Hosts is his name, the Holy One of Israel." Blessed be thou, O Lord, the Redeemer of Israel.

15. THE SEVENFOLD BENEDICTION.
(The Congregation rise and pray with the Reader in a low voice.)

I. We arise to praise thee, O Lord our God, and the God of our fathers—God of Abraham, Isaac, and Jacob. Great and mighty art thou, and wondrous are thy works, O Author of the Universe. In the abundance of thy mercy thou causest the virtues of the fathers to bring salvation to their children's children.

(During the Penitential Days.)
(Remember us and grant us life, O Eternal, who delightest in dispensing the blessings of life. Write us in the book of life, in order that we may proclaim thy mercy, O God of life.)

O Heavenly King! our Supporter, Savior, and Shield! Praised be thou, O Lord, the Shield of Abraham.

II. Thou art ever omnipotent, O Lord, leading us unto life eternal, in thy abundant salvation.

(Thou biddest the winds to blow and the rain to descend.)

Thou sustainest in beneficence all living, and thy infinite love will attend us in the regions of a blessed hereafter. As thou supportest the falling, healest the sick, and loosenest the bonds of the oppressed, so doth thy faithfulness not abandon those who sleep in the dust. Who is like unto thee, Master of mighty acts? Who can be compared unto thee, O King, who, whether dispensing death or life, wilt cause salvation to spring forth?

תפלת שחרית לשבת ולרגלים

(During the Penitential Days.)

מִי כָמֽוֹךָ אַב הָרַחֲמִים. זוֹכֵר יְצוּרָיו לַחַיִּים בְּרַחֲמִים:

וְנֶאֱמָן אַתָּה לְהַחֲיוֹת מֵתִים. בָּרוּךְ אַתָּה יְיָ מְחַיֵּה הַמֵּתִים:

(When praying alone.)

*III. אַתָּה קָדוֹשׁ וְשִׁמְךָ קָדוֹשׁ וּקְדוֹשִׁים בְּכָל־יוֹם יְהַלְלֽוּךָ סֶּֽלָה. בָּרוּךְ אַתָּה יְיָ הָאֵל הַקָּדוֹשׁ:

(At the Public Service.)

*III. נְקַדֵּשׁ אֶת שִׁמְךָ בָּעוֹלָם כְּשֵׁם שֶׁמַּקְדִּישִׁים אוֹתוֹ בִּשְׁמֵי מָרוֹם כַּכָּתוּב עַל יַד נְבִיאֶֽךָ וְקָרָא זֶה אֶל זֶה וְאָמַר:

קָדוֹשׁ ׀ קָדוֹשׁ קָדוֹשׁ יְיָ צְבָאוֹת מְלֹא כָל־הָאָֽרֶץ כְּבוֹדוֹ:

Read. אָז בְּקוֹל רַֽעַשׁ גָּדוֹל אַדִּיר וְחָזָק מַשְׁמִיעִים קוֹל מִתְנַשְּׂאִים לְעֻמַּת שְׂרָפִים לְעֻמָּתָם בָּרוּךְ יֹאמֵֽרוּ:

Choir and Congregation.

בָּרוּךְ כְּבוֹד יְיָ מִמְּקוֹמוֹ:

Read. מִמְּקוֹמְךָ מַלְכֵּֽנוּ תוֹפִֽיעַ וְתִמְלוֹךְ עָלֵֽינוּ. כִּי מְחַכִּים אֲנַֽחְנוּ לָךְ מָתַי תִּמְלוֹךְ עַל כָּל הָעוֹלָם כֻּלּוֹ בִּכְבוֹדֶֽךָ. תִּתְגַּדֵּל וְתִתְקַדֵּשׁ עַל מַקְדִּישֵׁי שְׁמֶֽךָ לְדוֹר וָדוֹר וּלְנֵֽצַח נְצָחִים. וְעֵינֵֽינוּ תִרְאֶֽינָה מַלְכוּתֶֽךָ כַּדָּבָר הָאָמוּר בְּשִׁירֵי עֻזֶּֽךָ:

Choir and Congregation.

יִמְלֹךְ יְיָ לְעוֹלָם אֱלֹהַֽיִךְ צִיּוֹן לְדֹר וָדֹר הַלְלוּיָהּ:

Read. לְדוֹר וָדוֹר נַגִּיד גָּדְלֶֽךָ. וּלְנֵֽצַח נְצָחִים קְדֻשָּׁתְךָ נַקְדִּישׁ. וְשִׁבְחֲךָ אֱלֹהֵֽינוּ מִפִּֽינוּ לֹא יָמוּשׁ לְעוֹלָם וָעֶד. כִּי אֵל מֶֽלֶךְ גָּדוֹל וְקָדוֹשׁ אָֽתָּה. בָּרוּךְ אַתָּה יְיָ הָאֵל הַקָּדוֹשׁ:

(The Congregation are seated.)

75   Service for the Morning of Sabbaths and Festivals.

(*During the Penitential Days.*)
(Yea, who is like unto thee, merciful Father, who in mercy rememberest thy creatures to life?)

We faithfully believe that thou wilt restore us from death unto life. Praised be thou, O Lord, who restorest the dead to life.

(When praying alone.)

*III. Thou art holy, and thy Name is holy, and it is a mission of holiness to praise thee daily. Praised be thou, O Lord, the Holy God.

---

*III. We, on earth, will sanctify thy Name as it is sanctified in the heavens above, accomplishing the words of the divine seer, and proclaiming one to the other:

Choir and Congregation.

Holy, holy, holy is the Lord of Hosts; the whole earth is full of his glory.

Reader. Yea, in echoes loud and mighty does thy praise resound throughout thy vast kingdom, where the messengers of thy grace and grandeur herald thy Majesty and proclaim thee blessed.

Choir and Congregation.

Blessed be the Majesty of the Lord in every place where it is manifested.

Reader. Let the refulgence of thy Majesty appear unto all who seek thy glory and place implicit trust in thee; and O! approximate the period when thou wilt be every where extolled from generation to generation, unto all eternity. Grant that we may behold this era, when thy kingdom will be so happily established, even as written by the sweet Psalmist of Israel:

Choir and Congregation.

The Lord shall reign for ever, even thy God, O Zion, for all generations. Hallelujah!

Reader. From generation to generation will we make known thy greatness, and for evermore proclaim thy holiness. Thy praise shall never depart from our lips, for great and holy art thou, O King. Praised be thou, O Lord, the Holy God!

(The Congregation are seated.)

תפלת שחרית לשבת ולרגלים

(On the Sabbath.)

IV. יִשְׂמַח מֹשֶׁה בְּמַתְּנַת חֶלְקוֹ. כִּי עֶבֶד נֶאֱמָן קָרָאתָ לּוֹ. כְּלִיל תִּפְאֶרֶת בְּרֹאשׁוֹ נָתַתָּ. בְּעָמְדוֹ לְפָנֶיךָ עַל הַר־סִינָי. וּשְׁנֵי לֻחֹת אֲבָנִים הוֹרִיד בְּיָדוֹ. וְכָתוּב בָּהֶם שְׁמִירַת שַׁבָּת. וְכֵן כָּתוּב בְּתוֹרָתֶךָ:

וְשָׁמְרוּ בְנֵי־יִשְׂרָאֵל אֶת־הַשַּׁבָּת לַעֲשׂוֹת אֶת־הַשַּׁבָּת לְדֹרֹתָם בְּרִית עוֹלָם: בֵּינִי וּבֵין בְּנֵי יִשְׂרָאֵל אוֹת הִוא לְעֹלָם. כִּי־שֵׁשֶׁת יָמִים עָשָׂה יְיָ אֶת־הַשָּׁמַיִם וְאֶת־הָאָרֶץ וּבַיּוֹם הַשְּׁבִיעִי שָׁבַת וַיִּנָּפַשׁ:

(On Festivals.)

IV. אַתָּה בְחַרְתָּנוּ מִכָּל־הָעַמִּים. אָהַבְתָּ אוֹתָנוּ. וְרָצִיתָ בָּנוּ. וְקִדַּשְׁתָּנוּ בְּמִצְוֹתֶיךָ. וְקֵרַבְתָּנוּ מַלְכֵּנוּ לַעֲבוֹדָתֶךָ. וְשִׁמְךָ הַגָּדוֹל וְהַקָּדוֹשׁ עָלֵינוּ קָרָאתָ:

וַתִּתֶּן־לָנוּ יְיָ אֱלֹהֵינוּ בְּאַהֲבָה (שַׁבָּתוֹת לִמְנוּחָה וּ) מוֹעֲדִים לְשִׂמְחָה חַגִּים וּזְמַנִּים לְשָׂשׂוֹן. אֶת־יוֹם (הַשַּׁבָּת הַזֶּה וְאֶת־יוֹם)

(Atzereth)	(Succoth)	(Shabuoth)	(Passover)
חַג הָעֲצֶרֶת הַשְּׁמִינִי	חַג הַסֻּכּוֹת הַזֶּה.	חַג הַשָּׁבֻעוֹת הַזֶּה.	חַג הַמַּצּוֹת הַזֶּה.
זְמַן שִׂמְחָתֵנוּ	זְמַן שִׂמְחָתֵנוּ	זְמַן מַתַּן תּוֹרָתֵנוּ	זְמַן חֵרוּתֵנוּ

(בְּאַהֲבָה) מִקְרָא קֹדֶשׁ זֵכֶר לִיצִיאַת מִצְרָיִם:

---

*) The words in parenthesis are said if the feast occurs on Sabbath.

(*On the Sabbath.*)

IV. As a gift of happiness didst thou vouchsafe unto us the Sabbath, and thy faithful servant Moses rejoiced in being the chosen messenger of thy ordinance unto Israel. He stood before thee on Sinai, and brought down from its heights the two tables of stone, on which the sacred precept of the Sabbath was inscribed. And further we read in thy Torah:

"The children of Israel shall keep the Sabbath, to observe it throughout their generations as a perpetual covenant. Between me and the children of Israel is it a sign for ever, that in six days the Lord created heaven and earth, and appointed the seventh day for rest and spiritual reflection."

(*On Festivals.*)

IV. Thou hast chosen us from among all nations, and in thy love hast assigned unto us the priestly mission of spreading the knowledge of thy Holy Name, so that we may not alone perform thy commandments, but consecrate ourselves to thy service.

And in the abundance of thy kindness hast thou given us *(Sabbaths for rest and) festive seasons for delight, even this *(Sabbath and this) day of the Feast of

Matzoth,	*Shebuoth,*	*Succoth,*	*Sh'mini Atzereth,*
the anniversary of our delivery from bondage,	reminding us of the revelation at Mount Sinai,	devoted to joy and thanks for thy merciful protection,	consecrated to joyful conclusion of the festive seasons,

a holy convocation, reminding us of our mission from our going out from Egypt.

---

*The words in parenthesis are said if the feast occurs on Sabbath.

תפלת שחרית לשבת ולרגלים

(On the Sabbath.)

וַתִּתֶּן אוֹתוֹ יְיָ אֱלֹהֵינוּ לְיִשְׂרָאֵל עַמְּךָ בְּאַהֲבָה. וּלְזֶרַע יַעֲקֹב אֲשֶׁר בָּם בָּחַרְתָּ. עַם מְקַדְּשֵׁי שְׁבִיעִי כֻּלָּם יִשְׂבְּעוּ וְיִתְעַנְּגוּ מִטּוּבֶךָ. וּבַשְּׁבִיעִי רָצִיתָ בּוֹ וְקִדַּשְׁתּוֹ. חֶמְדַּת יָמִים אוֹתוֹ קָרָאתָ. זֵכֶר לְמַעֲשֵׂה בְרֵאשִׁית:

אֱלֹהֵינוּ וֵאלֹהֵי אֲבוֹתֵינוּ. רְצֵה בִמְנוּחָתֵנוּ. קַדְּשֵׁנוּ בְּמִצְוֹתֶיךָ. וְתֵן חֶלְקֵנוּ בְּתוֹרָתֶךָ. שַׂבְּעֵנוּ מִטּוּבֶךָ. וְשַׂמְּחֵנוּ בִּישׁוּעָתֶךָ. וְטַהֵר לִבֵּנוּ לְעָבְדְּךָ בֶּאֱמֶת. וְהַנְחִילֵנוּ יְיָ אֱלֹהֵינוּ בְּאַהֲבָה וּבְרָצוֹן שַׁבַּת קָדְשֶׁךָ. וְיִשְׂמְחוּ בְךָ יִשְׂרָאֵל אֹהֲבֵי שְׁמֶךָ. בָּרוּךְ אַתָּה יְיָ מְקַדֵּשׁ הַשַּׁבָּת:

(On Festivals.)

אֱלֹהֵינוּ וֵאלֹהֵי אֲבוֹתֵינוּ. יַעֲלֶה וְיָבֹא זִכְרוֹנֵנוּ וְזִכְרוֹן אֲבוֹתֵינוּ. וְזִכְרוֹן כָּל עַמְּךָ בֵּית יִשְׂרָאֵל לְפָנֶיךָ. לְחֵן וּלְחֶסֶד וּלְרַחֲמִים לְחַיִּים וּלְשָׁלוֹם בְּיוֹם

(Atzereth.) (Succoth) (Shabuoth) (Passover)

חַג הַמַּצּוֹת הַזֶּה. חַג הַשָּׁבֻעוֹת הַזֶּה. חַג הַסֻּכּוֹת הַזֶּה. הַשְּׁמִינִי חַג הָעֲצֶרֶת הַזֶּה.

זָכְרֵנוּ יְיָ אֱלֹהֵינוּ בּוֹ לְטוֹבָה. וּפָקְדֵנוּ בוֹ לִבְרָכָה. וְהוֹשִׁיעֵנוּ בוֹ לְחַיִּים. וּבִדְבַר יְשׁוּעָה וְרַחֲמִים. חוּס וְחָנֵּנוּ. וְרַחֵם עָלֵינוּ וְהוֹשִׁיעֵנוּ. כִּי אֵלֶיךָ עֵינֵינוּ. כִּי אֵל מֶלֶךְ חַנּוּן וְרַחוּם אָתָּה:

(*On the Sabbath.*)

We thank thee, O Lord our God, for having bestowed this precious gift upon thy people Israel in abundant love,—that thou hast inspired the seed of Jacob to find pleasure and delight in keeping the seventh day holy. Yea, our hearts long for this sacred day, which crowns the week with spiritual joy, and gives us a foretaste of celestial bliss, in this earthly life, where we gaze on the wonderous works of thy creation.

O our God, and the God of our fathers! grant that our Sabbath rest may render us worthy of thy grace. Sanctify our lives for the performance of thy commandments. Satisfy us with thy abundant goodness, and grant us joy through thy salvation. Purify our hearts to serve thee in truth, and permit us to enjoy thy holy Sabbath, in full love for thy holy Name. Praised be thou, O Lord, who hast sanctified the Sabbath.

(*On Festivals.*)

O our God, and the God of our fathers! we beseech thee to permit our memorial and the memorial of our ancestors, and even of all thy people Israel, to ascend and come before thee, so that we may obtain grace, favor, and blessing, mercy, life and peace, on this day of

the Feast of Matzoth.	the Feast of Pentecost.	the Feast of Booths.	the Feast of Conclusion.

Vouchsafe unto us thy blessing, and save us from the sorrows and trials of life. And as thy Holy Word is full of the assurance of salvation and benign compassion, so mayest thou save and compassionate us, whose eyes are directed to thee, our Heavenly King, who rulest all mankind in mercy and love.

תפלת שחרית לשבת ולרגלים

ז. רְצֵה יְיָ אֱלֹהֵינוּ בְּעַמְּךָ יִשְׂרָאֵל. וְתִפְלָּתָם בְּאַהֲבָה תְקַבֵּל. וּתְהִי לְרָצוֹן תָּמִיד עֲבוֹדַת יִשְׂרָאֵל עַמֶּךָ.

(On the New Moon and in the Festival Week.)

(אֱלֹהֵינוּ וֵאלֹהֵי אֲבוֹתֵינוּ. יַעֲלֶה וְיָבֹא זִכְרוֹנֵנוּ וְזִכְרוֹן אֲבוֹתֵינוּ. וְזִכְרוֹן כָּל עַמְּךָ בֵּית יִשְׂרָאֵל לְפָנֶיךָ. לְחֵן וּלְחֶסֶד וּלְרַחֲמִים לְחַיִּים וּלְשָׁלוֹם בְּיוֹם

(Succoth.)   (Passover.)   (New Moon.)

רֹאשׁ הַחֹדֶשׁ הַזֶּה.   חַג הַמַּצּוֹת הַזֶּה.   חַג הַסֻּכּוֹת הַזֶּה.

זָכְרֵנוּ יְיָ אֱלֹהֵינוּ בּוֹ לְטוֹבָה. וּפָקְדֵנוּ בוֹ לִבְרָכָה. וְהוֹשִׁיעֵנוּ בוֹ לְחַיִּים. וּבִדְבַר יְשׁוּעָה וְרַחֲמִים. חוּס וְחָנֵּנוּ. וְרַחֵם עָלֵינוּ וְהוֹשִׁיעֵנוּ. כִּי אֵלֶיךָ עֵינֵינוּ. כִּי אֵל מֶלֶךְ חַנּוּן וְרַחוּם אָתָּה:)

בָּרוּךְ אַתָּה יְיָ שֶׁאוֹתְךָ לְבַדְּךָ בְּיִרְאָה נַעֲבוֹד:

(On Festivals.)

אֱלֹהֵינוּ וֵאלֹהֵי אֲבוֹתֵינוּ. (רְצֵה בִמְנוּחָתֵנוּ) קַדְּשֵׁנוּ בְּמִצְוֹתֶיךָ. וְתֵן חֶלְקֵנוּ בְּתוֹרָתֶךָ. שַׂבְּעֵנוּ מִטּוּבֶךָ. וְשַׂמְּחֵנוּ בִּישׁוּעָתֶךָ. וְטַהֵר לִבֵּנוּ לְעָבְדְּךָ בֶּאֱמֶת. וְהַנְחִילֵנוּ יְיָ אֱלֹהֵינוּ (בְּאַהֲבָה וּבְרָצוֹן) בְּשִׂמְחָה וּבְשָׂשׂוֹן (שַׁבַּת וְ) מוֹעֲדֵי קָדְשֶׁךָ. וְיִשְׂמְחוּ בְךָ יִשְׂרָאֵל אוֹהֲבֵי שְׁמֶךָ. בָּרוּךְ אַתָּה יְיָ מְקַדֵּשׁ (הַשַּׁבָּת וְ) יִשְׂרָאֵל וְהַזְּמַנִּים: (רְצֵה)

V. O Lord our God, bestow thy grace upon thy people Israel. Accept the prayers of those who approach thee in love, and let the worship of thy people Israel be ever pleasing unto thee.

(On the New Moon and in the Festival Week.)

(O our God, and the God of our fathers! especially do we beseech thee to permit our memorial and the memorial of our ancestors, and even of all thy people Israel, to ascend and come before thee, so that we may obtain grace, favor, and blessing, mercy, life and peace, on this day of

(New Moon).   (Feast of Matzoth).   (Feast of Succoth).

Vouchsafe unto us thy blessing, and save us from the sorrows and trials of life. And as thy Holy Word is full of the assurance of salvation and benign compassion, so mayest thou save and compassionate us, whose eyes are directed to thee, our Heavenly King, who rulest all mankind in mercy and love.

Praised be thou, O Lord, unto whom alone we offer reverence and adoration. Amen!

(On Festivals.)

O our God, and the God of our fathers! (Grant that our Sabbath rest may render us worthy of thy grace.) Sanctify our lives for the performance of thy commandments. Satisfy us with thy abundant goodness, and grant us joy through thy salvation. Purify our hearts to serve thee in truth, and permit us to enjoy thy holy (Sabbath and) Festivals, in full love for thy holy Name. Praised be thou, O Lord, who hast sanctified the (Sabbath and) Israel and the Festivals.

תפלת שחרית לשבת ולרגלים

VI. מוֹדִים אֲנַחְנוּ לָךְ. שָׁאַתָּה הוּא יְיָ אֱלֹהֵינוּ וֵאלֹהֵי אֲבוֹתֵינוּ לְעוֹלָם וָעֶד. צוּר חַיֵּינוּ. מָגֵן יִשְׁעֵנוּ. אַתָּה הוּא לְדוֹר וָדוֹר. נוֹדֶה לְךָ וּנְסַפֵּר תְּהִלָּתֶךָ. עַל חַיֵּינוּ הַמְּסוּרִים בְּיָדֶךָ. וְעַל נִשְׁמוֹתֵינוּ הַפְּקוּדוֹת לָךְ. וְעַל נִסֶּיךָ שֶׁבְּכָל־יוֹם עִמָּנוּ. וְעַל נִפְלְאוֹתֶיךָ וְטוֹבוֹתֶיךָ שֶׁבְּכָל־עֵת. עֶרֶב וָבֹקֶר וְצָהֳרָיִם. הַטּוֹב כִּי לֹא־כָלוּ רַחֲמֶיךָ. וְהַמְרַחֵם כִּי לֹא־תַמּוּ חֲסָדֶיךָ. מֵעוֹלָם קִוִּינוּ לָךְ:*

וְעַל־כֻּלָּם יִתְבָּרַךְ וְיִתְרוֹמַם שִׁמְךָ מַלְכֵּנוּ תָּמִיד לְעוֹלָם וָעֶד:

(During the Penitential Days.)

וּכְתוֹב לְחַיִּים טוֹבִים כָּל־בְּנֵי בְרִיתֶךָ:

וְכֹל הַחַיִּים יוֹדוּךָ סֶּלָה. וִיהַלְלוּ אֶת־שִׁמְךָ בֶּאֱמֶת. הָאֵל יְשׁוּעָתֵנוּ וְעֶזְרָתֵנוּ סֶלָה. בָּרוּךְ אַתָּה יְיָ הַטּוֹב שִׁמְךָ וּלְךָ נָאֶה לְהוֹדוֹת:

(On Chanuckah.)

*עַל הַנִּסִּים. וְעַל הַפֻּרְקָן. וְעַל הַגְּבוּרוֹת. וְעַל הַתְּשׁוּעוֹת. וְעַל הַמִּלְחָמוֹת. שֶׁעָשִׂיתָ לַאֲבוֹתֵינוּ בַּיָּמִים הָהֵם בַּזְּמַן הַזֶּה: בִּימֵי מַתִּתְיָהוּ בֶּן־יוֹחָנָן הַכֹּהֵן. חַשְׁמוֹנַאי וּבָנָיו. כְּשֶׁעָמְדָה מַלְכוּת יָוָן הָרְשָׁעָה עַל עַמְּךָ יִשְׂרָאֵל. לְהַשְׁכִּיחָם תּוֹרָתֶךָ. וּלְהַעֲבִירָם מֵחֻקֵּי רְצוֹנֶךָ. וְאַתָּה בְּרַחֲמֶיךָ הָרַבִּים. עָמַדְתָּ לָהֶם בְּעֵת צָרָתָם. רַבְתָּ אֶת־רִיבָם. דַּנְתָּ אֶת־דִּינָם. נָקַמְתָּ אֶת־נִקְמָתָם. מָסַרְתָּ גִבּוֹרִים בְּיַד חַלָּשִׁים. וְרַבִּים בְּיַד מְעַטִּים. וּטְמֵאִים בְּיַד טְהוֹרִים. וּרְשָׁעִים בְּיַד צַדִּיקִים. וְזֵדִים בְּיַד עוֹסְקֵי תוֹרָתֶךָ. וּלְךָ עָשִׂיתָ שֵׁם גָּדוֹל וְקָדוֹשׁ בְּעוֹלָמֶךָ. וּלְעַמְּךָ יִשְׂרָאֵל עָשִׂיתָ תְּשׁוּעָה גְדוֹלָה וּפֻרְקָן כְּהַיּוֹם הַזֶּה. וְאַחַר כֵּן בָּאוּ בָנֶיךָ לִדְבִיר בֵּיתֶךָ. וּפִנּוּ אֶת־הֵיכָלֶךָ. וְטִהֲרוּ אֶת־מִקְדָּשֶׁךָ. וְהִדְלִיקוּ נֵרוֹת בְּחַצְרוֹת קָדְשֶׁךָ. וְקָבְעוּ שְׁמוֹנַת יְמֵי חֲנֻכָּה אֵלּוּ. לְהוֹדוֹת וּלְהַלֵּל לְשִׁמְךָ הַגָּדוֹל: (וְעַל כֻּלָּם)

VII. We render our heartfelt thanks unto thee, our God and the God of our fathers, who art the firm stay of our existence, our shield of protection at all times. We, indeed, thank thee, and proclaim thy praise for our lives which are in thy hands, for our souls which are under thy guardianship, for the marks of thy providential care which we daily receive, and for the wonderful gifts which thou dost dispense unto us morning, noon, and night. Thou art good, for thy mercies never fail; and thy loving kindness never ceaseth from thy people, for thou hast been their hope and trust from the distant past to the present moment of our lives.*

And for all these mercies will we praise thy Holy Name, our King, now and for evermore.

(During the Penitential Days.)
(Vouchsafe a blissful life unto all the children of thy covenant.)

O that all the living would pay homage unto thee, and praise thy name in truth, O Lord, our help and assistance. Blessed be thou, O Lord, whose name is the All-bountiful, and unto whom the praises of man should be gratefully rendered. Amen!

(On Chanuckah.)
* Specially do we render thanks unto thee, O Lord, for our wonderful preservation from persecution and danger, and for the mighty deeds wrought on our behalf in ancient times at this particular season.

In the days of the Hasmonean priest Mattathias and his sons, when the wicked Grecian government, under Antiochus Epiphanes, sought to exterminate thy people Israel, to cast thy law into oblivion, and compel them to transgress thy statutes, thou didst protect them in thy abundant mercy. Thou didst defend their cause and restore their rights. Thou didst deliver the mighty into the hands of the weak; the many into the hands of the few; the wicked into the hands of the righteous; the defiled into the hands of the pure; and the arrogant into the hands of the followers of thy law. Thus didst thou make known thy power and thy Holy Name unto the nations of the earth by means of thy wondrous redemption and salvation of thy people Israel, which remains a memorable event even unto this day.

After this, thy children entered thy sanctuary at Jerusalem, cleansed it from all the defilement of idolatry, reëstablished thy service, illuminated the courts of thy temple, and appointed these eight days of Chanuckah for the praise and glorification of thy great Name!

תפלת שחרית לשבת ולרגלים

(אֱלֹהֵינוּ וֵאלֹהֵי אֲבוֹתֵינוּ. בָּרְכֵנוּ בַבְּרָכָה הַמְשֻׁלֶּשֶׁת בַּתּוֹרָה. הַכְּתוּבָה עַל יְדֵי מֹשֶׁה עַבְדֶּךָ. הָאֲמוּרָה מִפִּי אַהֲרֹן וּבָנָיו. כֹּהֲנִים עַם קְדוֹשֶׁךָ כָּאָמוּר. יְבָרֶכְךָ יְיָ וְיִשְׁמְרֶךָ: יָאֵר יְיָ ׀ פָּנָיו אֵלֶיךָ וִיחֻנֶּךָּ: יִשָּׂא יְיָ ׀ פָּנָיו אֵלֶיךָ וְיָשֵׂם לְךָ שָׁלוֹם:)

VII. שִׂים שָׁלוֹם טוֹבָה וּבְרָכָה חֵן וָחֶסֶד וְרַחֲמִים עָלֵינוּ וְעַל כָּל־יִשְׂרָאֵל עַמֶּךָ. בָּרְכֵנוּ אָבִינוּ כֻּלָּנוּ כְּאֶחָד בְּאוֹר פָּנֶיךָ. כִּי בְאוֹר פָּנֶיךָ נָתַתָּ לָּנוּ יְיָ אֱלֹהֵינוּ תּוֹרַת חַיִּים וְאַהֲבַת חֶסֶד וּצְדָקָה וּבְרָכָה וְרַחֲמִים וְחַיִּים וְשָׁלוֹם וְטוֹב בְּעֵינֶיךָ לְבָרֵךְ אֶת־עַמְּךָ יִשְׂרָאֵל בְּכָל־עֵת וּבְכָל־שָׁעָה בִּשְׁלוֹמֶךָ:

(During the Penitential Days.)

בְּסֵפֶר חַיִּים בְּרָכָה וְשָׁלוֹם וּפַרְנָסָה טוֹבָה נִזָּכֵר וְנִכָּתֵב לְפָנֶיךָ אֲנַחְנוּ וְכָל עַמְּךָ בֵּית יִשְׂרָאֵל לְחַיִּים טוֹבִים וּלְשָׁלוֹם.

בָּרוּךְ אַתָּה יְיָ עוֹשֵׂה הַשָּׁלוֹם:

(On ordinary Sabbaths the Torah is here taken out and read, page 92.)

(On the New Moon, Chanuckah and Festivals, HALLEL is read — On Succoth, the palm branch and the other species of the vegetable kingdom are here taken, and the following blessing said.)

בָּרוּךְ אַתָּה יְיָ אֱלֹהֵינוּ מֶלֶךְ הָעוֹלָם אֲשֶׁר קִדְּשָׁנוּ בְּמִצְוֹתָיו וְצִוָּנוּ עַל־נְטִילַת לוּלָב:

(On the first day, the following is added.)

בָּרוּךְ אַתָּה יְיָ אֱלֹהֵינוּ מֶלֶךְ הָעוֹלָם שֶׁהֶחֱיָנוּ וְקִיְּמָנוּ וְהִגִּיעָנוּ לַזְּמַן הַזֶּה:

Our God, and the God of our fathers! bless us with the threefold blessing mentioned in the law written by thy servant Moses, and solemnly pronounced by Aaron, and his sons, thy sanctified people, as it is said: "The Lord bless and preserve thee! The Lord make his face to shine upon thee, and be gracious unto thee! The Lord lift up his countenance unto thee, and give thee peace!"

VII. We now implore thee to grant us the precious gift of peace, and to instill within us a contented spirit, benevolence and love. Bless all of us together with the light of thy countenance, so that we may learn to practice charity and righteousness, and to perform deeds of benevolence and love, whereby peace and happiness may be spread around us, in like manner as thou hast blessed thy people Israel, amid all the vicissitudes of life.

(*During the Penitential Days.*)
(And especially on these solemn days of penitence do we pray thee to remenber and inscribe us, and all the people of the house of Israel, in the book of life, blessing, peace, and prosperity.)

Praised be thou, O Lord, the never-failing fount of peace. Amen!

(On ordinary Sabbaths the Torah is here taken out and read, page 92.)
(On the New Moon, Chanuckah and Festivals, HALLEL is read.— On Succoth, the palm branch and the other species of the vegetable kingdom, are here taken, and the following blessing said:)

Blessed be thou, O Lord our God, Ruler of the universe, who hast sanctified us with thy precepts, and commanded us to distinguish this festival with the palm branch.

(On the first day, the following is added:)

Blessed be thou, O Lord our God, Ruler of the universe, who hast vouchsafed unto us life and health, to behold the return of this festive season.

סדר הלל
לראש חדש חנוכה ולרגלים

(תהלים קי״ג)

16. הַלְלוּיָהּ. הַלְלוּ עַבְדֵי יְיָ הַלְלוּ אֶת־שֵׁם יְיָ: יְהִי שֵׁם יְיָ מְבֹרָךְ מֵעַתָּה וְעַד־עוֹלָם: מִמִּזְרַח־שֶׁמֶשׁ עַד־מְבוֹאוֹ מְהֻלָּל שֵׁם יְיָ: רָם עַל־כָּל־גּוֹיִם ׀ יְיָ עַל־הַשָּׁמַיִם כְּבוֹדוֹ: מִי כַּיְיָ אֱלֹהֵינוּ הַמַּגְבִּיהִי לָשָׁבֶת: הַמַּשְׁפִּילִי לִרְאוֹת בַּשָּׁמַיִם וּבָאָרֶץ: מְקִימִי מֵעָפָר דָּל מֵאַשְׁפֹּת יָרִים אֶבְיוֹן: לְהוֹשִׁיבִי עִם־נְדִיבִים עִם נְדִיבֵי עַמּוֹ: מוֹשִׁיבִי ׀ עֲקֶרֶת הַבַּיִת אֵם־הַבָּנִים שְׂמֵחָה הַלְלוּיָהּ:

(תהלים קי״ד)

17. בְּצֵאת יִשְׂרָאֵל מִמִּצְרָיִם בֵּית יַעֲקֹב מֵעַם לֹעֵז: הָיְתָה יְהוּדָה לְקָדְשׁוֹ יִשְׂרָאֵל מַמְשְׁלוֹתָיו: הַיָּם רָאָה וַיָּנֹס הַיַּרְדֵּן יִסֹּב לְאָחוֹר: הֶהָרִים רָקְדוּ כְאֵילִים גְּבָעוֹת כִּבְנֵי־צֹאן: מַה־לְּךָ הַיָּם כִּי תָנוּס הַיַּרְדֵּן תִּסֹּב לְאָחוֹר: הֶהָרִים תִּרְקְדוּ כְאֵילִים גְּבָעוֹת כִּבְנֵי־צֹאן: מִלִּפְנֵי אָדוֹן חוּלִי אָרֶץ מִלִּפְנֵי אֱלוֹהַּ יַעֲקֹב: הַהֹפְכִי הַצּוּר אֲגַם־מָיִם חַלָּמִישׁ לְמַעְיְנוֹ־מָיִם:

HALLEL;

OR

PSALMS OF PRAISE

FOR

FESTIVE OCCASIONS.

(Psalm 113.)

16. Hallelujah! Praise, ye servants of the Lord, praise ye the Name of the Lord! The Name of the Lord be blessed from now and for ever; from the rising of the sun to his going down praised be the Name of the Lord. High above all nations is the Lord, above the heavens his glory. Who is like the Lord our God, that dwells so high, that looks so deep, in the heavens and on the earth? He makes rise from the dust the poor, from the dunghill lifts up the needy, to place him with nobles, with the nobles of his people. He makes the childless in the house abide, a joyful mother of children. Hallelujah!

(Psalm 114.)

17. When Israel went out of Egypt, the house of Jacob from a people of strange tongue, Judah became his sanctuary, Israel his dominion. The sea saw it, and fled; the Jordan turned backward. The mountains skipped like rams, the hills like lambs. What ails thee, O sea, that thou fleest? thou Jordan, that thou turnest back? ye mountains, that ye skip like rams? ye hills, like lambs? Before the Lord tremble, O earth! before the God of Jacob, who changes the rock into a pool of water, the flint into a fountain of water.

סדר הלל

(תהלים קי״ז)

18. הַלְלוּ אֶת־יְיָ כָּל־גּוֹיִם שַׁבְּחוּהוּ כָּל־הָאֻמִּים:

כִּי גָבַר עָלֵינוּ · חַסְדּוֹ וֶאֱמֶת־יְיָ לְעוֹלָם.

הַלְלוּיָהּ:

(תהלים קי״ח)

(After each verse spoken by the Reader, the Choir and Congregation repeat the first verse.)

19. הוֹדוּ לַיְיָ כִּי־טוֹב	כִּי לְעוֹלָם חַסְדּוֹ:
יֹאמַר־נָא יִשְׂרָאֵל	כִּי לְעוֹלָם חַסְדּוֹ:
יֹאמְרוּ נָא בֵית אַהֲרֹן	כִּי לְעוֹלָם חַסְדּוֹ:
יֹאמְרוּ נָא יִרְאֵי יְיָ	כִּי לְעוֹלָם חַסְדּוֹ:

מִן־הַמֵּצַר קָרָאתִי יָּהּ עָנָנִי בַמֶּרְחַבְיָהּ: יְיָ לִי לֹא אִירָא

מַה־יַּעֲשֶׂה לִי אָדָם: יְיָ לִי בְּעֹזְרָי וַאֲנִי אֶרְאֶה בְשֹׂנְאָי:

טוֹב לַחֲסוֹת בַּיְיָ מִבְּטֹחַ בָּאָדָם: טוֹב לַחֲסוֹת בַּיְיָ מִבְּטֹחַ

בִּנְדִיבִים: כָּל־גּוֹיִם סְבָבוּנִי בְּשֵׁם יְיָ כִּי אֲמִילַם: סַבּוּנִי

גַם־סְבָבוּנִי בְּשֵׁם יְיָ כִּי אֲמִילַם: סַבּוּנִי כִדְבֹרִים דֹּעֲכוּ

כְּאֵשׁ קוֹצִים בְּשֵׁם יְיָ כִּי אֲמִילַם: דָּחֹה דְחִיתַנִי לִנְפֹּל

וַיְיָ עֲזָרָנִי: עָזִּי וְזִמְרָת יָהּ וַיְהִי־לִי לִישׁוּעָה: קוֹל · רִנָּה

Hallel.

(*Psalm* 117.)

18. Praise the Lord, all ye nations; praise him, all ye people. For mighty is his kindness toward us, and the truth of the Lord is everlasting. Hallelujah!

(*Psalm* 118.)
(After each verse spoken by the Reader, the Choir and Congregation repeat the first verse.)

19. Give thanks unto the Lord, for he is good;
For everlasting is his kindness!

Let Israel now say:
Yea, everlasting is his kindness!

Let the house of Aaron now say:
Yea, everlasting is his kindness!

Let those who fear the Lord now say:
Yea, everlasting is his kindness!

Out of distress I called on Jah: with enlargement Jah answered me. The Lord is mine, I will not fear: what can man do unto me? The Lord is mine, among my aids; and I will look upon my haters. It is better to shelter with the Lord than to trust in man. It is better to shelter with the Lord than to trust in nobles. All nations inclosed me: by the name of the Lord I cut them off. They moved round me; yea, they inclosed me: by the name of the Lord I cut them off. They moved round me like bees; they were quenched like a fire of thorns: by the name of the Lord I cut them off. Thou didst thrust me to make me fall, but the Lord has helped me. My strength and song is Jah; and he was mine, for my delivery. Hark!

סדר הלל

וִישׁוּעָה בְּאָהֳלֵי צַדִּיקִים יְמִין יְיָ עֹשָׂה חָיִל: יְמִין יְיָ רוֹמֵמָה יְמִין יְיָ עֹשָׂה חָיִל: לֹא־אָמוּת כִּי־אֶחְיֶה וַאֲסַפֵּר מַעֲשֵׂי יָהּ: יַסֹּר יִסְּרַנִּי יָּהּ וְלַמָּוֶת לֹא נְתָנָנִי: פִּתְחוּ־לִי שַׁעֲרֵי־צֶדֶק אָבֹא בָם אוֹדֶה יָהּ: זֶה־הַשַּׁעַר לַיְיָ צַדִּיקִים יָבֹאוּ בוֹ: אוֹדְךָ כִּי עֲנִיתָנִי וַתְּהִי־לִי לִישׁוּעָה: אֶבֶן מָאֲסוּ הַבּוֹנִים הָיְתָה לְרֹאשׁ פִּנָּה: מֵאֵת יְיָ הָיְתָה זֹּאת הִיא נִפְלָאת בְּעֵינֵינוּ: זֶה הַיּוֹם עָשָׂה יְיָ נָגִילָה וְנִשְׂמְחָה בוֹ:

Reader.	Ch. and Cong.
אָנָּא יְיָ הוֹשִׁיעָה נָּא	אָנָּא יְיָ הוֹשִׁיעָה נָּא
אָנָּא יְיָ הַצְלִיחָה נָּא:	אָנָּא יְיָ הַצְלִיחָה נָּא:

בָּרוּךְ הַבָּא בְּשֵׁם יְיָ בֵּרַכְנוּכֶם מִבֵּית יְיָ: אֵל ׀ יְיָ וַיָּאֶר לָנוּ אִסְרוּ־חַג בַּעֲבֹתִים עַד קַרְנוֹת הַמִּזְבֵּחַ: אֵלִי אַתָּה וְאוֹדֶךָּ אֱלֹהַי אֲרוֹמְמֶךָּ:

הוֹדוּ לַיְיָ כִּי־טוֹב כִּי לְעוֹלָם חַסְדּוֹ:

songs of rejoicing and delivery in the tents of the righteous! "The right hand of the Lord creates strength. The right hand of the Lord is exalted; the right hand of the Lord creates strength." I shall not die, but live and tell of the works of Jah. With chastisement Jah visited me, but unto death he has not given me over. Open unto me the gates of salvation: I will go in through them; I will give thanks unto Jah. This gate is the Lord's; the righteous may go in through it. I thank thee, for thou didst afflict me, but hast been mine, for my delivery. The stone the builders rejected has become the head of the corner. From the Lord this has come; it is marvellous in our eyes. This day, the Lord has made it; let us exalt and rejoice thereon.

Reader.	*Ch. and Congr.*
O Lord, give salvation!	O Lord, give salvation!
O Lord, give prosperity!	O Lord, give prosperity!

"Blessed who enters in the name of the Lord." Such is our blessing from the house of the Lord. Mighty is the Lord, and he shines upon us: bind ye the festive sacrifice with cords to the horns of the altar. My might art thou, and I will thank thee; my God, I will exalt thee.

Give thanks unto the Lord, for he is good; for everlasting is his kindness!

THE READING OF THE TORAH

FOR

SABBATHS AND FESTIVALS.

THE TAKING OUT OF THE TORAH.

(Before the Ark is opened, the Choir and Congregation say:)

None is like thee among all powers, O Lord, and nothing like thy works. Thy kingdom is a kingdom of all ages, and thy rule exists in every generation. The Lord reigns; the Lord did reign; the Lord will reign for ever and ever. The Lord will give strength unto his people, the Lord will bless his people with peace.

אֵין כָּמוֹךָ בָאֱלֹהִים אֲדֹנָי וְאֵין כְּמַעֲשֶׂיךָ: מַלְכוּתְךָ מַלְכוּת כָּל־עֹלָמִים וּמֶמְשַׁלְתְּךָ בְּכָל־דּוֹר וָדֹר: יְיָ מֶלֶךְ יְיָ מָלָךְ יְיָ יִמְלֹךְ לְעֹלָם וָעֶד: יְיָ עֹז לְעַמּוֹ יִתֵּן יְיָ יְבָרֵךְ אֶת־עַמּוֹ בַשָּׁלוֹם:

(The Ark is opened, and the Reader says:)

Arise, O Lord! let thy enemies be scattered and thy haters flee before thee. For from Zion comes forth the law, and the word of the Lord from Jerusalem.

קוּמָה יְיָ. וְיָפֻצוּ אֹיְבֶיךָ. וְיָנֻסוּ מְשַׂנְאֶיךָ מִפָּנֶיךָ: כִּי מִצִּיּוֹן תֵּצֵא תוֹרָה. וּדְבַר יְיָ מִירוּשָׁלָיִם:

93 The Reading of the Torah for Sabbaths and Festivals.

(The Rabbi before the Ark.)

Be praised, O Lord of the universe, for the priceless treasure of 'thy law which thou hast given us. We stand here before the open ark of thy Covenant, as humble and faithful worshipers at its sacred shrine. We bow before thee and thy law which is a reflection of thy holy spirit, and pay homage only to thee, for we put not our trust in man, nor rely on any being to whom divinity is ascribed, yea, but in thee alone, gracious Father, do we place our hopes. We know, O God, that thou art truth—that thy law is truth, thy prophets are proclaimers of truth, and that thy every action is founded on love and truth.

Be pleased, O Eternal, to open our hearts to receive thy sacred word, that we may understand its blissful ideas, and with love perform its injunctions. And as we, on this day of rest and holiness (of our Festival of Redemption—of the Giving of the Law—of Rejoicing) send up to thee our prayers from the depth of our hearts, O hearken unto us, and grant us whatever will ennoble our lives,—whatever will create and preserve the peace and serenity of our souls. Amen!

(The Torah is taken out, and the Reader, on elevating it, chants the following verses, which are repeated by the Choir and Congregation.)

Hear, O Israel, the Lord is our God, the Lord is one! שְׁמַע יִשְׂרָאֵל יְיָ אֱלֹהֵינוּ יְיָ אֶחָד:

One is our God, great our Lord, holy is his name! אֶחָד אֱלֹהֵינוּ גָּדוֹל אֲדוֹנֵינוּ קָדוֹשׁ שְׁמוֹ:

(*Reader* alone.)

Magnify the Lord with me, and let us together extol his name! גַּדְּלוּ לַיְיָ אִתִּי וּנְרוֹמְמָה שְׁמוֹ יַחְדָּו:

The Reading of the Torah for Sabbaths and Festivals. 94

Choir and Congregation.

Thine, O Lord, is the greatness and the power, the victory, glory and majesty, even all that is in the heaven and on the earth. Thine, O Lord, is the kingdom, and thou art exalted as Chief over all.

לְךָ יְיָ הַגְּדֻלָּה. וְהַגְּבוּרָה. וְהַתִּפְאֶרֶת. וְהַנֵּצַח. וְהַהוֹד. כִּי כֹל בַּשָּׁמַיִם וּבָאָרֶץ. לְךָ יְיָ הַמַּמְלָכָה. וְהַמִּתְנַשֵּׂא לְכֹל לְרֹאשׁ:

(The Reader having unfolded the Torah elevates it and says:)

This is the Torah which Moses set before the children of Israel, by command of the Lord.

וְזֹאת הַתּוֹרָה אֲשֶׁר שָׂם מֹשֶׁה לִפְנֵי בְּנֵי יִשְׂרָאֵל. עַל פִּי יְיָ:

Choir and Congregation.

Blessed be he, who in his holiness hath given the Torah to his people Israel!

בָּרוּךְ שֶׁנָּתַן תּוֹרָה לְעַמּוֹ יִשְׂרָאֵל בִּקְדֻשָּׁתוֹ:

(The Congregation assume their seats.)

BENEDICTIONS FOR THE READING OF THE TORAH.

(Before reading.)

Praise ye the Lord, unto whom all praise belongeth!
Praised be the Lord for ever and ever!
We praise thee, O Lord, Ruler of the universe, who hast chosen us from among all nations to give us thy law. Blessed be thou, O Lord, our divine lawgiver.

בָּרְכוּ אֶת־יְיָ הַמְבֹרָךְ:
בָּרוּךְ יְיָ הַמְבֹרָךְ לְעוֹלָם וָעֶד:
בָּרוּךְ אַתָּה יְיָ אֱלֹהֵינוּ מֶלֶךְ הָעוֹלָם. אֲשֶׁר בָּחַר־בָּנוּ מִכָּל־הָעַמִּים. וְנָתַן־לָנוּ אֶת־תּוֹרָתוֹ. בָּרוּךְ אַתָּה יְיָ נוֹתֵן הַתּוֹרָה:

95 The Reading of the Torah for Sabbaths and Festivals.

(The portion of the Torah having been read, the following is then said:)

We praise thee, O Lord our God! Ruler of the universe, for having given us a law of truth, whereby a tree of life is planted in our midst. Blessed be thou, O Lord, our divine lawgiver.

בָּרוּךְ אַתָּה יְיָ אֱלֹהֵינוּ מֶלֶךְ הָעוֹלָם. אֲשֶׁר נָתַן־לָנוּ תּוֹרַת אֱמֶת. וְחַיֵּי עוֹלָם נָטַע בְּתוֹכֵנוּ. בָּרוּךְ אַתָּה יְיָ נוֹתֵן הַתּוֹרָה:

BENEDICTIONS FOR THE HAFTARAH.

(Before the prophetical portion.)

We bless thee, O Lord our God, Ruler of the universe, who didst select holy prophets and wast pleased to inspire their words in truth and faithfulness.

We praise thee, O Lord our God, for having chosen thy servant Moses, and through him, thy people Israel, to perform the divine mission of spreading truth and justice.

(After the prophetical portion.)

We praise thee, O Lord our God, Ruler of the universe, the Rock of all ages, our Refuge in all times, the righteous Judge of all generations! Yea, thou art faithful in fulfilling thy word, in performing what thou hast promised, in accomplishing all thou hast spoken, because thou art the embodiment of truth and justice.

Faithful art thou, O Lord, and faithful is thy word which thou didst impart to us through the mouth of thy inspired seers. None of them shall return back fruitless, for thou art a righteous and merciful God.

We render thee our thanks, O Lord, not alone for the sacred teachings of thy holy prophets, but also for the festive days which thou hast sanctified, that we may enlighten and elevate ourselves, through thy blessed word. Amen!

ON SIMCHATH - TORAH.

שִׂישׂוּ וְגִילוּ בְּשִׂמְחַת תּוֹרָה. וּתְנוּ כָבוֹד לַתּוֹרָה.
כִּי טוֹב סַחֲרָהּ מִכָּל סְחוֹרָה. מִפָּז וּמִפְּנִינִים יְקָרָה:

נָגִיל וְנָשִׂישׂ בְּזֹאת הַתּוֹרָה. כִּי הִיא לָנוּ עֹז וְאוֹרָה:

תּוֹרַת יְיָ תְּמִימָה מְשִׁיבַת נָפֶשׁ.
עֵדוּת יְיָ נֶאֱמָנָה מַחְכִּימַת פֶּתִי: נָגִיל.
פִּקּוּדֵי יְיָ יְשָׁרִים מְשַׂמְּחֵי־לֵב.
מִצְוַת יְיָ בָּרָה מְאִירַת עֵינָיִם: נָגִיל.
יִרְאַת יְיָ טְהוֹרָה עוֹמֶדֶת לָעַד.
מִשְׁפְּטֵי־יְיָ אֱמֶת צָדְקוּ יַחְדָּו: נָגִיל.

אַשְׁרֵיכֶם יִשְׂרָאֵל. אַשְׁרֵיכֶם יִשְׂרָאֵל. אַשְׁרֵיכֶם יִשְׂרָאֵל. כִּי בָכֶם בָּחַר
אֵל. וְהִנְחִילְכֶם בְּאוֹר פָּנָיו תּוֹרָתוֹ. תּוֹרַת אֱמֶת. תּוֹרַת חַיִּים:

אַשְׁרֵינוּ מַה־טּוֹב חֶלְקֵנוּ. וּמַה־נָּעִים גּוֹרָלֵנוּ. וּמַה־יָּפָה יְרֻשָּׁתֵנוּ.
חֶלְקֵנוּ בֶּאֱמוּנָתוֹ. גּוֹרָלֵנוּ עֲבוֹדָתוֹ. יְרֻשָּׁתֵנוּ תּוֹרָתוֹ. תּוֹרַת אֱמֶת. תּוֹרַת חַיִּים:

תּוֹרָה הִיא עֵץ חַיִּים. לְכֻלָּם חַיִּים. כִּי עִמְּךָ מְקוֹר חַיִּים:

עֵץ חַיִּים הִיא לַמַּחֲזִיקִים בָּהּ וְתֹמְכֶיהָ מְאֻשָּׁר: דְּרָכֶיהָ דַרְכֵי־
נֹעַם וְכָל־נְתִיבוֹתֶיהָ שָׁלוֹם: אֹרֶךְ יָמִים בִּימִינָהּ בִּשְׂמֹאלָהּ עֹשֶׁר וְכָבוֹד:
יְיָ חָפֵץ לְמַעַן צִדְקוֹ יַגְדִּיל תּוֹרָה וְיַאְדִּיר: יְיָ עֹז לְעַמּוֹ יִתֵּן. יְיָ יְבָרֵךְ אֶת
עַמּוֹ בַשָּׁלוֹם:

אַשְׁרֵי הָעָם שֶׁכָּכָה לּוֹ. אַשְׁרֵי הָעָם שֶׁיְיָ אֱלֹהָיו.

FOR A MOTHER VISITING THE SYNAGOGUE AFTER HER CONFINEMENT.

Lord and Father! With feelings of profound thankfulness, appears the Mother ——— before thee, to whom thou hast given, in thine infinite mercy, a son (a daughter). Thou didst sustain her in her hour of trial, and now, she asks thy aid in performing the duties of a true mother, so that her child may be reared in piety and virtue, that the name ——— (now) given him (her) may ever be an honored one. And do thou, O Eternal Father, spare the tender infant, guard him (her) in the hour of temptation, grant him (her) health and strength, and let his (her) future be such as to bring happiness to the parents and a blessing unto all mankind. Amen! *Choir:* Amen!

FOR A BAR MITZVAH.

O Lord and Father, we beseech thy blessings on behalf of ——— who has this day pronounced the blessings of the Torah, by which he promises to devote himself to thy service. Be thou, O Lord, with him. Strengthen his every pious resolve, and aid him in the hour of temptation, that he may remain faithful to the Religion of Israel, observe all its divine inculcations, and thus promote the happiness of his parents and friends, as well as his own salvation. Amen. *Choir:* Amen.

FOR THOSE RECENTLY MARRIED.

O Lord and Father! During the past week have thy children...and..entered the holy bonds of matrimony. Grant them thy blessing, that their home may become the dwelling-place of love and affection, of truth and piety, so that they may be instrumental in preserving and promoting those domestic virtues which have been, up to this day, the inheritance of the Congregation of Jacob. Amen. *Choir:* Amen.

FOR SICK PERSONS.

Lord and Father, who art ever nigh unto those who call upon thee in truth, we approach thee humbly and sincerely, to implore thy mercy on behalf of our brother (sister) ——— now lying on the bed of pain and sickness. Show compassion unto thy servant, and send him (her) a perfect healing, so that he (she) may again be able to join in praises and thanksgivings for the bestowal of thy bountiful kindness. Amen. *Choir:* Amen.

FOR THOSE DECEASED DURING THE WEEK.

Lord and Father! In submission to thy holy will do we remember to-day the demise of one in our midst. Our brother . . . (sister . . .) has, during the last week, departed this life. His (Her) relatives and friends have appeared in this sanctuary to pour out their grief, and we deeply sympathize with them. O Father of compassion, grant heavenly peace and bliss to the soul that hath returned to her eternal home, and strengthen the mourners, that they may bear thy dispensation in faith and devotion, and let them be reminded of thy holy word, which promises eternal life and salvation hereafter. Amen. *Choir:* Amen.

FOR THE DECEASED, ON THE ANNIVERSARY OF THEIR DEATH.

O Lord and Father! We remember this day our departed brother . . (sister . .), on the anniversary of his (her) death. We beseech thee, cause him (her) to enjoy the happiness which thou hast reserved for those that trust in thee, in thy eternal kingdom, and send thy comfort and thy blessing to those that keep his (her) dear memory enshrined in their hearts, so that they may pass over the road of this life in happiness. Amen! *Choir:* Amen!

99 The Reading of the Torah for Sabbaths and Festivals.

ANNOUNCEMENT OF THE NEW MOON.

O Lord and Father! May it be thy will, that the approaching month of ———, whose beginning we will celebrate on the ——— day of the coming week, may be the harbinger of happiness and blessings unto us all. May it bring us the enjoyment of life and health, peace and rest, prosperity and contentment. O sustain us from thy bountiful hand, which is ever open to satisfy the wants of thy creatures; remove far from us all manner of trouble and sorrow, and so influence our hearts, that we may walk in the path that pleaseth thee, and devote ourselves to thy service. Amen. *Choir:* Amen.

REPLACING THE TORAH IN THE ARK.

(The Congregation rise, and the Reader, taking the Torah, says:)

Let us all praise the name of the Lord, for his name alone is excellent. יְהַלְלוּ אֶת־שֵׁם יְיָ כִּי־נִשְׂגָּב שְׁמוֹ לְבַדּוֹ:

Choir and Congregation.

His majesty extends over earth and heaven. He exalteth the horn of his people— a praise to all his pious servants, even to the children of Israel, the people he hath drawn nigh unto him. Hallelujah! הוֹדוֹ עַל־אֶרֶץ וְשָׁמָיִם. וַיָּרֶם קֶרֶן לְעַמּוֹ. תְּהִלָּה לְכָל־חֲסִידָיו. לִבְנֵי יִשְׂרָאֵל עַם קְרֹבוֹ. הַלְלוּיָהּ:

(The Torah being returned to the Ark, the Reader says:)

Return, O Lord, to the many thousands of Israel. Turn us, O Lord, towards thee, and we shall be turned; renew our days, as thou didst promise of old. שׁוּבָה יְיָ רִבְבוֹת אַלְפֵי יִשְׂרָאֵל: הֲשִׁיבֵנוּ יְיָ אֵלֶיךָ וְנָשׁוּבָה חַדֵּשׁ יָמֵינוּ כְּקֶדֶם:

(The Ark is closed, and the Congregation take their seats.)

תפלת מוסף
לשבת ולרגלים

20. יִתְגַּדַּל וְיִתְקַדַּשׁ שְׁמֵהּ רַבָּא בְּעָלְמָא דִי־בְרָא כִרְעוּתֵהּ וְיַמְלִיךְ מַלְכוּתֵהּ בְּחַיֵּיכוֹן וּבְיוֹמֵיכוֹן וּבְחַיֵּי דְכָל בֵּית יִשְׂרָאֵל בַּעֲגָלָא וּבִזְמַן קָרִיב וְאִמְרוּ אָמֵן.

CHOIR AND CONGREGATION.

אָמֵן יְהֵא שְׁמֵהּ רַבָּא מְבָרַךְ לְעָלַם וּלְעָלְמֵי עָלְמַיָּא. יִתְבָּרַךְ וְיִשְׁתַּבַּח וְיִתְפָּאַר וְיִתְרוֹמַם וְיִתְנַשֵּׂא וְיִתְהַדָּר וְיִתְעַלֶּה וְיִתְהַלָּל שְׁמֵהּ דְּקֻדְשָׁא בְּרִיךְ הוּא לְעֵלָּא מִן כָּל־בִּרְכָתָא וְשִׁירָתָא תֻּשְׁבְּחָתָא וְנֶחָמָתָא דַּאֲמִירָן בְּעָלְמָא וְאִמְרוּ אָמֵן:

21. ברכת שבע

(Reader, the Congregation arise and repeat in a low voice.)

I. בָּרוּךְ אַתָּה יְיָ אֱלֹהֵינוּ וֵאלֹהֵי אֲבוֹתֵינוּ. אֱלֹהֵי אַבְרָהָם אֱלֹהֵי יִצְחָק וֵאלֹהֵי יַעֲקֹב. הָאֵל הַגָּדוֹל הַגִּבּוֹר וְהַנּוֹרָא. אֵל עֶלְיוֹן. גּוֹמֵל חֲסָדִים טוֹבִים. וְקֹנֵה הַכֹּל. וְזוֹכֵר חַסְדֵי אָבוֹת. וּמֵבִיא גְאֻלָּה לִבְנֵי בְנֵיהֶם לְמַעַן שְׁמוֹ בְּאַהֲבָה:

(On the Penitential Days.)

זָכְרֵנוּ לַחַיִּים. מֶלֶךְ חָפֵץ בַּחַיִּים. וְכָתְבֵנוּ בְּסֵפֶר הַחַיִּים. לְמַעַנְךָ אֱלֹהִים חַיִּים:

מֶלֶךְ עוֹזֵר וּמוֹשִׁיעַ וּמָגֵן. בָּרוּךְ אַתָּה יְיָ מָגֵן אַבְרָהָם:

ADDITIONAL SERVICE
FOR SABBATHS AND FESTIVALS.

20. Let the great Name of the Eternal be exalted and sanctified throughout the whole universe, which he hath created according to his will. May his kingdom soon be established over the whole earth, and may ye and all Israel live to partake of the blessings of that happy period. Unto which say ye, Amen.

Choir and Congregation.

Amen! May his great Name be praised for ever and unto all eternity.

Reader.

Yea, let us praise and worship, magnify and exalt the Name of the Most Holy, (blessed be he,) whose glory exceedeth all the praises and hymns that may be rendered unto him by human lips. And let us say, Amen!

---

21. THE SEVENFOLD BENEDICTION.

(The Congregation rise, and pray with the Reader in a low voice.)

I. We arise to praise thee, O Lord our God, and the God of our fathers—God of Abraham, Isaac, and Jacob. Great and mighty art thou, and wondrous are thy works, O Author of the universe. In the abundance of thy mercy thou causest the virtues of the fathers to bring salvation to their children's children.

(During the Penitential Days.)

(Remember us and grant us life, O Eternal, who delightest in dispensing the blessings of life. Write us in the book of life, in order that we may proclaim thy mercy, O God of life.

O Heavenly King! our Supporter, Savior, and Shield! Praised be thou, O Lord, the Shield of Abraham.

תפלת מוסף לשבת ולרגלים

II. אַתָּה גִבּוֹר לְעוֹלָם אֲדֹנָי מְחַיֵה מֵתִים אַתָּה רַב לְהוֹשִׁיעַ.* (מַשִׁיב הָרוּחַ וּמוֹרִיד הַגֶּשֶׁם:) מְכַלְכֵּל חַיִים בְּחֶסֶד מְחַיֵה מֵתִים בְּרַחֲמִים רַבִּים סוֹמֵךְ נוֹפְלִים וְרוֹפֵא חוֹלִים וּמַתִּיר אֲסוּרִים וּמְקַיֵם אֱמוּנָתוֹ לִישֵׁנֵי עָפָר. מִי כָמוֹךָ בַּעַל גְבוּרוֹת וּמִי דוֹמֶה לָךְ מֶלֶךְ מֵמִית וּמְחַיֶה וּמַצְמִיחַ יְשׁוּעָה:

(During the Penitential Days.)

מִי כָמוֹךָ אַב הָרַחֲמִים. זוֹכֵר יְצוּרָיו לַחַיִים בְּרַחֲמִים:

וְנֶאֱמָן אַתָּה לְהַחֲיוֹת מֵתִים. בָּרוּךְ אַתָּה יְיָ מְחַיֵה הַמֵּתִים:

(When praying alone.)

III. אַתָּה קָדוֹשׁ וְשִׁמְךָ קָדוֹשׁ וּקְדוֹשִׁים בְּכָל־יוֹם יְהַלְלוּךָ סֶּלָה. בָּרוּךְ אַתָּה יְיָ הָאֵל הַקָדוֹשׁ:

*(On the First day of Passover, and on the Feast of Conclusion [Atzereth], the following is added:)

READER.

אַתָּה הוּא יְיָ אֱלֹהֵינוּ מַשִׁיב הָרוּחַ וּמוֹרִיד

הַטָל: (Atzereth) הַגֶּשֶׁם: (Passover)

Reader. אָנָא הוֹרִידֵהוּ Choir a. Congregation.

לִבְרָכָה וְלֹא לִקְלָלָה. אָמֵן:

לְשׂבַע וְלֹא לְרָזוֹן. אָמֵן:

לְחַיִים וְלֹא לַמָוֶת. אָמֵן:

II. Thou art ever omnipotent, O Lord, leading us unto life eternal, in thy abundant salvation.

*(Thou biddest the winds to blow and the rain to descend.)

Thou sustainest in beneficence all the living, and thy infinite love will attend us in the regions of a blessed hereafter. As thou supportest the falling, healest the sick, and loosenest the bonds of the oppressed, so doth thy faithfulness not abandon those who sleep in the dust. Who is like unto thee, Master of mighty acts? Who can be compared unto thee, O King, who, whether dispensing death or life, wilt cause salvation to spring forth?

(*During the Penitential Days.*)

(Yea, who is like unto thee, merciful Father, who in mercy rememberest thy creatures to life?)

We faithfully believe that thou wilt restore us from death unto life. Praised be thou, O Lord, who restorest the dead to life.

(When praying alone.)

III. Thou art holy, and thy Name is holy, and it is a mission of holiness to praise thee daily. Praised be thou, O Lord, the Holy God.

---

*(On the First day of Passover, and on the Feast of Conclusion [Atzereth], the following is added:)

It is thou, O Lord our God, who biddest the winds to blow and causest the

(Passover) dew

(Atzereth) rain

to descend.

O, SEND IT DOWN

For a blessing, and not for harm (*Choir & Cong.*) Amen.
For plenty, and not for want. (*Choir & Cong.*) Amen.
For life, and not for death. (*Choir & Cong.*) Amen.

תפלת מוסף לשבת ולרגלים

(At the public Service.)

Read. III. נַעֲרִיצְךָ וְנַקְדִּישְׁךָ כְּסוֹד שִׂיחַ שַׂרְפֵי קֹדֶשׁ. הַמַּקְדִּישִׁים שִׁמְךָ בַּקֹּדֶשׁ כַּכָּתוּב עַל יַד נְבִיאֶךָ. וְקָרָא זֶה אֶל זֶה וְאָמַר:

Choir and Congregation.

קָדוֹשׁ ׀ קָדוֹשׁ קָדוֹשׁ יְיָ צְבָאוֹת מְלֹא כָל־הָאָרֶץ כְּבוֹדוֹ:

Read. כְּבוֹדוֹ מָלֵא עוֹלָם. מְשָׁרְתָיו שׁוֹאֲלִים זֶה לָזֶה. אַיֵּה מְקוֹם כְּבוֹדוֹ. לְעֻמָּתָם בָּרוּךְ יֹאמֵרוּ:

Choir and Congregation.

בָּרוּךְ כְּבוֹד יְיָ מִמְּקוֹמוֹ:

Read. מִמְּקוֹמוֹ הוּא יִפֶן בְּרַחֲמִים. וְיָחוֹן עַם הַמְיַחֲדִים שְׁמוֹ. עֶרֶב וָבֹקֶר בְּכָל יוֹם תָּמִיד. פַּעֲמַיִם בְּאַהֲבָה שְׁמַע אוֹמְרִים:

Choir and Congregation.

שְׁמַע יִשְׂרָאֵל יְיָ אֱלֹהֵינוּ יְיָ אֶחָד:

Read. אֶחָד הוּא אֱלֹהֵינוּ. הוּא אָבִינוּ. הוּא מַלְכֵּנוּ. הוּא מוֹשִׁיעֵנוּ. וְהוּא יַשְׁמִיעֵנוּ בְּרַחֲמָיו שֵׁנִית לְעֵינֵי כָּל־חָי. לִהְיוֹת לָכֶם לֵאלֹהִים:

Choir and Congregation.

אֲנִי יְיָ אֱלֹהֵיכֶם:

Read. אַדִּיר אַדִּירֵנוּ. יְיָ אֲדוֹנֵינוּ. מָה אַדִּיר שִׁמְךָ בְּכָל הָאָרֶץ. וְהָיָה יְיָ לְמֶלֶךְ עַל כָּל הָאָרֶץ. בַּיּוֹם הַהוּא יִהְיֶה יְיָ אֶחָד וּשְׁמוֹ אֶחָד: וּבְדִבְרֵי קָדְשְׁךָ כָּתוּב לֵאמֹר:

Choir and Congregation.

יִמְלֹךְ יְיָ לְעוֹלָם אֱלֹהַיִךְ צִיּוֹן לְדֹר וָדֹר הַלְלוּיָהּ:

Read. לְדוֹר וָדוֹר נַגִּיד גָּדְלֶךָ. וּלְנֵצַח נְצָחִים קְדֻשָּׁתְךָ נַקְדִּישׁ. וְשִׁבְחֲךָ אֱלֹהֵינוּ מִפִּינוּ לֹא יָמוּשׁ לְעוֹלָם וָעֶד. כִּי אֵל מֶלֶךְ גָּדוֹל וְקָדוֹשׁ אָתָּה. בָּרוּךְ אַתָּה יְיָ הָאֵל הַקָּדוֹשׁ:

(The Congregation are seated.)

(At the public Service.)

III. *Reader.* In solemn chants will we give forth the songs of thy glory, and like the Seraphim of the prophetic vision, in united chorus will we sanctify thy holiness, calling one unto the other and saying:

Ch. & Cong. "Holy, Holy, Holy is the Lord of Hosts; the whole earth is full of his glory."

Reader. Yea, his majesty filleth the universe; in vain then would his servants ask, "Where is the seat of his glory?" All creation sounds the response, "Praised—

Ch. & Cong. "Praised be the Majesty of the Lord, it everywhere appeareth."

Reader. Like his majesty, so may his mercy ever appear unto us, and may he bestow grace unto the people, who proclaim the unity of his name evening and morning,—yea, twice daily, with love and devotion do they exclaim: "Hear—

Ch. & Cong. "Hear, O Israel, the Lord our God, the Lord is One!"

Reader. The one Eternal Being is our God! He is our Father! He is our King! He is our Savior! He will, in mercy, hearken unto us, and evince unto all mankind, that he is indeed our God.

Ch. & Cong. "I am the Lord your God."

Reader. Mighty and powerful is the Eternal, our God. Oh how excellent is his name throughout all the earth! He shall be known as sole King and Ruler by the people, all acknowledging on that day: "The Lord is one and his name one."

And thus do we exclaim in the words of the Holy Scriptures:

Ch. & Cong. "The Lord shall reign for ever and ever, even thy God, O Zion, for all generations, Hallelujah."

Reader. From generation to generation will we make known thy greatness, and for evermore proclaim thy holiness. Thy praise shall never depart from our lips, for great and holy art thou, O King. Praised be thou, O Lord, the Holy God.

(The Congregation take their seats.)

תפלת מוסף לשבת ולרגלים

(On the Sabbath.)

IV. אַתָּה יָצַרְתָּ עוֹלָמְךָ מִקֶּדֶם. כִּלִּיתָ מְלַאכְתְּךָ בַּיּוֹם הַשְּׁבִיעִי. אָהַבְתָּ אוֹתָנוּ. וְרָצִיתָ בָּנוּ. וְקִדַּשְׁתָּנוּ בְּמִצְוֹתֶיךָ. וְקֵרַבְתָּנוּ מַלְכֵּנוּ לַעֲבוֹדָתֶךָ. וְשִׁמְךָ הַגָּדוֹל וְהַקָּדוֹשׁ עָלֵינוּ קָרָאתָ. וַתִּתֶּן־לָנוּ יְיָ אֱלֹהֵינוּ בְּאַהֲבָה שַׁבָּתוֹת לִמְנוּחָה. זִכָּרוֹן לְמַעֲשֵׂה־בְרֵאשִׁית. כְּמוֹ שֶׁכָּתַבְתָּ עָלֵינוּ בְּתוֹרָתֶךָ. עַל יְדֵי מֹשֶׁה עַבְדֶּךָ:

(On Festivals.)

IV. אַתָּה בְחַרְתָּנוּ מִכָּל־הָעַמִּים. אָהַבְתָּ אוֹתָנוּ. וְרָצִיתָ בָּנוּ. וְקִדַּשְׁתָּנוּ בְּמִצְוֹתֶיךָ. וְקֵרַבְתָּנוּ מַלְכֵּנוּ לַעֲבוֹדָתֶךָ. וְשִׁמְךָ הַגָּדוֹל וְהַקָּדוֹשׁ עָלֵינוּ קָרָאתָ:

וַתִּתֶּן־לָנוּ יְיָ אֱלֹהֵינוּ בְּאַהֲבָה (*שַׁבָּתוֹת לִמְנוּחָה וּ) מוֹעֲדִים לְשִׂמְחָה חַגִּים וּזְמַנִּים לְשָׂשׂוֹן. אֶת־יוֹם (הַשַּׁבָּת הַזֶּה וְאֶת־יוֹם)

(Passover)	(Shabuoth)	(Succoth)	(Atzereth)
חַג הַמַּצּוֹת הַזֶּה.	חַג הַשָּׁבֻעוֹת הַזֶּה.	חַג הַסֻּכּוֹת הַזֶּה.	הַשְּׁמִינִי חַג הָעֲצֶרֶת
זְמַן חֵרוּתֵנוּ	זְמַן מַתַּן תּוֹרָתֵנוּ	זְמַן שִׂמְחָתֵנוּ	הַזֶּה. זְמַן שִׂמְחָתֵנוּ

(בְּאַהֲבָה) מִקְרָא קֹדֶשׁ זֵכֶר לִיצִיאַת מִצְרָיִם:

(On the Sabbath.)

(יִשְׂמְחוּ בְמַלְכוּתְךָ שׁוֹמְרֵי שַׁבָּת וְקוֹרְאֵי עֹנֶג עַם מְקַדְּשֵׁי שְׁבִיעִי. כֻּלָּם יִשְׂבְּעוּ וְיִתְעַנְּגוּ מִטּוּבֶךָ. וּבַשְּׁבִיעִי רָצִיתָ בּוֹ וְקִדַּשְׁתּוֹ חֶמְדַּת יָמִים אוֹתוֹ קָרָאתָ זֵכֶר לְמַעֲשֵׂה בְרֵאשִׁית:)

---

*) The words in parenthesis are said if the feast occurs on Sabbath.

(*On the Sabbath.*)

IV. When forming thy world in the beginning, thou didst crown thy work with the seventh day. In thy abundant love wast thou pleased to sanctify us with thy commandments, and enjoin on us the mission of thy service, in proclaiming thy great and holy name. Yea, we recognize thy unbounded love in giving us the Sabbath for spiritual joy and bodily repose, enabling us to reflect on thy wonderful works of creation. And thus do we read in thy law, handed us through Moses thy servant

(*On Festivals.*)

IV. Thou hast chosen us from among all nations, and in thy love hast assigned unto us the priestly mission of spreading the knowledge of thy Holy Name, so that we may not alone perform thy commandments, but consecrate ourselves to thy service.

And in the abundance of thy kindness hast thou given us *(Sabbaths for rest and) festive seasons for delight, even this *(Sabbath and this) day of the Feast of

Matzoth, the anniversary of our delivery from bondage,	*Shabuoth*, reminding us of the revelation at Mount Sinai,	*Succoth*, devoted to joy and thanks for thy merciful protection,	*Sh'mini Atzereth*, consecrated to a joyful conclusion of the festive season,

a holy convocation, reminding us of our mission from our going out from Egypt.

(*On Sabbath.*)

Grant that those who observe the Sabbath and call it a delight, may rejoice in the knowledge of thy beneficent government. Yea, the people who sanctify the seventh day may find joy and satisfaction from thy fount of goodness, and as thou wast pleased to sanctify the seventh day, making it the most desirable of all days, may its observance confirm our belief in thee, the Creator of the universe, the Father of all beings.

* The words in parenthesis are said if the feast occurs on Sabbath.

תפלת מוסף לשבת ולרגלים

(On the Sabbath.)

זָכוֹר אֶת־יוֹם הַשַּׁבָּת לְקַדְּשׁוֹ: שֵׁשֶׁת יָמִים תַּעֲבֹד וְעָשִׂיתָ כָּל־מְלַאכְתֶּךָ: וְיוֹם הַשְּׁבִיעִי שַׁבָּת לַיהוָֹה אֱלֹהֶיךָ לֹא־תַעֲשֶׂה כָל־מְלָאכָה אַתָּה וּבִנְךָ־וּבִתֶּךָ עַבְדְּךָ וַאֲמָתְךָ וּבְהֶמְתֶּךָ וְגֵרְךָ אֲשֶׁר בִּשְׁעָרֶיךָ: כִּי שֵׁשֶׁת־יָמִים עָשָׂה יְהוָה אֶת־הַשָּׁמַיִם וְאֶת־הָאָרֶץ אֶת־הַיָּם וְאֶת־כָּל־אֲשֶׁר־בָּם וַיָּנַח בַּיּוֹם הַשְּׁבִיעִי עַל־כֵּן בֵּרַךְ יְהוָה אֶת־יוֹם הַשַּׁבָּת וַיְקַדְּשֵׁהוּ:

יִשְׂמְחוּ בְמַלְכוּתְךָ שׁוֹמְרֵי שַׁבָּת וְקוֹרְאֵי עֹנֶג עַם מְקַדְּשֵׁי שְׁבִיעִי. כֻּלָּם יִשְׂבְּעוּ וְיִתְעַנְּגוּ מִטּוּבֶךָ. וּבַשְּׁבִיעִי רָצִיתָ בּוֹ וְקִדַּשְׁתּוֹ חֶמְדַּת יָמִים אוֹתוֹ קָרָאתָ זֵכֶר לְמַעֲשֵׂה בְרֵאשִׁית:

(On Festivals.)

אֱלֹהֵינוּ וֵאלֹהֵי אֲבוֹתֵינוּ. מֶלֶךְ רַחֲמָן. שׁוּבָה אֵלֵינוּ בַּהֲמוֹן רַחֲמֶיךָ. בִּגְלַל אָבוֹת שֶׁעָשׂוּ רְצוֹנֶךָ. בְּנֵה בֵיתְךָ בֵּית תְּפִלָּה לְכָל הָעַמִּים. וְיָבֹא כָל כָּשֵׁר לְהִשְׁתַּחֲווֹת לְפָנֶיךָ. כַּאֲשֶׁר בִּהְיוֹת מִקְדָּשְׁךָ עַל־מְכוֹנוֹ. וְכֹהֲנִים בַּעֲבוֹדָתָם. וּלְוִיִּם בְּשִׁירָם וְזִמְרָם. וְיִשְׂרָאֵל בְּנוֵיהֶם. עָלוּ בְחִירֶיךָ לֵרָאוֹת וּלְהִשְׁתַּחֲווֹת לְפָנֶיךָ. בְּשָׁלוֹשׁ פַּעֲמֵי רְגָלֵינוּ. כַּכָּתוּב בְּתוֹרָתֶךָ שָׁלוֹשׁ פְּעָמִים ׀ בַּשָּׁנָה יֵרָאֶה כָל־זְכוּרְךָ אֶת־פְּנֵי ׀ יְיָ אֱלֹהֶיךָ בַּמָּקוֹם אֲשֶׁר יִבְחָר בְּחַג הַמַּצּוֹת וּבְחַג הַשָּׁבֻעוֹת וּבְחַג הַסֻּכּוֹת וְלֹא יֵרָאֶה אֶת־פְּנֵי יְיָ רֵיקָם: אִישׁ כְּמַתְּנַת יָדוֹ כְּבִרְכַּת יְיָ אֱלֹהֶיךָ אֲשֶׁר נָתַן־לָךְ:

(*On the Sabbath.*)

Remember the Sabbath day to keep it holy. Six days shalt thou labor and do all thy work, but the seventh day is the Sabbath in honor of the Lord thy God. On it thou shalt not do any work, neither thou, nor thy son, nor thy daughter, thy man-servant, nor thy maid-servant, nor thy cattle, nor thy stranger that is within thy gates. For in six days the Lord made the heavens and the earth, the sea and all that is in them, and rested on the seventh day; therefore the Lord blessed the Sabbath day and hallowed it.

Grant that those who observe the Sabbath and call it a delight, may rejoice in the knowledge of thy beneficent government. Yea, the people who sanctify the seventh day may find joy and satisfaction from thy fount of goodness, and as thou wast pleased to sanctify the seventh day, making it the most desirable of all days, may its observance confirm our belief in thee, the Creator of the universe, the Father of all beings.

(*On Festivals.*)

Our God, and God of our Fathers! Turn unto us in the abundance of thy mercy, for the sake of our ancestors who were zealous in the performance of thy will. Make thy house a house of prayer for all nations, wherein all flesh may come and bow down before thee, with like reverence as when thy chosen ones went up to the Temple at Jerusalem on the three great Festivals; even when thy Sanctuary was standing in its pristine glory, and priests and levites officiated there with chants and songs, and Israel dwelt in their own land. For thus is it written in thy law, "Three times in the year shall all thy males appear before the Lord thy God in the place which he shall choose: on the feast of unleavened bread, on the feast of weeks, and on the feast of booths; and no one shall appear before the Lord empty; each according to what his hand can give, according to the blessing of the Lord thy God, which he hath given thee!"

תפלת מוסף לשבת ולרגלים

(On Sabbath.)

אֱלֹהֵינוּ וֵאלֹהֵי אֲבוֹתֵינוּ.
רְצֵה בִמְנוּחָתֵנוּ. קַדְּשֵׁנוּ
בְּמִצְוֹתֶיךָ. וְתֵן חֶלְקֵנוּ
בְּתוֹרָתֶךָ. שַׂבְּעֵנוּ מִטּוּבֶךָ.
וְשַׂמְּחֵנוּ בִּישׁוּעָתֶךָ. וְטַהֵר
לִבֵּנוּ לְעָבְדְּךָ בֶּאֱמֶת.
וְהַנְחִילֵנוּ יְיָ אֱלֹהֵינוּ בְּאַהֲבָה
וּבְרָצוֹן שַׁבַּת קָדְשֶׁךָ.
וְיִשְׂמְחוּ בְךָ יִשְׂרָאֵל אוֹהֲבֵי
שְׁמֶךָ. בָּרוּךְ אַתָּה יְיָ מְקַדֵּשׁ
הַשַּׁבָּת:

(On Sabbath-New Moon.)

אֱלֹהֵינוּ וֵאלֹהֵי אֲבוֹתֵינוּ.
רְצֵה בִמְנוּחָתֵנוּ. וְחַדֵּשׁ
עָלֵינוּ בְּיוֹם הַשַּׁבָּת הַזֶּה
אֶת־הַחֹדֶשׁ הַזֶּה. לְטוֹבָה
וְלִבְרָכָה. לְשָׂשׂוֹן וּלְשִׂמְחָה.
לִישׁוּעָה וּלְנֶחָמָה. לְפַרְנָסָה
וּלְכַלְכָּלָה. לְחַיִּים וּלְשָׁלוֹם.
לִמְחִילַת חֵטְא וְלִסְלִיחַת עָוֹן
(Leap-Year וּלְכַפָּרַת פָּשַׁע:
כִּי בְעַמְּךָ יִשְׂרָאֵל בָּחַרְתָּ.
וְשַׁבַּת קָדְשְׁךָ לָהֶם הוֹדָעְתָּ.
וְחֻקֵּי רָאשֵׁי חֳדָשִׁים לָהֶם
קָבָעְתָּ. בָּרוּךְ אַתָּה יְיָ
מְקַדֵּשׁ הַשַּׁבָּת וְיִשְׂרָאֵל
וְרָאשֵׁי חֳדָשִׁים:

(On the Festivals.)

אֱלֹהֵינוּ וֵאלֹהֵי אֲבוֹתֵינוּ. (רְצֵה בִמְנוּחָתֵנוּ) קַדְּשֵׁנוּ
בְּמִצְוֹתֶיךָ. וְתֵן חֶלְקֵנוּ בְּתוֹרָתֶךָ. שַׂבְּעֵנוּ מִטּוּבֶךָ.
וְשַׂמְּחֵנוּ בִּישׁוּעָתֶךָ. וְטַהֵר לִבֵּנוּ לְעָבְדְּךָ בֶּאֱמֶת.
וְהַנְחִילֵנוּ יְיָ אֱלֹהֵינוּ (בְּאַהֲבָה וּבְרָצוֹן) בְּשִׂמְחָה וּבְשָׂשׂוֹן
(שַׁבָּת וּ) מוֹעֲדֵי קָדְשֶׁךָ. וְיִשְׂמְחוּ בְךָ יִשְׂרָאֵל אוֹהֲבֵי שְׁמֶךָ.
בָּרוּךְ אַתָּה יְיָ מְקַדֵּשׁ (הַשַּׁבָּת וְ) יִשְׂרָאֵל וְהַזְּמַנִּים:

111 · Additional Service for Sabbaths and Festivals.

(*On Sabbath and New Moon.*)

O our God, and the God of our fathers! Grant that our Sabbath-rest may render us worthy of thy grace, and may this New Moon bring unto us bliss and happiness, joy and gladness, salvation and comfort, sustenance and support, life and peace, forgiveness and remission of our sins and transgressions. For thou hast chosen thy people Israel to be thy servants, and thou didst appoint thy holy Sabbath and establish the ordinance of the New Moon, that they might be reminded of their mission. Blessed be thou, O Lord, who hast sanctified the Sabbath, Israel, and the New Moons.

(*On the Sabbath.*)

O our God, and the God of our fathers! grant that our Sabbath rest may render us worthy of thy grace. Sanctify our lives for the performance of thy commandments. Satisfy us with thy abundant goodness, and grant us joy through thy salvation. Purify our hearts to serve thee in truth, and permit us to enjoy thy holy Sabbath, in full love for thy holy Name. Praised be thou, O Lord, who hast sanctified the Sabbath.

(*On Festivals.*)

O our God, and the God of our Fathers! (Grant that our Sabbath rest may render us worthy of thy grace.) Sanctify our lives for the performance of thy commandments. Satisfy us with thy abundant goodness, and grant us joy through thy salvation. Purify our hearts to serve thee in truth, and permit us to enjoy thy holy (Sabbath and) Festivals, in full love for thy holy Name. Praised be thou, O Lord, who hast sanctified the (Sabbath and) Israel and the Festivals.

תפלת מוסף לשבת ולרגלים

v. רְצֵה יְיָ אֱלֹהֵינוּ בְּעַמְּךָ יִשְׂרָאֵל. וּתְפִלָּתָם בְּאַהֲבָה תְקַבֵּל. וּתְהִי לְרָצוֹן תָּמִיד עֲבוֹדַת יִשְׂרָאֵל עַמֶּךָ. בָּרוּךְ אַתָּה יְיָ שֶׁאוֹתְךָ לְבַדְּךָ בְּיִרְאָה נַעֲבוֹד:

vi. מוֹדִים אֲנַחְנוּ לָךְ. שָׁאַתָּה הוּא יְיָ אֱלֹהֵינוּ וֵאלֹהֵי אֲבוֹתֵינוּ לְעוֹלָם וָעֶד. צוּר חַיֵּינוּ. מָגֵן יִשְׁעֵנוּ. אַתָּה הוּא לְדוֹר וָדוֹר. נוֹדֶה לְּךָ וּנְסַפֵּר תְּהִלָּתֶךָ. עַל חַיֵּינוּ הַמְּסוּרִים בְּיָדֶךָ. וְעַל נִשְׁמוֹתֵינוּ הַפְּקוּדוֹת לָךְ. וְעַל נִסֶּיךָ שֶׁבְּכָל-יוֹם עִמָּנוּ. וְעַל נִפְלְאוֹתֶיךָ וְטוֹבוֹתֶיךָ שֶׁבְּכָל-עֵת. עֶרֶב וָבֹקֶר וְצָהֳרָיִם. הַטּוֹב כִּי לֹא-כָלוּ רַחֲמֶיךָ. וְהַמְרַחֵם כִּי לֹא-תַמּוּ חֲסָדֶיךָ. מֵעוֹלָם קִוִּינוּ לָךְ:*

(On Hanuccah.)

*עַל הַנִּסִּים. וְעַל הַפֻּרְקָן. וְעַל הַגְּבוּרוֹת. וְעַל הַתְּשׁוּעוֹת. וְעַל הַמִּלְחָמוֹת. שֶׁעָשִׂיתָ לַאֲבוֹתֵינוּ בַּיָּמִים הָהֵם בַּזְּמַן הַזֶּה:

בִּימֵי מַתִּתְיָהוּ בֶּן-יוֹחָנָן הַכֹּהֵן. חַשְׁמוֹנַי וּבָנָיו. כְּשֶׁעָמְדָה מַלְכוּת יָוָן הָרְשָׁעָה עַל עַמְּךָ יִשְׂרָאֵל. לְהַשְׁכִּיחָם תּוֹרָתֶךָ. וּלְהַעֲבִירָם מֵחֻקֵּי רְצוֹנֶךָ. וְאַתָּה בְּרַחֲמֶיךָ הָרַבִּים. עָמַדְתָּ לָהֶם בְּעֵת צָרָתָם. רַבְתָּ אֶת-רִיבָם. דַּנְתָּ אֶת-דִּינָם. נָקַמְתָּ אֶת-נִקְמָתָם. מָסַרְתָּ גִבּוֹרִים בְּיַד חַלָּשִׁים. וְרַבִּים בְּיַד מְעַטִּים. וּטְמֵאִים בְּיַד טְהוֹרִים. וּרְשָׁעִים בְּיַד צַדִּיקִים. וְזֵדִים בְּיַד עוֹסְקֵי תוֹרָתֶךָ. וּלְךָ עָשִׂיתָ שֵׁם גָּדוֹל וְקָדוֹשׁ בְּעוֹלָמֶךָ. וּלְעַמְּךָ יִשְׂרָאֵל עָשִׂיתָ תְּשׁוּעָה גְדוֹלָה וּפֻרְקָן כְּהַיּוֹם הַזֶּה. וְאַחַר כֵּן בָּאוּ בָנֶיךָ לִדְבִיר בֵּיתֶךָ. וּפִנּוּ אֶת-הֵיכָלֶךָ. וְטִהֲרוּ אֶת-מִקְדָּשֶׁךָ. וְהִדְלִיקוּ נֵרוֹת בְּחַצְרוֹת קָדְשֶׁךָ. וְקָבְעוּ שְׁמוֹנַת יְמֵי חֲנֻכָּה אֵלּוּ. לְהוֹדוֹת וּלְהַלֵּל לְשִׁמְךָ הַגָּדוֹל: (וְעַל כֻּלָּם)

V. O Lord our God! Bestow thy grace upon thy people Israel; accept the prayers of those who approach thee in love, and let the worship of thy people Israel be ever pleasing unto thee.

Praised be thou, O Lord, unto whom alone do we offer reverence and adoration. Amen!

VI. We render our heartfelt thanks unto thee, our God and the God of our fathers, who art the firm stay of our existence, our shield of protection at all times. We, indeed, thank thee, and proclaim thy praise for our lives which are in thy hands, for our souls which are under thy guardianship, for the marks of thy providential care which we daily receive, and for the wonderful gifts which thou dost dispense unto us morning, noon, and night. Thou art good, for thy mercies never fail; and thy loving kindness never ceaseth from thy people, for thou hast been their hope and trust from the distant past to the present moment of our lives.*

(*On Chanuckah.*)

* Specially do we render thanks unto thee, O Lord, for our wonderful preservation from persecution and danger, and for the mighty deeds wrought on our behalf in ancient times at this particular season.

In the days of the Hasmonean priest Mattathias and his sons, when the wicked Grecian government, under Antiochus Epiphanes, sought to exterminate thy people Israel, to cast thy law into oblivion, and compel them to transgress thy statutes, thou didst protect them in thy abundant mercy. Thou didst defend their cause and restore their rights. Thou didst deliver the mighty into the hands of the weak; the many into the hands of the few; the wicked into the hands of the righteous; the defiled into the hands of the pure; and the arrogant into the hands of the followers of thy law. Thus didst thou make known thy power and thy Holy Name unto the nations of the earth by means of thy wondrous redemption and salvation of thy people Israel, which remains a memorable event even unto this day.

After this, thy children entered thy sanctuary at Jerusalem, cleansed it from all the defilement of idolatry, reëstablished thy service, illuminated the courts of thy temple, and appointed these eight days of Chanuckah for the praise and glorification of thy great Name!

תפלת מוסף לשבת ולרגלים

וְעַל־כֻּלָּם יִתְבָּרַךְ וְיִתְרוֹמַם שִׁמְךָ מַלְכֵּנוּ תָּמִיד לְעוֹלָם וָעֶד:

(During the Penitential Days.)
וּכְתוֹב לְחַיִּים טוֹבִים כָּל־בְּנֵי בְרִיתֶךָ:

וְכֹל הַחַיִּים יוֹדוּךָ סֶּלָה. וִיהַלְלוּ אֶת־שִׁמְךָ בֶּאֱמֶת. הָאֵל יְשׁוּעָתֵנוּ וְעֶזְרָתֵנוּ סֶלָה. בָּרוּךְ אַתָּה יְיָ הַטּוֹב שִׁמְךָ וּלְךָ נָאֶה לְהוֹדוֹת:

(אֱלֹהֵינוּ וֵאלֹהֵי אֲבוֹתֵינוּ. בָּרְכֵנוּ בַבְּרָכָה הַמְשֻׁלֶּשֶׁת בַּתּוֹרָה. הַכְּתוּבָה עַל יְדֵי מֹשֶׁה עַבְדֶּךָ. הָאֲמוּרָה מִפִּי אַהֲרֹן וּבָנָיו. כֹּהֲנִים עַם קְדוֹשֶׁךָ כָּאָמוּר. יְבָרֶכְךָ יְיָ וְיִשְׁמְרֶךָ: יָאֵר יְיָ · פָּנָיו אֵלֶיךָ וִיחֻנֶּךָּ: יִשָּׂא יְיָ · פָּנָיו אֵלֶיךָ וְיָשֵׂם לְךָ שָׁלוֹם:)

VII. שִׂים שָׁלוֹם טוֹבָה וּבְרָכָה חֵן וָחֶסֶד וְרַחֲמִים עָלֵינוּ וְעַל־כָּל־יִשְׂרָאֵל עַמֶּךָ. בָּרְכֵנוּ אָבִינוּ כֻּלָּנוּ כְּאֶחָד בְּאוֹר פָּנֶיךָ. כִּי בְאוֹר פָּנֶיךָ נָתַתָּ לָּנוּ יְיָ אֱלֹהֵינוּ תּוֹרַת חַיִּים וְאַהֲבַת חֶסֶד וּצְדָקָה וּבְרָכָה וְרַחֲמִים וְחַיִּים וְשָׁלוֹם וְטוֹב בְּעֵינֶיךָ לְבָרֵךְ אֶת־עַמְּךָ יִשְׂרָאֵל בְּכָל־עֵת וּבְכָל־שָׁעָה בִּשְׁלוֹמֶךָ:

(During the Penitential Days.)
בְּסֵפֶר חַיִּים בְּרָכָה וְשָׁלוֹם וּפַרְנָסָה טוֹבָה נִזָּכֵר וְנִכָּתֵב לְפָנֶיךָ אֲנַחְנוּ וְכָל־עַמְּךָ בֵּית יִשְׂרָאֵל לְחַיִּים טוֹבִים וּלְשָׁלוֹם.

בָּרוּךְ אַתָּה יְיָ עוֹשֵׂה הַשָּׁלוֹם:

(On Succoth, instead of אֵין כֵּאלֹהֵינוּ, Hoshanoth; Appendix No. 1.)

And for all these mercies will we praise thy Holy Name, our King, now and for evermore.

(During the Penitential Days.)
(Vouchsafe a blissful life unto all the children of thy covenant.)

O that all the living would pay homage unto thee, and praise thy name in truth, O Lord, our help and assistance. Blessed be thou, O Lord, whose name is the All-bountiful, and unto whom the praises of man should be gratefully rendered. Amen!

(At the public Service.)

(Our God, and the God of our fathers! bless us with the threefold blessing mentioned in the law written by thy servant Moses, and solemnly pronounced by Aaron, and his sons, thy sanctified people, as it is said: "The Lord bless and preserve thee! The Lord make his face to shine upon thee, and be gracious unto thee! The Lord lift up his countenance unto thee, and give thee peace!"

VII. We now implore thee to grant us the precious gift of peace, and to instill within us a contented spirit, benevolence and love. Bless all of us together with the light of thy countenance, so that we may learn to practice charity and righteousness, and to perform deeds of benevolence and love, whereby peace and happiness may be spread around us, in like manner as thou hast blessed thy people Israel, amid all the vicissitudes of life.

(During the Penitential Days.)

(And especially on these solemn days of penitence do we pray thee to remenber and inscribe us, and all the people of the house of Israel, in the book of life, blessing, peace, and prosperity.)

Praised be thou, O Lord, the never-failing fount of peace. Amen!

(On Succoth say, instead of En-kelohanu, Hoshanoth; Appendix No. 1.)

Additional Service for Sabbaths and Festivals.

Choir and Congregation.   Reader. 22.

There is none like our God!	אֵין כֵּאלֹהֵינוּ.
There is none like our Lord!	אֵין כַּאדוֹנֵינוּ.
There is none like our King!	אֵין כְּמַלְכֵּנוּ.
There is none like our Savior!	אֵין כְּמוֹשִׁיעֵנוּ:
Who is like our God?	מִי כֵאלֹהֵינוּ.
Who is like our Lord?	מִי כַאדוֹנֵינוּ.
Who is like our King?	מִי כְמַלְכֵּנוּ.
Who is like our Savior?	מִי כְמוֹשִׁיעֵנוּ:
We will give thanks unto our God!	נוֹדֶה לֵאלֹהֵינוּ.
We will give thanks unto our Lord!	נוֹדֶה לַאדוֹנֵינוּ.
We will give thanks unto our King!	נוֹדֶה לְמַלְכֵּנוּ.
We will give thanks unto our Savior!	נוֹדֶה לְמוֹשִׁיעֵנוּ:
Blessed be our God!	בָּרוּךְ אֱלֹהֵינוּ.
Blessed be our Lord!	בָּרוּךְ אֲדוֹנֵינוּ.
Blessed be our King!	בָּרוּךְ מַלְכֵּנוּ.
Blessed be our Savior!	בָּרוּךְ מוֹשִׁיעֵנוּ:
Thou art our God!	אַתָּה הוּא אֱלֹהֵינוּ.
Thou art our Lord!	אַתָּה הוּא אֲדוֹנֵינוּ.
Thou art our King!	אַתָּה הוּא מַלְכֵּנוּ.
Thou art our Savior!	אַתָּה הוּא מוֹשִׁיעֵנוּ:

28. PRAYERS IN MEMORY OF THE DEAD.

Reader.

Every believer in God, whose unity it is the mission of Israel to proclaim, will partake of the everlasting life of futurity, as we read in the Holy Scriptures: "Thy people are all the righteous, and will inherit the eternal kingdom." Happy is he who adheres to the law and performs the will of his Creator; he will gain a good name while living, and will depart from earth with a good name. Of him it is said: "Better is the fragrance of a good name than the perfume of precious oil; even better is the day of death (to him) than the day of birth." In the paths of virtue there is life, and in its ways there is immortality.

Yea, there is a future where thy hope will not be cut off; for know that it is in the world to come that the righteous will find their complete reward.

כָּל־יִשְׂרָאֵל יֵשׁ לָהֶם חֵלֶק לְעוֹלָם הַבָּא. שֶׁנֶּאֱמַר וְעַמֵּךְ כֻּלָּם צַדִּיקִים. לְעוֹלָם יִירְשׁוּ אָרֶץ: אַשְׁרֵי מִי שֶׁעֲמָלוֹ בַתּוֹרָה. וְעָשָׂה רְצוֹן יוֹצְרוֹ. גָּדֵל בְּשֵׁם טוֹב. וְנִפְטַר בְּשֵׁם טוֹב מִן הָעוֹלָם. וְעָלָיו נֶאֱמַר טוֹב שֵׁם מִשֶּׁמֶן טוֹב וְיוֹם הַמָּוֶת מִיוֹם הִוָּלְדוֹ: בְּאֹרַח צְדָקָה חַיִּים וְדֶרֶךְ נְתִיבָה אַל־מָוֶת: כִּי אִם־יֵשׁ אַחֲרִית וְתִקְוָתְךָ לֹא תִכָּרֵת: וְדַע שֶׁמַּתַּן שְׂכָרָם שֶׁל צַדִּיקִים לֶעָתִיד לָבֹא:

(Mourners, and those observing the anniversary of a parent's death, will rise and say with the Reader, in a low voice, the *Kaddish* on the following page.)

תפלת מוסף לשבת ולרגלים

Reader and Mourners.

24. יִתְגַּדַּל וְיִתְקַדַּשׁ שְׁמֵהּ רַבָּא. בְּעָלְמָא דִּי־בְרָא כִרְעוּתֵהּ וְיַמְלִיךְ מַלְכוּתֵהּ בְּחַיֵּיכוֹן וּבְיוֹמֵיכוֹן וּבְחַיֵּי דְכָל בֵּית יִשְׂרָאֵל בַּעֲגָלָא וּבִזְמַן קָרִיב וְאִמְרוּ אָמֵן:

Congregation.

אָמֵן יְהֵא שְׁמֵהּ רַבָּא מְבָרַךְ לְעָלַם וּלְעָלְמֵי עָלְמַיָּא.

Reader and Mourners.

יִתְבָּרַךְ וְיִשְׁתַּבַּח וְיִתְפָּאַר וְיִתְרוֹמַם וְיִתְנַשֵּׂא וְיִתְהַדָּר וְיִתְעַלֶּה וְיִתְהַלָּל שְׁמֵהּ דְּקֻדְשָׁא בְּרִיךְ הוּא לְעֵלָּא מִן כָּל־בִּרְכָתָא וְשִׁירָתָא תֻּשְׁבְּחָתָא וְנֶחָמָתָא דַּאֲמִירָן בְּעָלְמָא וְאִמְרוּ אָמֵן:

Read. תִּתְקַבַּל צְלוֹתְהוֹן וּבָעוּתְהוֹן דְּכָל יִשְׂרָאֵל. קֳדָם אֲבוּהוֹן דִּי בִשְׁמַיָּא. וְאִמְרוּ אָמֵן:)

Reader and Mourners.

עַל יִשְׂרָאֵל וְעַל צַדִּיקַיָּא. וְעַל כָּל מָן דְּאִתְפְּטַר מִן עָלְמָא הָדֵין כִּרְעוּתֵהּ דֶּאֱלָהָא. יְהֵא לְהוֹן שְׁלָמָא רַבָּא. וְחוּלָקָא טָבָא לְחַיֵּי עָלְמָא דְּאָתֵי. וְחִסְדָּא וְרַחֲמֵי מִן קֳדָם מָרֵא שְׁמַיָּא וְאַרְעָא. וְאִמְרוּ אָמֵן:

יְהֵא שְׁלָמָא רַבָּא מִן־שְׁמַיָּא וְחַיִּים טוֹבִים עָלֵינוּ וְעַל־כָּל־יִשְׂרָאֵל. וְאִמְרוּ אָמֵן:

עֹשֶׂה שָׁלוֹם בִּמְרוֹמָיו. הוּא בְּרַחֲמָיו יַעֲשֶׂה שָׁלוֹם עָלֵינוּ. וְעַל כָּל־יִשְׂרָאֵל. וְאִמְרוּ אָמֵן:

Reader and Mourners.

24. Let the great Name of the Eternal be exalted and sanctified throughout the whole universe, which he hath created according to his will. May his kingdom soon be established in the whole earth, and may you and all Israel live to partake of the blessings of that happy period. Unto which say ye, Amen!

Congregation.

Amen! May his great Name be praised for ever and unto all eternity.

Reader and Mourners.

Yea, let us praise and worship, magnify and exalt the Name of the Most Holy, (blessed be he,) whose glory exceedeth all the praises and hymns that may be rendered unto him by human lips. And let us say, Amen!

Reader.

May the prayer and supplications of the whole house of Israel be accepted in the presence of their Father in heaven. And say ye, Amen!

Reader and Mourners.

O that Israel and all the righteous who have departed from this world, and all those who bow with submission to God's inscrutable will, may enjoy the fullness of peace and happiness in the world to come. May they obtain mercy and forgiveness from the Lord of heaven and earth. And say ye, Amen!

And may the fullness of heavenly peace and a happy life on earth be granted unto us and all Israel. And say ye, Amen!

May he who causeth peace to reign on high, cause peace to prevail among us and all Israel. And say ye, Amen!

Additional Service for Sabbaths and Festivals. 120

CONCLUDING PRAYER.

It is a duty incumbent on us to praise the Sovereign Lord of the universe, to give honor unto him, who is the Creator of heaven and earth, who hath removed us from idolatry and superstition, and brought us to the knowledge of light and truth, which have become our happy portion in his service.

(Choir and Congregation rise.)

WE BEND THE KNEE, BOW DOWN, AND GIVE HOMAGE TO THE SUPREME KING, THE MOST HOLY. BLESSED BE HE.

(The Congregation take their seats.)

He hath stretched out the heavens and established the earth, and the residence of his glory is most exalted, even in the heavens above. He is God, and none besides.

Choir and Congregation.

HE IS GOD, AND NONE BESIDES.

Yea, it is an eternal truth that he is our King, and none besides him; for thus is it written in the law: "Know thou this day, and take to heart, that the Eternal is God in the heavens above and on the earth beneath, and there is none else."

We therefore trust speedily to behold thy triumphant glory, O Lord our God, when idolatry will be exterminated from the earth, and the clouds of doubt and error be entirely dispelled. Then will the whole universe recognize thy glorious kingdom, all mankind will acknowledge and call upon thy Name, and every sinner turn in penitence to thee. Yea, all will then know and understand, that before thee alone must every knee bend, to thee alone must every tongue swear fealty, all prostrating themselves and giving honor to thy most Holy Name. All will acknowledge thy dominion, and thou wilt be their Sovereign Ruler for evermore. For thine is the kingdom, and for ever wilt thou reign in glory, as it is written in thy law, "The Lord will reign for ever and ever;" and furthermore is it written, "The Everlasting will be King over all the earth; on that day will it be acknowledged that the Lord is ONE, and his name ONE."

Choir and Congregation.

ON THAT DAY THE LORD EVERLASTING
WILL BE ONE AND HIS NAME ONE.

BENEDICTION.

May the blessing of Divine Providence rest upon you all, O congregation.

"The Lord bless and preserve thee. The Lord cause his countenance to shine upon thee, and be gracious unto thee. The Lord lift up his countenance unto thee, and grant thee peace."

"May peace abide within thy walls, prosperity within thy habitations."

May the Eternal bless the President of the United States and all the constituted authorities, the Governor and officers of this State and this city, that through them order may be preserved, and right and liberty be fostered.

May the Almighty God send unto you and your dear ones the blessings of his day of rest (the delight of his festivals), that the sacred observance of the Sabbath (of this festive day) may impress you with increased faith and fill your souls with heavenly peace. O Lord, give strength unto thy people, bless thy people with peace! Amen!

Choir and Congregation.

HIS PEOPLE'S STRENGTH WILL HE INCREASE,
AND BLESS THEM EVERMORE WITH PEACE! AMEN.

תפלת מנחה
לשבת ולרגלים.

אַשְׁרֵי יוֹשְׁבֵי בֵיתֶךָ עוֹד יְהַלְלוּךָ סֶּלָה:

Happy are they that dwell in thy house, they praise thee continually. Selah.

אַשְׁרֵי הָעָם שֶׁכָּכָה לּוֹ אַשְׁרֵי הָעָם שֶׁיְיָ אֱלֹהָיו:

Happy the people unto whom such is vouchsafed; yea, happy the people whose God is the Lord.

(Psalm 145, page 56, after which the following is said.)

בָּרוּךְ אֱלֹהֵינוּ. שֶׁבְּרָאָנוּ לִכְבוֹדוֹ. וְהִבְדִּילָנוּ מִן הַתּוֹעִים וְנָתַן לָנוּ תּוֹרַת אֱמֶת. וְחַיֵּי עוֹלָם נָטַע בְּתוֹכֵנוּ. הוּא יִפְתַּח לִבֵּנוּ בְּתוֹרָתוֹ. וְיָשֵׂם בְּלִבֵּנוּ אַהֲבָתוֹ וְיִרְאָתוֹ. וְלַעֲשׂוֹת רְצוֹנוֹ. וּלְעָבְדוֹ בְּלֵבָב שָׁלֵם. לְמַעַן לֹא נִיגַע לָרִיק. וְלֹא נֵלֵד לַבֶּהָלָה: יְהִי רָצוֹן מִלְּפָנֶיךָ יְיָ אֱלֹהֵינוּ וֵאלֹהֵי אֲבוֹתֵינוּ. שֶׁנִּשְׁמוֹר חֻקֶּיךָ

Blessed be our God, who hath created us to proclaim his glory, who hath removed us from the path of ignorance and superstition, and hath given us the law of truth—the imperishable source of existence. May he open our hearts to receive his holy law, and impress therein love and reverence, so that we may faithfully perform his will, and serve him with undivided spirit. Then will our toil in this life not be in vain, nor the creations of our mind without value. Vouchsafe then, O Lord our God and God of our fathers, that we may so observe thy law in

Afternoon Service for Sabbaths and Festivals.

בָּעוֹלָם הַזֶּה. וְנִזְכֶּה
טוֹבָה וּבְרָכָה לְחַיֵּי
הָעוֹלָם הַבָּא: לְמַעַן יְזַמֶּרְךָ
כָבוֹד וְלֹא יִדֹּם יְיָ אֱלֹהַי
לְעוֹלָם אוֹדֶךָ: וְיִבְטְחוּ בְךָ
יוֹדְעֵי שְׁמֶךָ כִּי לֹא עָזַבְתָּ
דֹרְשֶׁיךָ יְיָ: יְיָ חָפֵץ לְמַעַן
צִדְקוֹ יַגְדִּיל תּוֹרָה וְיַאְדִּיר:

this sphere as to qualify ourselves for the happiness and blessing of the world to come. And may we never be weary of chanting thy praises, but extol thee, O Lord, continually. Yea, let all who know thy name put their trust in thee, for thou dost not abandon those who truly seek thee. The Lord was pleased to elevate and glorify his law, in order that his righteousness might be known to all.

(On Sabbaths and Festivals occurring on the Sabbath, the Law is here read. See page 93 to 99. For the Benedictions until Kedushah, see p. 72 No. 15, after which the following Kedushah.)

נְקַדֵּשׁ אֶת שִׁמְךָ בָּעוֹלָם כְּשֵׁם שֶׁמַּקְדִּישִׁים אוֹתוֹ
בִּשְׁמֵי מָרוֹם ככתוב על יַד נְבִיאֶךָ וְקָרָא זֶה אֶל זֶה וְאָמַר.
קָדוֹשׁ · קָדוֹשׁ קָדוֹשׁ יְיָ צְבָאוֹת מְלֹא כָל־הָאָרֶץ כְּבוֹדוֹ:
לְעֻמָּתָם בָּרוּךְ יֹאמֵרוּ:
בָּרוּךְ כְּבוֹד יְיָ מִמְּקוֹמוֹ:
וּבְדִבְרֵי קָדְשְׁךָ כָּתוּב לֵאמֹר:
יִמְלֹךְ יְיָ לְעוֹלָם אֱלֹהַיִךְ צִיּוֹן לְדֹר וָדֹר הַלְלוּיָהּ:
לְדוֹר וָדוֹר נַגִּיד גָּדְלֶךָ וּלְנֵצַח נְצָחִים קְדֻשָּׁתְךָ נַקְדִּישׁ
וְשִׁבְחֲךָ אֱלֹהֵינוּ מִפִּינוּ לֹא יָמוּשׁ לְעוֹלָם וָעֶד כִּי אֵל
מֶלֶךְ גָּדוֹל וְקָדוֹשׁ אָתָּה. בָּרוּךְ אַתָּה יְיָ הָאֵל הַקָּדוֹשׁ:

תפלת מנחה לשבת ולרגלים

(On **Festivals** continue on page 74, No. IV, below the line, to page 84.—On Sabbaths say this:)

IV. Thou art one, and thy name is one. And where is one nation on earth crowned like thy people Israel, with a diadem of glory and salvation, even with this day of holy rest, which renews our love and devotion to thee, strengthens our belief and faith in thee, and gives us celestial peace and happiness, calmness and serenity? Such is the rest in which thou delightest. O may thy children ever prize this thy gift, and sanctify thy name in the Sabbath's rest!

IV. אַתָּה אֶחָד וְשִׁמְךָ אֶחָד. וּמִי כְּעַמְּךָ יִשְׂרָאֵל גּוֹי אֶחָד בָּאָרֶץ. תִּפְאֶרֶת גְּדֻלָּה. וַעֲטֶרֶת יְשׁוּעָה. יוֹם מְנוּחָה וּקְדֻשָּׁה לְעַמְּךָ נָתָתָּ. מְנוּחַת אַהֲבָה וּנְדָבָה. מְנוּחַת אֱמֶת וֶאֱמוּנָה. מְנוּחַת שָׁלוֹם וְשַׁלְוָה וְהַשְׁקֵט וָבֶטַח. מְנוּחָה שְׁלֵמָה שֶׁאַתָּה רוֹצֶה בָּהּ. יַכִּירוּ בָנֶיךָ וְיֵדְעוּ כִּי מֵאִתְּךָ הִיא מְנוּחָתָם וְעַל מְנוּחָתָם יַקְדִּישׁוּ אֶת שְׁמֶךָ:

אֱלֹהֵינוּ וֵאלֹהֵי אֲבוֹתֵינוּ רְצֵה בִמְנוּחָתֵנוּ קַדְּשֵׁנוּ בְּמִצְוֹתֶיךָ וְתֵן חֶלְקֵנוּ בְּתוֹרָתֶךָ שַׂבְּעֵנוּ מִטּוּבֶךָ וְשַׂמְּחֵנוּ בִּישׁוּעָתֶךָ וְטַהֵר לִבֵּנוּ לְעָבְדְּךָ בֶּאֱמֶת וְהַנְחִילֵנוּ יְיָ אֱלֹהֵינוּ בְּאַהֲבָה וּבְרָצוֹן שַׁבַּת קָדְשֶׁךָ וְיִשְׂמְחוּ בְךָ יִשְׂרָאֵל אֹהֲבֵי שְׁמֶךָ. בָּרוּךְ אַתָּה יְיָ מְקַדֵּשׁ הַשַּׁבָּת:

(Continue the Benediction, p. 80, V–VII.—Kol Yisrael, and Kaddish, pp. 117–118, No. 23–24.)

FOURTH PART.

PRAYERS
FOR
Week Days.

CONTENTS OF THE FOURTH PART.

Prayers for Week Days.

	PAGE
Introductory Prayer	529
Morning Service	530
Prayer for the New Moon	560
Afternoon Service	565
Evening Service	567
Prayer for the Deceased in the house of Mourning	576

Introductory Prayer.

מַה־טֹּבוּ אֹהָלֶיךָ יַעֲקֹב מִשְׁכְּנֹתֶיךָ יִשְׂרָאֵל: וַאֲנִי בְּרֹב חַסְדְּךָ אָבֹא בֵיתֶךָ אֶשְׁתַּחֲוֶה אֶל־הֵיכַל קָדְשְׁךָ בְּיִרְאָתֶךָ ׀ יְיָ אָהַבְתִּי מְעוֹן בֵּיתֶךָ וּמְקוֹם מִשְׁכַּן כְּבוֹדֶךָ: וַאֲנִי אֶשְׁתַּחֲוֶה וְאֶכְרָעָה אֶבְרְכָה לִפְנֵי־יְיָ עֹשִׂי: וַאֲנִי תְפִלָּתִי לְךָ ׀ יְיָ עֵת רָצוֹן אֱלֹהִים בְּרָב־חַסְדֶּךָ עֲנֵנִי בֶּאֱמֶת יִשְׁעֶךָ:

בָּרוּךְ אַתָּה יְיָ אֱלֹהֵינוּ מֶלֶךְ הָעוֹלָם. אֲשֶׁר קִדְּשָׁנוּ בְּמִצְוֹתָיו וְצִוָּנוּ עַל מִצְוַת צִיצִת:

בָּרוּךְ אַתָּה יְיָ אֱלֹהֵינוּ מֶלֶךְ הָעוֹלָם. אֲשֶׁר קִדְּשָׁנוּ בְּמִצְוֹתָיו וְצִוָּנוּ לְהָנִיחַ תְּפִלִּין:

בָּרוּךְ אַתָּה יְיָ אֱלֹהֵינוּ מֶלֶךְ הָעוֹלָם. אֲשֶׁר קִדְּשָׁנוּ בְּמִצְוֹתָיו וְצִוָּנוּ עַל מִצְוַת תְּפִלִּין:

בָּרוּךְ שֵׁם כְּבוֹד מַלְכוּתוֹ לְעוֹלָם וָעֶד:

תפלת שחרית לחול

1. אֱלֹהַי נְשָׁמָה שֶׁנָּתַתָּ בִּי טְהוֹרָה הִיא. אַתָּה בְרָאתָהּ. אַתָּה יְצַרְתָּהּ. אַתָּה נְפַחְתָּהּ בִּי. וְאַתָּה מְשַׁמְּרָהּ בְּקִרְבִּי. וְאַתָּה עָתִיד לִטְּלָהּ מִמֶּנִּי. וּלְהַחֲזִירָהּ בִּי לֶעָתִיד לָבֹא: כָּל־זְמַן שֶׁהַנְּשָׁמָה בְקִרְבִּי מוֹדֶה אֲנִי לְפָנֶיךָ. יְיָ אֱלֹהַי וֵאלֹהֵי אֲבוֹתַי. בָּרוּךְ אַתָּה יְיָ רִבּוֹן כָּל־הַמַּעֲשִׂים אֲדוֹן כָּל־הַנְּשָׁמוֹת:

2. בָּרוּךְ אַתָּה יְיָ אֱלֹהֵינוּ מֶלֶךְ הָעוֹלָם. אֲשֶׁר נָתַן לַשֶּׂכְוִי בִינָה לְהַבְחִין בֵּין יוֹם וּבֵין לָיְלָה:

בָּרוּךְ אַתָּה יְיָ אֱלֹהֵינוּ מֶלֶךְ הָעוֹלָם. שֶׁעָשַׂנִי יִשְׂרָאֵל:

בָּרוּךְ אַתָּה יְיָ אֱלֹהֵינוּ מֶלֶךְ הָעוֹלָם. פּוֹקֵחַ עִוְרִים:

בָּרוּךְ אַתָּה יְיָ אֱלֹהֵינוּ מֶלֶךְ הָעוֹלָם. מַתִּיר אֲסוּרִים:

בָּרוּךְ אַתָּה יְיָ אֱלֹהֵינוּ מֶלֶךְ הָעוֹלָם. זוֹקֵף כְּפוּפִים:

בָּרוּךְ אַתָּה יְיָ אֱלֹהֵינוּ מֶלֶךְ הָעוֹלָם. אוֹזֵר יִשְׂרָאֵל בִּגְבוּרָה:

בָּרוּךְ אַתָּה יְיָ אֱלֹהֵינוּ מֶלֶךְ הָעוֹלָם. עוֹטֵר יִשְׂרָאֵל בְּתִפְאָרָה:

SERVICE FOR THE MORNING OF WEEK DAYS.

1. My God, the soul which thou hast placed in my body is pure, for it is a portion of thy Holy Spirit, an emanation from thee, who art the fountain of purity. Thou hast created it and formed it. Thou hast breathed it into me, and dost carefully guard it within me. When thou seest fit, thou wilt take it from me, but wilt restore it in the eternal happiness of the future world. Whilst this soul shall continue within me will I adore thee, O Lord my God, and God of my fathers. Blessed be thou, O Lord, Author of all works, Source of all souls.

2. Blessed be thou, O Lord our God, Ruler of the universe, who hast given to man intelligence to distinguish between day and night.

Blessed be thou, O Lord our God, Ruler of the universe, who didst grant me the privilege of being born in the faith of Israel.

Blessed be thou, O Lord our God, Ruler of the universe, who removest the bonds of darkness from the eyes of the blind.

Blessed be thou, O Lord our God, Ruler of the universe, who loosenest the fetters of the oppressed.

Blessed be thou, O Lord our God, Ruler of the universe, who raisest up those who are cast down.

Blessed be thou, O Lord our God, Ruler of the universe, who girdest Israel with the strength of faith.

Blessed be thou, O Lord our God, Ruler of the universe, who crownest Israel with the diadem of their priestly mission.

תפלת שחרית לחול

יְהִי רָצוֹן מִלְּפָנֶיךָ יְיָ אֱלֹהֵינוּ וֵאלֹהֵי אֲבוֹתֵינוּ. שֶׁתַּרְגִּילֵנוּ בְּתוֹרָתֶךָ. וְדַבְּקֵנוּ בְּמִצְוֹתֶיךָ. וְאַל תְּבִיאֵנוּ לֹא לִידֵי נִסָּיוֹן וְלֹא לִידֵי בִזָּיוֹן. וְהַרְחִיקֵנוּ מֵאָדָם רַע וּמֵחָבֵר רָע. וְדַבְּקֵנוּ בְּיֵצֶר הַטּוֹב וּבְמַעֲשִׂים טוֹבִים. וְכוֹף אֶת־יִצְרֵנוּ לְהִשְׁתַּעְבֶּד־לָךְ. וּתְנֵנוּ הַיּוֹם וּבְכָל־יוֹם לְחֵן וּלְחֶסֶד וּלְרַחֲמִים בְּעֵינֶיךָ וּבְעֵינֵי כָל־רוֹאֵינוּ. וְתִגְמְלֵנוּ חֲסָדִים טוֹבִים. בָּרוּךְ אַתָּה יְיָ גּוֹמֵל חֲסָדִים טוֹבִים:

---

3. בָּרוּךְ שֶׁאָמַר וְהָיָה הָעוֹלָם. בָּרוּךְ עוֹשֶׂה בְרֵאשִׁית. בָּרוּךְ אוֹמֵר וְעוֹשֶׂה. בָּרוּךְ גּוֹזֵר וּמְקַיֵּם. בָּרוּךְ מְרַחֵם עַל הָאָרֶץ. בָּרוּךְ מְרַחֵם עַל הַבְּרִיּוֹת. בָּרוּךְ מְשַׁלֵּם שָׂכָר טוֹב לִירֵאָיו. בָּרוּךְ חַי לָעַד וְקַיָּם לָנֶצַח. בָּרוּךְ פּוֹדֶה וּמַצִּיל. בָּרוּךְ הוּא וּבָרוּךְ שְׁמוֹ:

בָּרוּךְ אַתָּה יְיָ אֱלֹהֵינוּ מֶלֶךְ הָעוֹלָם. הָאֵל הָאָב הָרַחֲמָן הַמְהֻלָּל בְּפִי עַמּוֹ מְשֻׁבָּח וּמְפֹאָר בִּלְשׁוֹן חֲסִידָיו וַעֲבָדָיו. וּבְשִׁירֵי דָוִד עַבְדְּךָ נְהַלֶּלְךָ יְיָ אֱלֹהֵינוּ בִּשְׁבָחוֹת וּבִזְמִירוֹת נְגַדֶּלְךָ וּנְשַׁבֵּחֲךָ וּנְפָאֶרְךָ וְנַזְכִּיר שִׁמְךָ וְנַמְלִיכְךָ מַלְכֵּנוּ אֱלֹהֵינוּ יָחִיד חֵי הָעוֹלָמִים. מֶלֶךְ מְשֻׁבָּח וּמְפֹאָר עֲדֵי־עַד שְׁמוֹ הַגָּדוֹל. בָּרוּךְ אַתָּה יְיָ מֶלֶךְ מְהֻלָּל בַּתִּשְׁבָּחוֹת:

Be pleased to assist us, O Lord! that we may be instrumental in furthering the glorious aims of Israel, by walking in thy law and firmly adhering to thy precepts. Suffer us not to fall into temptation or disgrace, but do thou animate our hearts with holy impulses, and endue us with strength to subject our inclinations to thy divine will. Grant that our purity of life may obtain for us grace, favor, and benevolence in thy sight and in the sight of all mankind, and that we may enjoy the abundance of thy beneficence. Blessed be thou, O Lord! who bestowest bountifully goodness and beneficence. Amen.

8. Blessed be he, at whose word the world was called into existence. Blessed be he who fulfills what he promises, and establishes what he ordains. Blessed be he who provides the earth with marks of his mercy for all who dwell thereon. Blessed be he who bestows a good reward upon those who fear him. Blessed be the ever-living and all powerful God, the deliverer and redeemer of all mankind. *Blessed be he, and blessed be his name!*

Blessed be thou, O Lord our God, Ruler of the universe, the almighty and all-merciful Father, who accordest unto thy people and those who fear thee the privilege of praising thy loving kindness. And with the psalms of David, thy faithful servant, will we extol thy great name; with songs and hymns will we render homage unto our King, the only God, the Source of all life! unto whom be praise and glory now and for ever more. Blessed be thou, O Lord and King, for the blissful privilege we enjoy of chanting thy praises and glory. Amen.

(תהלים קמ״ה)

4. אֲרוֹמִמְךָ אֱלוֹהַי הַמֶּלֶךְ וַאֲבָרְכָה שִׁמְךָ לְעוֹלָם וָעֶד: בְּכָל־יוֹם אֲבָרְכֶךָּ וַאֲהַלְלָה שִׁמְךָ לְעוֹלָם וָעֶד: גָּדוֹל יְיָ וּמְהֻלָּל מְאֹד וְלִגְדֻלָּתוֹ אֵין חֵקֶר: דּוֹר לְדוֹר יְשַׁבַּח מַעֲשֶׂיךָ וּגְבוּרֹתֶיךָ יַגִּידוּ: הֲדַר כְּבוֹד הוֹדֶךָ וְדִבְרֵי נִפְלְאֹתֶיךָ אָשִׂיחָה: וֶעֱזוּז נוֹרְאֹתֶיךָ יֹאמֵרוּ וּגְדֻלָּתְךָ אֲסַפְּרֶנָּה: זֵכֶר רַב־טוּבְךָ יַבִּיעוּ וְצִדְקָתְךָ יְרַנֵּנוּ: חַנּוּן וְרַחוּם יְיָ אֶרֶךְ אַפַּיִם וּגְדָל־חָסֶד: טוֹב־יְיָ לַכֹּל וְרַחֲמָיו עַל־כָּל־מַעֲשָׂיו: יוֹדוּךָ יְיָ כָּל־מַעֲשֶׂיךָ וַחֲסִידֶיךָ יְבָרְכוּכָה: כְּבוֹד מַלְכוּתְךָ יֹאמֵרוּ וּגְבוּרָתְךָ יְדַבֵּרוּ: לְהוֹדִיעַ לִבְנֵי הָאָדָם גְּבוּרֹתָיו וּכְבוֹד הֲדַר מַלְכוּתוֹ: מַלְכוּתְךָ מַלְכוּת כָּל־עֹלָמִים וּמֶמְשַׁלְתְּךָ בְּכָל־דּוֹר וָדֹר: סוֹמֵךְ יְיָ לְכָל־הַנֹּפְלִים וְזוֹקֵף לְכָל־הַכְּפוּפִים: עֵינֵי כֹל אֵלֶיךָ יְשַׂבֵּרוּ וְאַתָּה נוֹתֵן־לָהֶם אֶת־אָכְלָם בְּעִתּוֹ: פּוֹתֵחַ אֶת־יָדֶךָ וּמַשְׂבִּיעַ לְכָל־חַי רָצוֹן: צַדִּיק יְיָ בְּכָל־דְּרָכָיו וְחָסִיד בְּכָל־מַעֲשָׂיו: קָרוֹב יְיָ לְכָל־קֹרְאָיו לְכֹל אֲשֶׁר יִקְרָאֻהוּ בֶאֱמֶת: רְצוֹן־יְרֵאָיו יַעֲשֶׂה וְאֶת־שַׁוְעָתָם יִשְׁמַע וְיוֹשִׁיעֵם: שׁוֹמֵר יְיָ אֶת־כָּל־אֹהֲבָיו וְאֵת כָּל־הָרְשָׁעִים יַשְׁמִיד: תְּהִלַּת יְיָ יְדַבֵּר פִּי וִיבָרֵךְ כָּל־בָּשָׂר שֵׁם קָדְשׁוֹ לְעוֹלָם וָעֶד: וַאֲנַחְנוּ ׀ נְבָרֵךְ יָהּ מֵעַתָּה וְעַד־עוֹלָם הַלְלוּיָהּ:

(*Psalm* 145.)

1. I'll praise thee, Lord, my God and King, || And ever bless thy name, || Day after day untiring sing; || and loud extol thy fame. || "Great is the Lord, no search can reach || His might, no word his praise" || Past ages of thy doings preach || And sound thy grand displays. || Like them, thy glorious majesty, || Thy wonders tune *my* song; || And as *they* tell thy victory || So claims thy might my tongue. || Their memory just claims thy grace, || And of thy deeds they sing || "The Lord is gracious to each race, || Kind and long suffering. || The Lord is good to all abroad, || Pity shines on all his rays." || Oh, may all creatures praise thee, God, || As thy true servants praise! || Let them proclaim thy glorious reign, || To men thy deeds commend. || Thy Kingdom ever shall remain, || Thy rule shall never end. || God lifts the feeble when they fall, || And makes the helpless stand; || He sends supplies of food to all || Who wait upon his hand. || He sends content to all that live, || His treasure ne'er decays, || His works abundant mercy give, || And righteous are his ways. || To answer prayer he's ever nigh || For all who seek aright; || He sends redemption when they cry || Who in his truth delight. || He safely keeps his servants all, || Destroys all wickedness; || His praise, therefore, my lips shall call; || His Name all flesh may bless!

But as to us, we will adore
His Holy Name for evermore. Hallelujah.

תפלת שחרית לחול

5. יִשְׁתַּבַּח שִׁמְךָ לָעַד מַלְכֵּנוּ. הָאֵל הַמֶּלֶךְ הַגָּדוֹל וְהַקָּדוֹשׁ בַּשָּׁמַיִם וּבָאָרֶץ. כִּי לְךָ נָאֶה יְיָ אֱלֹהֵינוּ וֵאלֹהֵי אֲבוֹתֵינוּ. שִׁיר וּשְׁבָחָה. הַלֵּל וְזִמְרָה. עֹז וּמֶמְשָׁלָה. קְדֻשָּׁה וּמַלְכוּת. בְּרָכוֹת וְהוֹדָאוֹת. מֵעַתָּה וְעַד־עוֹלָם: בָּרוּךְ אַתָּה יְיָ. אֵל מֶלֶךְ גָּדוֹל בַּתִּשְׁבָּחוֹת. אֵל הַהוֹדָאוֹת. אֲדוֹן הַנִּפְלָאוֹת. הַבּוֹחֵר בְּשִׁירֵי זִמְרָה. מֶלֶךְ אֵל חֵי הָעוֹלָמִים:

6. יִתְגַּדַּל וְיִתְקַדַּשׁ שְׁמֵהּ רַבָּא. בְּעָלְמָא דִי־בְרָא כִרְעוּתֵהּ. וְיַמְלִיךְ מַלְכוּתֵהּ בְּחַיֵּיכוֹן וּבְיוֹמֵיכוֹן. וּבְחַיֵּי דְכָל בֵּית יִשְׂרָאֵל. בַּעֲגָלָא וּבִזְמַן קָרִיב. וְאִמְרוּ אָמֵן: אָמֵן יְהֵא שְׁמֵהּ רַבָּא מְבָרַךְ לְעָלַם וּלְעָלְמֵי עָלְמַיָּא: יִתְבָּרַךְ וְיִשְׁתַּבַּח וְיִתְפָּאַר וְיִתְרוֹמַם וְיִתְנַשֵּׂא וְיִתְהַדָּר וְיִתְעַלֶּה וְיִתְהַלָּל שְׁמֵהּ דְּקוּדְשָׁא בְּרִיךְ הוּא. לְעֵלָּא מִן כָּל־בִּרְכָתָא וְשִׁירָתָא תֻּשְׁבְּחָתָא וְנֶחָמָתָא דַּאֲמִירָן בְּעָלְמָא. וְאִמְרוּ אָמֵן:)

בָּרְכוּ אֶת־יְיָ הַמְבֹרָךְ:
בָּרוּךְ יְיָ הַמְבֹרָךְ לְעוֹלָם וָעֶד:)

7. בָּרוּךְ אַתָּה יְיָ אֱלֹהֵינוּ מֶלֶךְ הָעוֹלָם יוֹצֵר אוֹר וּבוֹרֵא חֹשֶׁךְ עֹשֶׂה שָׁלוֹם וּבוֹרֵא אֶת־הַכֹּל: הַמֵּאִיר לָאָרֶץ וְלַדָּרִים עָלֶיהָ בְּרַחֲמִים. וּבְטוּבוֹ מְחַדֵּשׁ בְּכָל־יוֹם תָּמִיד מַעֲשֵׂה־בְרֵאשִׁית: מָה רַבּוּ מַעֲשֶׂיךָ

5. Yea, for evermore, O our King, be thy Name praised as the great and holy God, the Ruler of heaven and earth; for unto thee appertain all songs and praises, all hymns and psalms, and in blessings and thanksgivings all must acknowledge that thine are the power and dominion, thine the government in holiness and justice, from hence and for evermore. Blessed be thou, O Lord, Almighty King! magnified in hymns of praise and thanksgiving. Thy wondrous deeds are unspeakable, and yet art thou pleased to accept the songs and chants of psalmody with which we approach thy throne. O ever-living King of the universe.

6. Let the great Name of the Eternal be exalted and sanctified throughout the whole universe, which he hath created according to his will. May his kingdom soon be established over the whole earth, and may ye and all Israel live to partake of the blessings of that happy period. Unto which say ye, Amen.

Amen! May his great Name be praised for ever and unto all eternity.

Yea, let us praise and worship, magnify and exalt the Name of the Most Holy, (blessed be he,) whose glory exceedeth all the praises and hymns that may be rendered unto him by human lips. And let us say, Amen!

(*Praise ye the Lord, unto whom all praise belongeth.*
Praised be the Lord, unto whom all praise belongeth, now and for evermore.)

7. Yea, we praise thee, O Lord our God, Ruler of the universe, who causest light and darkness to alternate, and promotest the peace and harmony of all creation.

Thou givest light unto the earth, gladdening those who dwell thereon, greeting us day after day with thy kindness and renewing the wonders of thy crea-

תפלת שחרית לחול

יְיָ. כֻּלָּם בְּחָכְמָה עָשִֹיתָ. מָלְאָה הָאָרֶץ קִנְיָנֶךָ: הַמֶּלֶךְ הַמְרוֹמָם לְבַדּוֹ מֵאָז. הַמְשֻׁבָּח וְהַמְפֹאָר וְהַמִּתְנַשֵּׂא מִימוֹת עוֹלָם: אֱלֹהֵי עוֹלָם בְּרַחֲמֶיךָ הָרַבִּים רַחֵם עָלֵינוּ. אֲדוֹן עֻזֵּנוּ צוּר מִשְׂגַּבֵּנוּ. מָגֵן יִשְׁעֵנוּ מִשְׂגָּב בַּעֲדֵנוּ:

תִּתְבָּרַךְ יְיָ אֱלֹהֵינוּ עַל־שֶׁבַח מַעֲשֵׂה יָדֶיךָ. וְעַל־מְאוֹרֵי־אוֹר שֶׁעָשִֹיתָ יְפָאֲרוּךָ סֶּלָה. בָּרוּךְ אַתָּה יְיָ יוֹצֵר הַמְּאוֹרוֹת:

---

8. אַהֲבָה רַבָּה אֲהַבְתָּנוּ יְיָ אֱלֹהֵינוּ. חֶמְלָה גְדוֹלָה וִיתֵרָה חָמַלְתָּ עָלֵינוּ. אָבִינוּ מַלְכֵּנוּ. בַּעֲבוּר אֲבוֹתֵינוּ שֶׁבָּטְחוּ בָךְ. וַתְּלַמְּדֵם חֻקֵּי חַיִּים. כֵּן תְּחָנֵּנוּ וּתְלַמְּדֵנוּ: אָבִינוּ הָאָב הָרַחֲמָן. רַחֵם עָלֵינוּ. וְתֵן בְּלִבֵּנוּ לְהָבִין וּלְהַשְׂכִּיל. לִשְׁמוֹעַ לִלְמוֹד וּלְלַמֵּד. לִשְׁמוֹר וְלַעֲשׂוֹת. וּלְקַיֵּם אֶת־כָּל־דִּבְרֵי תַלְמוּד תּוֹרָתֶךָ בְּאַהֲבָה: וְהָאֵר עֵינֵינוּ בְּתוֹרָתֶךָ. וְדַבֵּק לִבֵּנוּ בְּמִצְוֹתֶיךָ. וְיַחֵד לְבָבֵנוּ לְאַהֲבָה וּלְיִרְאָה שְׁמֶךָ. וְלֹא־נֵבוֹשׁ לְעוֹלָם וָעֶד. כִּי בְשֵׁם קָדְשְׁךָ הַגָּדוֹל וְהַנּוֹרָא בָּטָחְנוּ. נָגִילָה וְנִשְׂמְחָה בִּישׁוּעָתֶךָ: כִּי אֵל פּוֹעֵל יְשׁוּעוֹת אָתָּה. וּבָנוּ בָחַרְתָּ מִכָּל־עַם וְלָשׁוֹן. וְקֵרַבְתָּנוּ לְשִׁמְךָ הַגָּדוֹל סֶלָה בֶּאֱמֶת. לְהוֹדוֹת לְךָ וּלְיַחֶדְךָ בְּאַהֲבָה. בָּרוּךְ אַתָּה יְיָ הַבּוֹחֵר בְּעַמּוֹ יִשְׂרָאֵל בְּאַהֲבָה:

tion. "How great are thy works, O Lord! in wisdom hast thou made them all; the earth is full of thy treasures." Thou art exalted, O King! and to thee alone is reverential praise and glory due; for the beginning of all things manifesteth thy greatness. O Lord Eternal, in thy infinite mercy have compassion on us, like as from old thou hast been our defence and our fortress, our shield and our refuge.

O that we could exceed in uttering thy praise, beyond all that thy handiwork declares; yea, more than the heavenly luminaries unceasingly announce. Blessed be thou, O Lord, Author of refulgent light. Amen.

---

8. In thy inexhaustible love, O Lord our God! didst thou give us spiritual light, causing it to shine upon us through thy benignity and grace. Our Father and King, as thou didst give thy law as a tree of life to our ancestors who trusted in thee, so be gracious unto us also, and incline our hearts to its sacred teachings, and instill within us the desire for knowledge and understanding, that we may perceive and comprehend all its inculcations, and be enabled to learn and teach, to observe and practise them in devoted love. O! illumine our eyes with thy Torah! Cause us to love thy precepts, and let us so act in the love and fear of thy Name, that we may never be put to shame for our deeds. Unwavering is our trust in thy holy Name, that thou wilt gladden us through thy salvation. For thou, O God! seekest the salvation of all mankind, and hast selected us from all nations and tongues to perform thy service, by proclaiming thy unity in truth and love. Blessed be thou, O Lord, who hast chosen thy people Israel for a mission of love. Amen.

תפלת שחרית לחול

קריאת שמע

שְׁמַע יִשְׂרָאֵל יְהוָה אֱלֹהֵינוּ יְהוָה אֶחָד:

בָּרוּךְ שֵׁם כְּבוֹד מַלְכוּתוֹ לְעוֹלָם וָעֶד:

(דברים ו ד י״א י״ג במדבר ט״ו ל״ז)

וְאָהַבְתָּ אֵת יְיָ אֱלֹהֶיךָ בְּכָל־לְבָבְךָ וּבְכָל־נַפְשְׁךָ וּבְכָל־מְאֹדֶךָ: וְהָיוּ הַדְּבָרִים הָאֵלֶּה אֲשֶׁר אָנֹכִי מְצַוְּךָ הַיּוֹם עַל־לְבָבֶךָ: וְשִׁנַּנְתָּם לְבָנֶיךָ וְדִבַּרְתָּ בָּם בְּשִׁבְתְּךָ בְּבֵיתֶךָ וּבְלֶכְתְּךָ בַדֶּרֶךְ וּבְשָׁכְבְּךָ וּבְקוּמֶךָ: וּקְשַׁרְתָּם לְאוֹת עַל־יָדֶךָ וְהָיוּ לְטֹטָפֹת בֵּין עֵינֶיךָ: וּכְתַבְתָּם עַל־מְזוּזֹת בֵּיתֶךָ וּבִשְׁעָרֶיךָ:

וְהָיָה אִם־שָׁמֹעַ תִּשְׁמְעוּ אֶל־מִצְוֹתַי אֲשֶׁר אָנֹכִי מְצַוֶּה אֶתְכֶם הַיּוֹם לְאַהֲבָה אֶת־יְיָ אֱלֹהֵיכֶם וּלְעָבְדוֹ בְּכָל־לְבַבְכֶם וּבְכָל־נַפְשְׁכֶם: וְנָתַתִּי מְטַר־אַרְצְכֶם בְּעִתּוֹ יוֹרֶה וּמַלְקוֹשׁ וְאָסַפְתָּ דְגָנֶךָ וְתִירֹשְׁךָ וְיִצְהָרֶךָ: וְנָתַתִּי עֵשֶׂב בְּשָׂדְךָ לִבְהֶמְתֶּךָ וְאָכַלְתָּ וְשָׂבָעְתָּ: הִשָּׁמְרוּ לָכֶם פֶּן־יִפְתֶּה לְבַבְכֶם וְסַרְתֶּם וַעֲבַדְתֶּם אֱלֹהִים אֲחֵרִים וְהִשְׁתַּחֲוִיתֶם לָהֶם: וְחָרָה אַף־יְיָ בָּכֶם וְעָצַר אֶת־

9. THE CONFESSION OF FAITH.

Hear, O Israel! The Lord is our God; the Lord is One!

Blessed be the name of his glorious kingdom for evermore.

(Deut. vi. 4–9, xi. 13–21; Numb. xv. 37–41.)

And thou shalt love the Lord thy God with all thy heart, and with all thy soul, and with all thy might. And these words, which I command thee this day, shall be in thy heart. And thou shalt teach them diligently unto thy children, and shalt speak of them when thou sittest in thy house, and when thou walkest by the way; when thou liest down, and when thou risest up. And thou shalt bind them for a sign upon thy hand, and they shall be as frontlets between thy eyes. And thou shalt write them upon the door-posts of thy house, and upon thy gates.

And it shall come to pass, that if ye will hearken diligently unto my commandments which I command you this day, to love the Lord your God, and to serve him with all your heart and all your soul, then will I send rain for your land in its due season, the first rain and the latter rain, that thou mayest gather in thy corn, thy wine, and thy oil. And I will give grass in thy field for thy cattle, and thou shalt eat and be satisfied. Take heed of yourselves, lest your heart be deceived, and ye turn aside, and serve other gods, and worship them. For then the Lord's wrath will be kindled

הַשָּׁמַיִם וְלֹא־יִהְיֶה מָטָר וְהָאֲדָמָה לֹא תִתֵּן אֶת־יְבוּלָהּ וַאֲבַדְתֶּם מְהֵרָה מֵעַל הָאָרֶץ הַטֹּבָה אֲשֶׁר יְיָ נֹתֵן לָכֶם: וְשַׂמְתֶּם אֶת־דְּבָרַי אֵלֶּה עַל־לְבַבְכֶם וְעַל־נַפְשְׁכֶם וּקְשַׁרְתֶּם אֹתָם לְאוֹת עַל־יֶדְכֶם וְהָיוּ לְטוֹטָפֹת בֵּין עֵינֵיכֶם: וְלִמַּדְתֶּם אֹתָם אֶת־בְּנֵיכֶם לְדַבֵּר בָּם בְּשִׁבְתְּךָ בְּבֵיתֶךָ וּבְלֶכְתְּךָ בַדֶּרֶךְ וּבְשָׁכְבְּךָ וּבְקוּמֶךָ: וּכְתַבְתָּם עַל־מְזוּזוֹת בֵּיתֶךָ וּבִשְׁעָרֶיךָ: לְמַעַן יִרְבּוּ יְמֵיכֶם וִימֵי בְנֵיכֶם עַל הָאֲדָמָה אֲשֶׁר נִשְׁבַּע יְיָ לַאֲבֹתֵיכֶם לָתֵת לָהֶם כִּימֵי הַשָּׁמַיִם עַל־הָאָרֶץ:

וַיֹּאמֶר יְיָ אֶל־מֹשֶׁה לֵּאמֹר: דַּבֵּר אֶל־בְּנֵי יִשְׂרָאֵל וְאָמַרְתָּ אֲלֵהֶם וְעָשׂוּ לָהֶם צִיצִת עַל־כַּנְפֵי בִגְדֵיהֶם לְדֹרֹתָם וְנָתְנוּ עַל־צִיצִת הַכָּנָף פְּתִיל תְּכֵלֶת: וְהָיָה לָכֶם לְצִיצִת וּרְאִיתֶם אֹתוֹ וּזְכַרְתֶּם אֶת־כָּל־מִצְוֹת יְיָ וַעֲשִׂיתֶם אֹתָם וְלֹא תָתוּרוּ אַחֲרֵי לְבַבְכֶם וְאַחֲרֵי עֵינֵיכֶם אֲשֶׁר־אַתֶּם זֹנִים אַחֲרֵיהֶם: לְמַעַן תִּזְכְּרוּ וַעֲשִׂיתֶם אֶת־כָּל־מִצְוֹתָי וִהְיִיתֶם קְדֹשִׁים לֵאלֹהֵיכֶם: אֲנִי יְיָ אֱלֹהֵיכֶם אֲשֶׁר הוֹצֵאתִי אֶתְכֶם מֵאֶרֶץ מִצְרַיִם לִהְיוֹת לָכֶם לֵאלֹהִים אֲנִי יְיָ אֱלֹהֵיכֶם:

יְיָ אֱלֹהֵיכֶם אֱמֶת:

against you, and he will shut up the heavens, that there be no rain, and the land will not yield her fruit, and ye shall perish quickly from off the goodly land which the Lord giveth you. Therefore shall ye lay up these my words in your heart and in your soul, and bind them for a sign upon your hand, and they shall be as frontlets between your eyes. And ye shall teach them to your children, speaking of them when thou sittest in thy house, and when thou walkest by the way; when thou liest down, and when thou risest up. And thou shalt write them upon the door-posts of thy house, and upon thy gates. That your days may be multiplied, and the days of your children, in the land which the Lord swore unto your fathers to give them, as the days of heaven over the earth.

And the Lord spoke unto Moses, saying, Speak unto the children of Israel, and bid them to make themselves fringes in the borders of their garments, throughout their generations, and that they put upon the fringes of the borders a thread of blue. And it shall be unto you for a fringe, that ye may look upon it, and remember all the commandments of the Lord, and do them; and that ye seek not after the inclinations of your own heart and the delight of your eyes, in pursuit of which ye have been led astray. That ye may remember, and do all my commandments, and be holy unto your God. I am the Lord your God, who brought you out of the land of Egypt, to be your God: I am the Lord your God.

The Lord your God is ever true and faithful!

תפלת שחרית לחול

10. אֱמֶת וְיַצִּיב וְנָכוֹן וְקַיָּם. הַדָּבָר הַזֶּה עָלֵינוּ לְעוֹלָם וָעֶד. אֱמֶת וֶאֱמוּנָה חֹק וְלֹא יַעֲבוֹר:

אֱמֶת שָׁאַתָּה הוּא יְיָ אֱלֹהֵינוּ וֵאלֹהֵי אֲבוֹתֵינוּ. מַלְכֵּנוּ מֶלֶךְ אֲבוֹתֵינוּ. גּוֹאֲלֵנוּ גּוֹאֵל אֲבוֹתֵינוּ. יוֹצְרֵנוּ צוּר יְשׁוּעָתֵנוּ. פּוֹדֵנוּ וּמַצִּילֵנוּ מֵעוֹלָם שְׁמֶךָ. אֵין אֱלֹהִים זוּלָתֶךָ:

אֱמֶת אַתָּה הוּא רִאשׁוֹן וְאַתָּה הוּא אַחֲרוֹן. וּמִבַּלְעָדֶיךָ אֵין לָנוּ מֶלֶךְ גּוֹאֵל וּמוֹשִׁיעַ. מִמִּצְרַיִם גְּאַלְתָּנוּ יְיָ אֱלֹהֵינוּ. וּמִבֵּית עֲבָדִים פְּדִיתָנוּ. וְיַם־סוּף בָּקַעְתָּ. וִידִידִים הֶעֱבַרְתָּ בְּתוֹכוֹ לַחֲרָבָה:

עַל־זֹאת שִׁבְּחוּ אֲהוּבִים וְרוֹמְמוּ אֵל. וְנָתְנוּ יְדִידִים זְמִירוֹת שִׁירוֹת וְתִשְׁבָּחוֹת. בְּרָכוֹת וְהוֹדָאוֹת לְמֶלֶךְ אֵל חַי וְקַיָּם. רָם וְנִשָּׂא. גָּדוֹל וְנוֹרָא. מַשְׁפִּיל גֵּאִים. וּמַגְבִּיהַּ שְׁפָלִים. מוֹצִיא אֲסִירִים. וּפוֹדֶה עֲנָוִים. וְעוֹזֵר דַּלִּים. וְעוֹנֶה לְעַמּוֹ בְּעֵת שַׁוְּעָם אֵלָיו:

תְּהִלּוֹת לָאֵל עֶלְיוֹן. בָּרוּךְ הוּא וּמְבֹרָךְ. מֹשֶׁה וּבְנֵי יִשְׂרָאֵל לְךָ עָנוּ שִׁירָה. בְּשִׂמְחָה רַבָּה. וְאָמְרוּ כֻלָּם:

מִי־כָמֹכָה בָּאֵלִם יְיָ מִי כָּמֹכָה נֶאְדָּר בַּקֹּדֶשׁ נוֹרָא תְהִלֹּת עֹשֵׂה פֶלֶא:

10. True, firm, unshaken, and stable is this word unto us for ever and ever! yea, a truth unchangeable, a statute unalterable!

The past lays before us the truth, and makes us confident that what thou hast been to our fathers, thou wilt be to us, even a guide, protector, and redeemer, the Rock of our salvation, our Savior and Deliverer. From old such is thy name, and there is no almighty power save thine.

It is a truth that thou art the first and the last, and without thee we have neither King, Redeemer, nor Savior. Thou didst give evidence of this in redeeming us from Egypt, and bringing us out of the house of bondage; and wonderful was thy salvation at the Red Sea, when thou didst lead thy chosen ones safely through its foaming billows.

The hearts of our ancestors were filled with emotions of gratitude for all this, and gave forth songs and chants, benedictions and thanksgivings unto thee, Fountain of life, Ever-existing God! They witnessed thy lofty and sublime acts, thy great and awe-inspiring deeds! They beheld that thou didst overthrow the haughty and raise up the lowly, that thou didst free the enslaved and redeem the depressed, O Helper of the needy and Hearer of the supplications of thy people whenever their petitions come before thee.

Therefore did they utter praises to the God on High, blessed be he, yea, ever blessed. Even Moses and the children of Israel, in accents of joy, chanted the song of praise in unison, shouting:

WHO AMONG THE MIGHTY IS LIKE UNTO THEE, O LORD! WHO IS LIKE UNTO THEE, GLORIFIED IN HOLINESS, FEARFUL IN PRAISED DEEDS, PERFORMING WONDERS!

תפלת שחרית לחול

שִׁירָה חֲדָשָׁה שִׁבְּחוּ גְאוּלִים לְשִׁמְךָ עַל־שְׂפַת הַיָּם יַחַד כֻּלָּם הוֹדוּ וְהִמְלִיכוּ וְאָמְרוּ:

יְיָ יִמְלֹךְ לְעֹלָם וָעֶד:

וְנֶאֱמַר גֹּאֲלֵנוּ יְיָ צְבָאוֹת שְׁמוֹ קְדוֹשׁ יִשְׂרָאֵל. בָּרוּךְ אַתָּה יְיָ גָּאַל יִשְׂרָאֵל:

II. שמונה עשרה

I. בָּרוּךְ אַתָּה יְיָ אֱלֹהֵינוּ וֵאלֹהֵי אֲבוֹתֵינוּ. אֱלֹהֵי אַבְרָהָם אֱלֹהֵי יִצְחָק וֵאלֹהֵי יַעֲקֹב. הָאֵל הַגָּדוֹל הַגִּבּוֹר וְהַנּוֹרָא. אֵל עֶלְיוֹן. גּוֹמֵל חֲסָדִים טוֹבִים. וְקֹנֵה הַכֹּל. וְזוֹכֵר חַסְדֵי אָבוֹת. וּמֵבִיא גְאֻלָּה לִבְנֵי בְנֵיהֶם לְמַעַן שְׁמוֹ בְּאַהֲבָה:

(On the Penitential Days.)
זָכְרֵנוּ לַחַיִּים. מֶלֶךְ חָפֵץ בַּחַיִּים.
וְכָתְבֵנוּ בְּסֵפֶר הַחַיִּים. לְמַעֲנָךְ אֱלֹהִים חַיִּים:

מֶלֶךְ עוֹזֵר וּמוֹשִׁיעַ וּמָגֵן. בָּרוּךְ אַתָּה יְיָ מָגֵן אַבְרָהָם:

II. אַתָּה גִבּוֹר לְעוֹלָם אֲדֹנָי מְחַיֵּה מֵתִים אַתָּה רַב לְהוֹשִׁיעַ. (מַשִּׁיב הָרוּחַ וּמוֹרִיד הַגֶּשֶׁם:)

מְכַלְכֵּל חַיִּים בְּחֶסֶד מְחַיֵּה מֵתִים בְּרַחֲמִים רַבִּים סוֹמֵךְ נוֹפְלִים וְרוֹפֵא חוֹלִים וּמַתִּיר אֲסוּרִים וּמְקַיֵּם אֱמוּנָתוֹ

Yea, the redeemed ones chanted a new song at the seashore when recognizing thy providence, and in united chorus did they acknowledge thy sovereignty, exclaiming:

THE LORD WILL REIGN FOR EVER AND EVER!

And thus it is recorded in the Holy Scriptures, "Our Redeemer, the Lord of Hosts is his name, the Holy One of Israel." Blessed be thou, O Lord, the Redeemer of Israel.

11. THE EIGHTEENFOLD BENEDICTION.

I. We arise to praise thee, O Lord our God, and the God of our fathers—God of Abraham, Isaac, and Jacob. Great and mighty art thou, and wondrous are thy works, O Author of the universe. In the abundance of thy mercy thou causest the virtues of the fathers to bring salvation to their children's children.

(During the Penitential Days.)
(Remember us and grant us life, O Eternal, who delightest in dispensing the blessings of life. Write us in the book of life, in order that we may proclaim thy mercy, O God of life.)

O Heavenly King! our Supporter, Savior, and Shield! Praised be thou, O Lord, the Shield of Abraham.

II. Thou art ever omnipotent, O Lord, leading us unto life eternal, in thy abundant salvation.

(Thou biddest the winds to blow and the rain to descend.)

Thou sustainest in beneficence all living, and thy infinite love will attend us in the regions of a blessed hereafter. As thou supportest the falling, healest the sick, and loosenest the bonds of the oppressed, so doth

תפלת שחרית לחול

לִישֵׁנֵי עָפָר. מִי כָמְוֹךָ בַּעַל גְּבוּרוֹת וּמִי דוֹמֶה לָּךְ מֶלֶךְ מֵמִית וּמְחַיֶּה וּמַצְמִיחַ יְשׁוּעָה:

(On the Penitential Days.)

מִי כָמְוֹךָ אַב הָרַחֲמִים. זוֹכֵר יְצוּרָיו לַחַיִּים בְּרַחֲמִים:

וְנֶאֱמָן אַתָּה לְהַחֲיוֹת מֵתִים. בָּרוּךְ אַתָּה יְיָ מְחַיֵּה הַמֵּתִים:

(When praying alone.)

*III. אַתָּה קָדוֹשׁ וְשִׁמְךָ קָדוֹשׁ וּקְדוֹשִׁים בְּכָל־יוֹם יְהַלְלוּךָ סֶּלָה. בָּרוּךְ אַתָּה יְיָ הָאֵל הַקָּדוֹשׁ:

(At the Public Service.)

*III. נְקַדֵּשׁ אֶת שִׁמְךָ בָּעוֹלָם כְּשֵׁם שֶׁמַּקְדִּישִׁים אוֹתוֹ בִּשְׁמֵי מָרוֹם כַּכָּתוּב עַל יַד נְבִיאֶךָ וְקָרָא זֶה אֶל זֶה וְאָמַר.

CONGREGATION.

קָדוֹשׁ ׀ קָדוֹשׁ קָדוֹשׁ יְיָ צְבָאוֹת מְלֹא כָל־הָאָרֶץ כְּבוֹדוֹ:

Read. לְעֻמָּתָם בָּרוּךְ יֹאמֵרוּ:

Cong. בָּרוּךְ כְּבוֹד יְיָ מִמְּקוֹמוֹ:

Read. וּבְדִבְרֵי קָדְשְׁךָ כָּתוּב לֵאמֹר:

CONGREGATION.

יִמְלֹךְ יְיָ לְעוֹלָם אֱלֹהַיִךְ צִיּוֹן לְדֹר וָדֹר הַלְלוּיָהּ:

READER.

לְדוֹר וָדוֹר נַגִּיד גָּדְלֶךָ וּלְנֵצַח נְצָחִים קְדֻשָּׁתְךָ נַקְדִּישׁ וְשִׁבְחֲךָ אֱלֹהֵינוּ מִפִּינוּ לֹא יָמוּשׁ לְעוֹלָם וָעֶד כִּי אֵל מֶלֶךְ גָּדוֹל וְקָדוֹשׁ אָתָּה. בָּרוּךְ אַתָּה יְיָ הָאֵל הַקָּדוֹשׁ:

thy faithfulness not abandon those who sleep in the dust. Who is like unto thee, Master of mighty acts? Who can be compared unto thee, O King, who, whether dispensing death or life, wilt cause salvation to spring forth?

(*During the Penitential Days.*)

(Yea, who is like unto thee, merciful Father, who in mercy rememberest thy creatures to life?)

We faithfully believe that thou wilt restore us from death unto life. Praised be thou, O Lord, who restorest the death to life.

(When praying alone.)

*III. Thou art holy, and thy Name is holy, and it is a mission of holiness to praise thee daily. Praised be thou, O Lord, the Holy God.

---

*III. We, on earth, will sanctify thy Name as it is sanctified in the heavens above, accomplishing the words of the divine seer, and proclaiming one to the other:

Congregation.

Holy, holy, holy is the Lord of Hosts; the whole earth is full of his glory.

(*Reader.*) Yea, in echoes loud and mighty, thy messengers proclaim thee blessed.

Congregation.

Blessed be the Majesty of the Lord in every place where it is manifested.

(*Reader.*) And thus do we exclaim in the words of the Psalmist:

Congregation.

The Lord shall reign for ever, even thy God, O Zion, for all generations. Hallelujah!

(*Reader.*) From generation to generation will we make known thy greatness, and for evermore proclaim thy holiness. Thy praise shall never depart from our lips, for great and holy art thou, O King. Praised be thou, O Lord, the Holy God!

תפלת שחרית לחול

IV. אַתָּה חוֹנֵן לְאָדָם דַּעַת. וּמְלַמֵּד לֶאֱנוֹשׁ בִּינָה. חָנֵּנוּ מֵאִתְּךָ דֵּעָה בִּינָה וְהַשְׂכֵּל. בָּרוּךְ אַתָּה יְיָ חוֹנֵן הַדָּעַת:

V. הֲשִׁיבֵנוּ אָבִינוּ לְתוֹרָתֶךָ. וְקָרְבֵנוּ מַלְכֵּנוּ לַעֲבוֹדָתֶךָ. וְהַחֲזִירֵנוּ בִּתְשׁוּבָה שְׁלֵמָה לְפָנֶיךָ. בָּרוּךְ אַתָּה יְיָ הָרוֹצֶה בִּתְשׁוּבָה:

VI. סְלַח-לָנוּ אָבִינוּ כִּי חָטָאנוּ. מְחַל-לָנוּ מַלְכֵּנוּ כִּי פָשָׁעְנוּ. כִּי מוֹחֵל וְסוֹלֵחַ אָתָּה. בָּרוּךְ אַתָּה יְיָ חַנּוּן הַמַּרְבֶּה לִסְלוֹחַ:

VII. רְאֵה בְעָנְיֵנוּ וְרִיבָה רִיבֵנוּ. וּגְאָלֵנוּ מְהֵרָה לְמַעַן שְׁמֶךָ. כִּי גּוֹאֵל חָזָק אָתָּה. בָּרוּךְ אַתָּה יְיָ גּוֹאֵל יִשְׂרָאֵל:

VIII. רְפָאֵנוּ יְיָ וְנֵרָפֵא. הוֹשִׁיעֵנוּ וְנִוָּשֵׁעָה. כִּי תְהִלָּתֵנוּ אָתָּה. וְהַעֲלֵה רְפוּאָה שְׁלֵמָה לְכָל תַּחֲלוּאֵינוּ וּלְכָל מַכְאוֹבֵינוּ. כִּי אֵל מֶלֶךְ רוֹפֵא נֶאֱמָן וְרַחֲמָן אָתָּה. בָּרוּךְ אַתָּה יְיָ רוֹפֵא חוֹלִים:

IX. בָּרֵךְ עָלֵינוּ יְיָ אֱלֹהֵינוּ אֶת-הַשָּׁנָה הַזֹּאת. וְאֶת-כָּל-מִינֵי תְבוּאָתָהּ לְטוֹבָה. וְתֵן טַל וּמָטָר לִבְרָכָה עַל פְּנֵי הָאֲדָמָה. וְשַׂבְּעֵנוּ מִטּוּבָךְ. וּבָרֵךְ שְׁנָתֵנוּ כַּשָּׁנִים הַטּוֹבוֹת. בָּרוּךְ אַתָּה יְיָ מְבָרֵךְ הַשָּׁנִים:

IV. O Lord, who in thy grace hast bestowed on man the gift of intelligence, and endowed mortals with the faculty of reason, we pray thee, that we may daily increase in true wisdom and understanding, so that we may fulfill the mission for which we have been placed on earth. Blessed be thou, O Lord, the Fount of all wisdom.

V. And as our daily pursuits may make us forgetful of our high vocation, be thou pleased, our Father, to lead us unto thee and draw us near unto thy service, and whenever we deviate from the right path, O give us strength to return to thee in true penitence. Blessed be thou, O Lord, who graciously acceptest the repentant.

VI. Forgive us, O our Father, our sins; pardon, O our King, our transgressions; for thy mercy never ceases and thy forgiveness is unending. Blessed be thou, O Lord, who abundantly bestowest pardon.

VII. Look with compassion on all the afflicted among us; be thou our guardian and our advocate, and redeem us speedily from all evil, for in thee do we trust as our mighty Redeemer. Blessed be thou, O Lord, who hast at all times been a Redeemer to the house of Israel.

VIII. Heal, we pray thee, all who are diseased, strengthen all that are feeble, and send us relief from affliction and woes, for thou dost faithfully compassionate and tend those who suffer. Blessed be thou, O Lord, the Source of health and strength.

IX. O Lord our God, let this year be blessed with the various products of the ground, whereby our earthly welfare will be advanced. Send dew and rain in their season, so that the soil may be fructified. Bless the work of our hands, and satisfy us from thy abundant treasures. Blessed be thou, O Lord, the Author of all prosperity.

תפלת שחרית לחול

X. תְּקַע בְּשׁוֹפָר גָּדוֹל לְחֵרוּתֵנוּ וְשָׂא נֵס לְקַבֵּץ גָּלֻיּוֹתֵינוּ וְקַבְּצֵנוּ יַחַד מֵאַרְבַּע כַּנְפוֹת הָאָרֶץ. בָּרוּךְ אַתָּה יְיָ מְקַבֵּץ נִדְחֵי עַמּוֹ יִשְׂרָאֵל:

XI. הָשִׁיבָה שׁוֹפְטֵינוּ כְּבָרִאשׁוֹנָה. וְיוֹעֲצֵינוּ כְּבַתְּחִלָּה. וְהָסֵר מִמֶּנּוּ יָגוֹן וַאֲנָחָה. וּמְלוֹךְ עָלֵינוּ אַתָּה יְיָ לְבַדְּךָ בְּחֶסֶד וּבְרַחֲמִים. וְצַדְּקֵנוּ בַּמִּשְׁפָּט. בָּרוּךְ אַתָּה יְיָ מֶלֶךְ אוֹהֵב צְדָקָה וּמִשְׁפָּט:

XII. עַל־הַצַּדִּיקִים. וְעַל־הַחֲסִידִים. וְעַל־זִקְנֵי עַמְּךָ בֵּית יִשְׂרָאֵל. וְעַל־פְּלֵטַת סוֹפְרֵיהֶם. וְעַל־גֵּרֵי הַצֶּדֶק וְעָלֵינוּ יֶהֱמוּ רַחֲמֶיךָ יְיָ אֱלֹהֵינוּ. וְתֵן שָׂכָר טוֹב לְכָל הַבּוֹטְחִים בְּשִׁמְךָ בֶּאֱמֶת. וְשִׂים חֶלְקֵנוּ עִמָּהֶם לְעוֹלָם. וְלֹא נֵבוֹשׁ כִּי־בְךָ בָטָחְנוּ. בָּרוּךְ אַתָּה יְיָ מִשְׁעָן וּמִבְטָח לַצַּדִּיקִים:

XIII. וְלִירוּשָׁלַיִם עִירְךָ בְּרַחֲמִים תָּשׁוּב. וְיָה. וְלִכְבוֹד תִּהְיֶה בְתוֹכָהּ כַּאֲשֶׁר דִּבַּרְתָּ. כִּי מִצִּיּוֹן תֵּצֵא תוֹרָה. וּדְבַר יְיָ מִירוּשָׁלָיִם. בָּרוּךְ אַתָּה יְיָ בּוֹנֵה יְרוּשָׁלָיִם:

XIV. אֶת־צֶמַח עַבְדְּךָ מְהֵרָה תַצְמִיחַ. וְקַרְנוֹ תָּרוּם בִּישׁוּעָתֶךָ. כִּי לִישׁוּעָתְךָ קִוִּינוּ כָּל־הַיּוֹם. בָּרוּךְ אַתָּה יְיָ מַצְמִיחַ קֶרֶן יְשׁוּעָה:

X. May liberty be enjoyed throughout the whole earth, and grant that thy people Israel, in all quarters of the globe, may be recognized and appreciated for their efforts towards the advancement of truth and enlightenment. Blessed be thou, O Lord, who exaltest on high the banner of Israel.

XI. Vouchsafe that those who are intrusted with the government of our public affairs may be inspired with a sense of justice and righteousness. Remove all oppression and wrongs from among us. Let thy kingdom of love and mercy be established on earth, and may we be found guiltless before thy judgment-seat. Blessed be thou, O Lord, who delightest in justice and righteousness.

XII. Have compassion, O Lord our God, on all the righteous and pious, on the leaders of the house of Israel, thy people, on all who spread knowledge and truth, as well as on all those who join our ranks from pure motives and conviction. Let all who trust in thy name be rewarded with the fulfillment of their hopes and aspirations. May we partake of their happiness, and never be ashamed of our faith in thee. Blessed be thou, O Lord, the Staff and Trust of the righteous.

XIII. May the glory of Jerusalem, thy city, be restored as the spiritual centre whence sprung forth all divine ideas, in accordance with thy promise, that from Zion the law should go forth, and the word of the Lord out of Jerusalem. Blessed be thou, O Lord, who didst rear up Jerusalem as the centre of religious ideas.

XIV. Let the salvation of thy servants speedily flourish, and may our dignity be uplifted through thy aid, for it is our trust in thee alone that sustains us day by day. Blessed be thou. O Lord, who raisest the horn of salvation.

תפלת שחרית לחול

XV. שְׁמַע קוֹלֵנוּ יְיָ אֱלֹהֵינוּ. חוּס וְרַחֵם עָלֵינוּ. וְקַבֵּל בְּרַחֲמִים וּבְרָצוֹן אֶת־תְּפִלָּתֵנוּ. וּכִלְּפָנֶיךָ מַלְכֵּנוּ רֵיקָם אַל־תְּשִׁיבֵנוּ. כִּי אַתָּה שׁוֹמֵעַ תְּפִלַּת כָּל־פֶּה בְּרַחֲמִים בָּרוּךְ אַתָּה יְיָ שׁוֹמֵעַ תְּפִלָּה:

XVI. רְצֵה יְיָ אֱלֹהֵינוּ בְּעַמְּךָ יִשְׂרָאֵל. וְתִפִלָּתָם בְּאַהֲבָה תְקַבֵּל. וּתְהִי לְרָצוֹן תָּמִיד עֲבוֹדַת יִשְׂרָאֵל עַמֶּךָ.

(On the New Moon and in the Festival Week.)

אֱלֹהֵינוּ וֵאלֹהֵי אֲבוֹתֵינוּ. יַעֲלֶה וְיָבֹא זִכְרוֹנֵנוּ וְזִכְרוֹן אֲבוֹתֵינוּ. וְזִכְרוֹן כָּל עַמְּךָ בֵּית יִשְׂרָאֵל לְפָנֶיךָ. לְחֵן וּלְחֶסֶד וּלְרַחֲמִים לְחַיִּים וּלְשָׁלוֹם בְּיוֹם

(New Moon.)   (Passover.)   (Succoth.)

רֹאשׁ הַחֹדֶשׁ הַזֶּה.   חַג הַמַּצּוֹת הַזֶּה.   חַג הַסֻּכּוֹת הַזֶּה.

זָכְרֵנוּ יְיָ אֱלֹהֵינוּ בּוֹ לְטוֹבָה. וּפָקְדֵנוּ בוֹ לִבְרָכָה. וְהוֹשִׁיעֵנוּ בוֹ לְחַיִּים. וּבִדְבַר יְשׁוּעָה וְרַחֲמִים. חוּס וְחָנֵּנוּ. וְרַחֵם עָלֵינוּ וְהוֹשִׁיעֵנוּ. כִּי אֵלֶיךָ עֵינֵינוּ. כִּי אֵל מֶלֶךְ חַנּוּן וְרַחוּם אָתָּה:

בָּרוּךְ אַתָּה יְיָ שֶׁאוֹתְךָ לְבַדְּךָ בְּיִרְאָה נַעֲבוֹד:

XVII. מוֹדִים אֲנַחְנוּ לָךְ. שָׁאַתָּה הוּא יְיָ אֱלֹהֵינוּ וֵאלֹהֵי אֲבוֹתֵינוּ לְעוֹלָם וָעֶד. צוּר חַיֵּינוּ. מָגֵן יִשְׁעֵנוּ. אַתָּה הוּא

XV. Having poured forth our petitions before thee, O Lord our God, we pray thee to accept our prayers with favor and mercy, and send us not away empty from thy presence, for thou art not unmindful of the prayer of every lip. Blessed be thou, O Lord, the hearer of prayer.

XVI. O Lord our God, bestow thy grace upon thy people Israel. Accept the prayers of those who approach thee in love, and let the worship of thy people Israel be ever pleasing unto thee.

(*On the New Moon and in the Festival Week.*)

(O our God, and the God of our fathers! especially do we beseech thee to permit our memorial and the memorial of our ancestors, and even of all thy people Israel, to ascend and come before thee, so that we may obtain grace, favor, and blessing, mercy, life and peace, on this day of

(New Moon.)   (Feast of Matzoth.)   (Feast of Succoth.)

Vouchsafe unto us thy blessing, and save us from the sorrows and trials of life. And as thy Holy Word is full of the assurance of salvation and benign compassion, so mayest thou save and compassionate us, whose eyes are directed to thee, our Heavenly King, who rulest all mankind in mercy and love.)

Praised be thou, O Lord, unto whom alone we offer reverence and adoration. Amen!

XVII. We render our heartfelt thanks unto thee, our God and the God of our fathers, who art the firm stay of our existence, our shield of protection at all times. We, indeed, thank thee, and proclaim thy praise for our lives which are in thy hands, for our souls which

תפלת שחרית לחול

לְדוֹר וָדוֹר. נוֹדֶה לְּךָ וּנְסַפֵּר תְּהִלָּתֶךָ. עַל חַיֵּינוּ הַמְּסוּרִים בְּיָדֶךָ. וְעַל נִשְׁמוֹתֵינוּ הַפְּקוּדוֹת לָךְ. וְעַל נִסֶּיךָ שֶׁבְּכָל־יוֹם עִמָּנוּ. וְעַל נִפְלְאוֹתֶיךָ וְטוֹבוֹתֶיךָ שֶׁבְּכָל־עֵת. עֶרֶב וָבֹקֶר וְצָהֳרָיִם. הַטּוֹב כִּי לֹא־כָלוּ רַחֲמֶיךָ. וְהַמְרַחֵם כִּי לֹא־תַמּוּ חֲסָדֶיךָ. מֵעוֹלָם קִוִּינוּ לָךְ:*

(On Chanuckah and on Purim.)

*עַל הַנִּסִּים. וְעַל הַפֻּרְקָן. וְעַל הַגְּבוּרוֹת. וְעַל הַתְּשׁוּעוֹת. וְעַל הַמִּלְחָמוֹת. שֶׁעָשִׂיתָ לַאֲבוֹתֵינוּ בַּיָּמִים הָהֵם בַּזְּמַן הַזֶּה:

(On Chanuckah.)	(On Purim.)
בִּימֵי מַתִּתְיָהוּ בֶּן־יוֹחָנָן הַכֹּהֵן.	בִּימֵי מָרְדְּכַי וְאֶסְתֵּר בְּשׁוּשַׁן הַבִּירָה.
חַשְׁמוֹנַי וּבָנָיו. כְּשֶׁעָמְדָה מַלְכוּת יָוָן	כְּשֶׁעָמַד עֲלֵיהֶם הָמָן הָרָשָׁע. בִּקֵּשׁ
הָרְשָׁעָה עַל עַמְּךָ יִשְׂרָאֵל. לְהַשְׁכִּיחָם	לְהַשְׁמִיד לַהֲרוֹג וּלְאַבֵּד אֶת־כָּל־
תּוֹרָתֶךָ. וּלְהַעֲבִירָם מֵחֻקֵּי רְצוֹנֶךָ.	הַיְּהוּדִים. מִנַּעַר וְעַד־זָקֵן טַף וְנָשִׁים
וְאַתָּה בְּרַחֲמֶיךָ הָרַבִּים. עָמַדְתָּ לָהֶם	בְּיוֹם אֶחָד. בִּשְׁלוֹשָׁה עָשָׂר לְחֹדֶשׁ
בְּעֵת צָרָתָם. רַבְתָּ אֶת־רִיבָם.	שְׁנֵים־עָשָׂר. הוּא חֹדֶשׁ אֲדָר וּשְׁלָלָם
דַּנְתָּ אֶת־דִּינָם. נָקַמְתָּ אֶת־נִקְמָתָם.	לָבוֹז: וְאַתָּה בְּרַחֲמֶיךָ הָרַבִּים
מָסַרְתָּ גִבּוֹרִים בְּיַד	
חַלָּשִׁים. וְרַבִּים בְּיַד מְעַטִּים. וּטְמֵאִים	הֵפַרְתָּ אֶת־עֲצָתוֹ. וְקִלְקַלְתָּ אֶת־
בְּיַד טְהוֹרִים. וּרְשָׁעִים בְּיַד צַדִּיקִים.	מַחֲשַׁבְתּוֹ. וַהֲשֵׁבוֹתָ גְּמוּלוֹ בְּרֹאשׁוֹ.
וְזֵדִים בְּיַד עוֹסְקֵי תוֹרָתֶךָ. וּלְךָ עָשִׂיתָ	וְתָלוּ אוֹתוֹ וְאֶת־בָּנָיו עַל הָעֵץ.
שֵׁם גָּדוֹל וְקָדוֹשׁ בְּעוֹלָמֶךָ. וּלְעַמְּךָ יִשְׂרָאֵל עָשִׂיתָ תְּשׁוּעָה גְדוֹלָה וּפֻרְקָן כְּהַיּוֹם	
הַזֶּה. וְאַחַר כֵּן בָּאוּ בָנֶיךָ לִדְבִיר בֵּיתֶךָ. וּפִנּוּ אֶת־הֵיכָלֶךָ. וְטִהֲרוּ אֶת־	
מִקְדָּשֶׁךָ. וְהִדְלִיקוּ נֵרוֹת בְּחַצְרוֹת קָדְשֶׁךָ. וְקָבְעוּ שְׁמוֹנַת יְמֵי חֲנֻכָּה	
אֵלּוּ. לְהוֹדוֹת וּלְהַלֵּל לְשִׁמְךָ הַגָּדוֹל:	עַל כֵּן נוֹדֶה לְשִׁמְךָ הַגָּדוֹל:

are under thy guardianship, for the marks of thy providential care which we daily receive, and for the wonderful gifts which thou dost dispense unto us morning, noon, and night. Thou art good, for thy mercies never fail; and thy loving kindness never ceaseth from thy people, for thou hast been their hope and trust from the distant past to the present moment of our lives.*

(*On Chanuckah and Purim.*)

* Specially do we render thanks unto thee, O Lord, for our wonderful preservation from persecution and danger, and for the mighty deeds wrought on our behalf in ancient times at this particular season.

(*On Chanuckah.*)

In the days of the Hasmonean priest Mattathias and his sons, when the wicked Grecian government, under Antiochus Epiphanes, sought to exterminate thy people Israel, to cast thy law into oblivion, and compel them to transgress thy statutes, thou didst protect them in thy abundant mercy. Thou didst defend their cause and restore their rights. Thou didst deliver the mighty into the hands of the weak; the many into the hands of the few; the wicked into the hands of the righteous; the defiled into the hands of the pure; and the arrogant into the hands of the followers of thy law. Thus didst thou make known thy power and thy Holy Name unto the nations of the earth by means of thy wondrous redemption and salvation of thy people Israel, which remains a memorable event even unto this day.

(*On Purim.*)

In the days of Mordecai and Esther in the royal City of Shushan, when the wicked Haman rose against us with the intention of destroying and rooting out all the Jews in the Persian dominions, sparing neither young nor old, women nor children, all on one day, the thirteenth of Adar, and despoiling them of their property: it was thou, O Lord, who in thy abundant mercy didst frustrate his designs and defeat his plans, causing the evil to fall on his own head. Therefore be praises and thankgivings rendered unto thy great Name.

After this, thy children entered thy sanctuary at Jerusalem, cleansed it from all the defilements of idolatry, reëstablished thy service, illuminated the courts of thy temple, and appointed these eight days of Chanuckah for the praise and glorification of thy great Name!

תפלת שחרית לחול

וְעַל־כֻּלָּם יִתְבָּרַךְ וְיִתְרוֹמַם שִׁמְךָ מַלְכֵּנוּ תָּמִיד לְעוֹלָם וָעֶד:

(On the Penitential Days.)
וּכְתוֹב לְחַיִּים טוֹבִים כָּל־בְּנֵי בְרִיתֶךָ:

וְכֹל הַחַיִּים יוֹדוּךָ סֶּלָה. וִיהַלְלוּ אֶת־שִׁמְךָ בֶּאֱמֶת. הָאֵל יְשׁוּעָתֵנוּ וְעֶזְרָתֵנוּ סֶלָה. בָּרוּךְ אַתָּה יְיָ הַטּוֹב שִׁמְךָ וּלְךָ נָאֶה לְהוֹדוֹת:

(At the Public Service.)

(אֱלֹהֵינוּ וֵאלֹהֵי אֲבוֹתֵינוּ. בָּרְכֵנוּ בַּבְּרָכָה הַמְשֻׁלֶּשֶׁת בַּתּוֹרָה. הַכְּתוּבָה עַל יְדֵי מֹשֶׁה עַבְדֶּךָ. הָאֲמוּרָה מִפִּי אַהֲרֹן וּבָנָיו. כֹּהֲנִים עַם קְדוֹשֶׁךָ כָּאָמוּר. יְבָרֶכְךָ יְיָ וְיִשְׁמְרֶךָ: יָאֵר יְיָ פָּנָיו אֵלֶיךָ וִיחֻנֶּךָּ: יִשָּׂא יְיָ פָּנָיו אֵלֶיךָ וְיָשֵׂם לְךָ שָׁלוֹם:)

XVIII. שִׂים שָׁלוֹם טוֹבָה וּבְרָכָה חֵן וָחֶסֶד וְרַחֲמִים עָלֵינוּ וְעַל־כָּל־יִשְׂרָאֵל עַמֶּךָ. בָּרְכֵנוּ אָבִינוּ כֻּלָּנוּ כְּאֶחָד בְּאוֹר פָּנֶיךָ. כִּי בְאוֹר פָּנֶיךָ נָתַתָּ לָּנוּ יְיָ אֱלֹהֵינוּ תּוֹרַת חַיִּים וְאַהֲבַת חֶסֶד וּצְדָקָה וּבְרָכָה וְרַחֲמִים וְחַיִּים וְשָׁלוֹם וְטוֹב בְּעֵינֶיךָ לְבָרֵךְ אֶת־עַמְּךָ יִשְׂרָאֵל בְּכָל־עֵת וּבְכָל־שָׁעָה בִּשְׁלוֹמֶךָ:

(On the Penitential Days.)
בְּסֵפֶר חַיִּים בְּרָכָה וְשָׁלוֹם וּפַרְנָסָה טוֹבָה נִזָּכֵר וְנִכָּתֵב לְפָנֶיךָ אֲנַחְנוּ וְכָל־עַמְּךָ בֵּית יִשְׂרָאֵל לְחַיִּים טוֹבִים וּלְשָׁלוֹם.

בָּרוּךְ אַתָּה יְיָ עוֹשֵׂה הַשָּׁלוֹם:

And for all these mercies will we praise thy Holy Name, our King, now and for evermore.

(During the Penitential Days.)

(Vouchsafe a blissful life unto all the children of thy covenant.)

O that all the living would pay homage unto thee, and praise thy name in truth, O Lord, our help and assistance. Blessed be thou, O Lord, whose name is the All-bountiful, and unto whom the praises of man should be gratefully rendered. Amen!

(At the public Service.)

(Our God, and the God of our fathers! bless us with the threefold blessing mentioned in the law written by thy servant Moses, and solemnly pronounced by Aaron, and his sons, thy sanctified people, as it is said: "The Lord bless and preserve thee! The Lord make his face to shine upon thee, and be gracious unto thee! The Lord lift up his countenance unto thee, and give thee peace!"

XVIII. We now implore thee to grant us the precious gift of peace, and to instill within us a contented spirit, benevolence and love. Bless all of us together with the light of thy countenance, so that we may learn to practice charity and righteousness, and to perform deeds of benevolence and love, whereby peace and happiness may be spread around us, in like manner as thou hast blessed thy people Israel, amid all the vicissitudes of life.

(During the Penitential Days.)

(And especially on these solemn days of penitence do we pray thee to remember and inscribe us, and all the people of the house of Israel, in the book of life, blessing, peace, and prosperity.)

Praised be thou, O Lord, the never-failing fount of peace. Amen!

תפלת שחרית לחול

אֱלֹהַי נְצוֹר לְשׁוֹנִי מֵרָע וּשְׂפָתַי מִדַּבֵּר מִרְמָה. וְלִמְקַלְלַי נַפְשִׁי תִדּוֹם. וְנַפְשִׁי כֶּעָפָר לַכֹּל תִּהְיֶה: פְּתַח לִבִּי בְּתוֹרָתֶךָ וּבְמִצְוֹתֶיךָ תִּרְדּוֹף נַפְשִׁי. וְכֹל הַחוֹשְׁבִים עָלַי רָעָה מְהֵרָה הָפֵר עֲצָתָם וְקַלְקֵל מַחֲשַׁבְתָּם: עֲשֵׂה לְמַעַן שְׁמֶךָ. עֲשֵׂה לְמַעַן יְמִינֶךָ. עֲשֵׂה לְמַעַן קְדֻשָּׁתֶךָ. עֲשֵׂה לְמַעַן תּוֹרָתֶךָ. לְמַעַן יֵחָלְצוּן יְדִידֶיךָ הוֹשִׁיעָה יְמִינְךָ וַעֲנֵנִי: יִהְיוּ לְרָצוֹן אִמְרֵי-פִי וְהֶגְיוֹן לִבִּי לְפָנֶיךָ יְיָ צוּרִי וְגוֹאֲלִי: עֹשֶׂה שָׁלוֹם בִּמְרוֹמָיו הוּא יַעֲשֶׂה שָׁלוֹם עָלֵינוּ וְעַל כָּל-יִשְׂרָאֵל. אָמֵן:

(On the New Moon, Chanuckah, and in the Festival Weeks of Passover and Succoth, HALLEL is here read; page 86, No. 16.—On the Penitential Days, ABENU MALKANU, p. 190, No. 14. In the Festival Weeks, on the Ninth of Ab, Purim, and Chanuckah, as well as on Mondays and Thursdays of every week, the TORAH is read; see p. 454.)

(On the New Moon and in the Festival Weeks, the Reading of the Torah is followed by the Mussaf-Benedictions. For those of the Festival Weeks see page 100, No. 20. On the New Moon read the three first Benedictions (p. 546-48; No. I-III), after which say this:

אֱלֹהֵינוּ וֵאלֹהֵי אֲבוֹתֵינוּ. חַדֵּשׁ עָלֵינוּ אֶת-הַחֹדֶשׁ הַזֶּה. לְטוֹבָה וְלִבְרָכָה. לְשָׂשׂוֹן וּלְשִׂמְחָה. לִישׁוּעָה וּלְנֶחָמָה. לְפַרְנָסָה וּלְכַלְכָּלָה. לְחַיִּים וּלְשָׁלוֹם. לִמְחִילַת חֵטְא. וְלִסְלִיחַת עָוֹן (In a Leap Year.) וּלְכַפָּרַת פָּשַׁע. כִּי-בְעַמְּךָ יִשְׂרָאֵל בָּחַרְתָּ. וְחֻקֵּי רָאשֵׁי חֳדָשִׁים לָהֶם קָבָעְתָּ. בָּרוּךְ אַתָּה יְיָ מְקַדֵּשׁ יִשְׂרָאֵל וְרָאשֵׁי חֳדָשִׁים:

(For the three last Benedictions see p. 554, No. XVI-XVIII.)

Service for the Morning of Week Days.

O my God! guard my tongue from evil and my lips from uttering deceit. Grant me forbearance unto those who deal ill towards me, and a calm and meek disposition unto all my fellow-beings. Open my heart to receive thy sacred teachings, so that my conduct may evidence the fulfillment of thy commandments. Frustrate the plans and destroy the devices of all those who meditate evil against me, for the sake of thy Holy Name. May the words I have uttered and the meditations of my heart be acceptable before thee, O Lord, my Rock and my Redeemer; and mayest thou, who causest peace to reign on high, grant peace unto us and all Israel. Amen!

(On the New Moon, Chanuckah, and in the Festival Weeks of Passover and Succoth, HALLEL is here read; page 87, No. 19.—On the Penitential Days, ABENU MALKANU, p. 191, No. 14. In the Festival Weeks, on the Ninth of Ab, Purim, and Chanuckah, as well as on Mondays and Thursdays of every week, the TORAH is read; see p. 454.)

(On the New Moon and in the Festival Weeks, the Reading of the Torah is followed by the Mussaf-Benedictions. For those of the Festival Weeks see page 101, No. 20. On the New Moon read the three first Benedictions (p. 547-49; No. I-III), after which say this:

Our God and God of our fathers! May this new month bring unto us a renewal of thy abundant blessings. Give us a cheerful and contented heart; relieve the distressed and comfort the afflicted; sustain us that we may suffer no want; grant us a life full of peace, and purify us from all sins and transgressions. For thou hast chosen thy people Israel to be thy servants,—and that they might be reminded of their sacred mission, thou didst establish the ordinance of the New Moon. Blessed be thou, O Lord, who hast sanctified Israel and the New-Moon.

(For the three last Benedictions see p. 555, No. XVI-XVIII.)

תפלת שחרית לחול

12. בָּרוּךְ אֱלֹהֵינוּ. שֶׁבְּרָאָנוּ לִכְבוֹדוֹ. וְהִבְדִּילָנוּ מִן הַתּוֹעִים. וְנָתַן־לָנוּ תּוֹרַת אֱמֶת. וְחַיֵּי עוֹלָם נָטַע בְּתוֹכֵנוּ. הוּא יִפְתַּח לִבֵּנוּ בְּתוֹרָתוֹ. וְיָשֵׂם בְּלִבֵּנוּ אַהֲבָתוֹ וְיִרְאָתוֹ. וְלַעֲשׂוֹת רְצוֹנוֹ. וּלְעָבְדוֹ בְּלֵבָב שָׁלֵם. לְמַעַן לֹא נִיגַע לָרִיק. וְלֹא נֵלֵד לַבֶּהָלָה: יְהִי רָצוֹן מִלְּפָנֶיךָ יְיָ אֱלֹהֵינוּ וֵאלֹהֵי אֲבוֹתֵינוּ. שֶׁנִּשְׁמוֹר חֻקֶּיךָ בָּעוֹלָם הַזֶּה. וְנִירַשׁ טוֹבָה וּבְרָכָה לְחַיֵּי הָעוֹלָם הַבָּא: לְמַעַן יְזַמֶּרְךָ כָבוֹד וְלֹא יִדֹּם יְיָ אֱלֹהַי לְעוֹלָם אוֹדֶךָּ: וְיִבְטְחוּ בְךָ יוֹדְעֵי שְׁמֶךָ כִּי לֹא עָזַבְתָּ דֹרְשֶׁיךָ יְיָ: יְיָ חָפֵץ לְמַעַן צִדְקוֹ יַגְדִּיל תּוֹרָה וְיַאְדִּיר:

13. כָּל־יִשְׂרָאֵל יֵשׁ לָהֶם חֵלֶק לָעוֹלָם הַבָּא. שֶׁנֶּאֱמַר וְעַמֵּךְ כֻּלָּם צַדִּיקִים. לְעוֹלָם יִירְשׁוּ אָרֶץ: אַשְׁרֵי מִי שֶׁעָמְלוֹ בַתּוֹרָה. וְעָשָׂה רְצוֹן יוֹצְרוֹ. גָּדַל בְּשֵׁם טוֹב. וְנִפְטַר בְּשֵׁם טוֹב מִן הָעוֹלָם. וְעָלָיו נֶאֱמַר טוֹב שֵׁם מִשֶּׁמֶן טוֹב וְיוֹם הַמָּוֶת מִיּוֹם הִוָּלְדוֹ: בְּאֹרַח צְדָקָה חַיִּים וְדֶרֶךְ נְתִיבָה אַל־מָוֶת: כִּי אִם־יֵשׁ אַחֲרִית וְתִקְוָתְךָ לֹא תִכָּרֵת: וְדַע שֶׁמַּתַּן שְׂכָרָם שֶׁל צַדִּיקִים לֶעָתִיד לָבֹא:

תפלת שחרית לחול

Reader and Mourners.

14. יִתְגַּדַּל וְיִתְקַדַּשׁ שְׁמֵהּ רַבָּא. בְּעָלְמָא דִּי־בְרָא כִרְעוּתֵהּ וְיַמְלִיךְ מַלְכוּתֵהּ בְּחַיֵּיכוֹן וּבְיוֹמֵיכוֹן וּבְחַיֵּי דְכָל בֵּית יִשְׂרָאֵל בַּעֲגָלָא וּבִזְמַן קָרִיב וְאִמְרוּ אָמֵן:

Congregation.

אָמֵן יְהֵא שְׁמֵהּ רַבָּא מְבָרַךְ לְעָלַם וּלְעָלְמֵי עָלְמַיָּא.

Reader and Mourners.

יִתְבָּרַךְ וְיִשְׁתַּבַּח וְיִתְפָּאַר וְיִתְרוֹמַם וְיִתְנַשֵּׂא וְיִתְהַדָּר וְיִתְעַלֶּה וְיִתְהַלָּל שְׁמֵהּ דְּקוּדְשָׁא בְּרִיךְ הוּא לְעֵלָּא מִן כָּל־בִּרְכָתָא וְשִׁירָתָא תֻּשְׁבְּחָתָא וְנֶחֱמָתָא דַּאֲמִירָן בְּעָלְמָא וְאִמְרוּ אָמֵן:

Read.) תִּתְקַבַּל צְלוֹתְהוֹן וּבָעוּתְהוֹן דְּכָל יִשְׂרָאֵל. קֳדָם אֲבוּהוֹן דִּי בִשְׁמַיָּא. וְאִמְרוּ אָמֵן:)

Reader and Mourners.

עַל יִשְׂרָאֵל וְעַל צַדִּיקַיָּא. וְעַל כָּל מַן דְּאִתְפְּטַר מִן עָלְמָא הָדֵין כִּרְעוּתֵהּ דֶּאֱלָהָא. יְהֵא לְהוֹן שְׁלָמָא רַבָּא. וְחוּלָקָא טָבָא לְחַיֵּי עָלְמָא דְאָתֵי. וְחִסְדָּא וְרַחֲמֵי מִן קֳדָם מָרֵא שְׁמַיָּא וְאַרְעָא. וְאִמְרוּ אָמֵן:

יְהֵא שְׁלָמָא רַבָּא מִן־שְׁמַיָּא וְחַיִּים טוֹבִים עָלֵינוּ וְעַל־כָּל־יִשְׂרָאֵל. וְאִמְרוּ אָמֵן:

עֹשֶׂה שָׁלוֹם בִּמְרוֹמָיו. הוּא בְּרַחֲמָיו יַעֲשֶׂה שָׁלוֹם עָלֵינוּ. וְעַל כָּל־יִשְׂרָאֵל. וְאִמְרוּ אָמֵן:

Concluding Prayer.

15. O Lord our God! be with us as thou wert with our fathers; forsake us not, nor abandon us. Incline our hearts unto thee, that we may walk in all thy ways, and keep all the commands and statutes which thou hast delivered unto our fathers. And let these my supplications be nigh unto thee, O Lord, and do thou ever maintain the cause of thy servants, that all the people of the earth may know, that the Lord is God, and none besides!

15. יְהִי יְיָ אֱלֹהֵינוּ עִמָּנוּ כַּאֲשֶׁר הָיָה עִם־אֲבֹתֵינוּ אַל־יַעַזְבֵנוּ וְאַל־יִטְּשֵׁנוּ: לְהַטּוֹת לְבָבֵנוּ אֵלָיו לָלֶכֶת בְּכָל־דְּרָכָיו וְלִשְׁמֹר מִצְוֺתָיו וְחֻקָּיו וּמִשְׁפָּטָיו אֲשֶׁר צִוָּה אֶת־אֲבֹתֵינוּ: וְיִהְיוּ דְבָרַי אֵלֶּה אֲשֶׁר הִתְחַנַּנְתִּי לִפְנֵי יְיָ קְרֹבִים אֶל־יְיָ אֱלֹהֵינוּ יוֹמָם וָלָיְלָה לַעֲשׂוֹת מִשְׁפַּט עַבְדּוֹ וּמִשְׁפַּט עַמּוֹ יִשְׂרָאֵל דְּבַר־יוֹם בְּיוֹמוֹ: לְמַעַן דַּעַת כָּל־עַמֵּי הָאָרֶץ כִּי יְיָ הוּא הָאֱלֹהִים אֵין עוֹד:

תפלת מנחה לחול

אַשְׁרֵי יוֹשְׁבֵי בֵיתֶךָ עוֹד יְהַלְלוּךָ סֶּלָה:
אַשְׁרֵי הָעָם שֶׁכָּכָה־לּוֹ אַשְׁרֵי הָעָם שֶׁיְיָ אֱלֹהָיו:

(תהלים קמ״ה)

1. אֲרוֹמִמְךָ אֱלוֹהַי הַמֶּלֶךְ וַאֲבָרְכָה שִׁמְךָ לְעוֹלָם וָעֶד: בְּכָל־יוֹם אֲבָרְכֶךָ וַאֲהַלְלָה שִׁמְךָ לְעוֹלָם וָעֶד: גָּדוֹל יְיָ וּמְהֻלָּל מְאֹד וְלִגְדֻלָּתוֹ אֵין חֵקֶר: דּוֹר לְדוֹר יְשַׁבַּח מַעֲשֶׂיךָ וּגְבוּרֹתֶיךָ יַגִּידוּ: הֲדַר כְּבוֹד הוֹדֶךָ וְדִבְרֵי נִפְלְאֹתֶיךָ אָשִׂיחָה: וֶעֱזוּז נוֹרְאֹתֶיךָ יֹאמֵרוּ וּגְדֻלָּתְךָ אֲסַפְּרֶנָּה: זֵכֶר רַב־טוּבְךָ יַבִּיעוּ וְצִדְקָתְךָ יְרַנֵּנוּ: חַנּוּן וְרַחוּם יְיָ אֶרֶךְ אַפַּיִם וּגְדָל־חָסֶד: טוֹב־יְיָ לַכֹּל וְרַחֲמָיו עַל־כָּל־מַעֲשָׂיו: יוֹדוּךָ יְיָ כָּל־מַעֲשֶׂיךָ וַחֲסִידֶיךָ יְבָרְכוּכָה: כְּבוֹד מַלְכוּתְךָ יֹאמֵרוּ וּגְבוּרָתְךָ יְדַבֵּרוּ: לְהוֹדִיעַ לִבְנֵי

Afternoon Service for Week Days. 566

הָאָדָם גְּבוּרֹתָיו וּכְבוֹד הֲדַר מַלְכוּתוֹ: מַלְכוּתְךָ מַלְכוּת
כָּל־עֹלָמִים וּמֶמְשַׁלְתְּךָ בְּכָל־דּוֹר וָדֹר: סוֹמֵךְ יְיָ לְכָל־
הַנֹּפְלִים וְזוֹקֵף לְכָל־הַכְּפוּפִים: עֵינֵי כֹל אֵלֶיךָ יְשַׂבֵּרוּ
וְאַתָּה נוֹתֵן־לָהֶם אֶת־אָכְלָם בְּעִתּוֹ: פּוֹתֵחַ אֶת־יָדֶךָ
וּמַשְׂבִּיעַ לְכָל־חַי רָצוֹן: צַדִּיק יְיָ בְּכָל־דְּרָכָיו וְחָסִיד
בְּכָל־מַעֲשָׂיו: קָרוֹב יְיָ לְכָל־קֹרְאָיו לְכֹל אֲשֶׁר יִקְרָאֻהוּ
בֶאֱמֶת: רְצוֹן־יְרֵאָיו יַעֲשֶׂה וְאֶת־שַׁוְעָתָם יִשְׁמַע וְיוֹשִׁיעֵם:
שׁוֹמֵר יְיָ אֶת־כָּל־אֹהֲבָיו וְאֵת כָּל־הָרְשָׁעִים יַשְׁמִיד:
תְּהִלַּת יְיָ יְדַבֶּר־פִּי וִיבָרֵךְ כָּל־בָּשָׂר שֵׁם קָדְשׁוֹ לְעוֹלָם וָעֶד:
וַאֲנַחְנוּ ׀ נְבָרֵךְ יָהּ מֵעַתָּה וְעַד־עוֹלָם הַלְלוּיָהּ:

2. (The Eighteen Benedictions, p. 546, No 11. During the Penitential Days, ABINU MALKENU [אבינו מלכנו] is said after the Benedictions; for which see p. 364, No. 26. — Unless the Evening Service immediately follow, the Afternoon Service closes with the Prayer for the Departed, p. 576, No. 7 and Kaddish, p. 563, No. 14.)

Service for the Evening of Week Days.

תפלת ערבית לחול

(On Sabbath-Nights the following Psalm is said before the Evening Service.)

(Psalm 67.) — (תהלים ס״ז.)

1. God graces us and blesses us, lets his face shine among us. Selah.

1. אֱלֹהִים יְחָנֵּנוּ וִיבָרְכֵנוּ יָאֵר פָּנָיו אִתָּנוּ סֶלָה: לָדַעַת

Let there be known thy way in the land, among all nations thy victory!

בָּאָרֶץ דַּרְכֶּךָ בְּכָל־גּוֹיִם יְשׁוּעָתֶךָ: יוֹדוּךָ עַמִּים ׀

People acknowledge thee as God, people acknowledge thee, — all of them.

אֱלֹהִים יוֹדוּךָ עַמִּים כֻּלָּם:

Masses rejoice and shout, when thou judgest nations in righteousness; yea, masses in the land whom thou leadest. Selah.

יִשְׂמְחוּ וִירַנְּנוּ לְאֻמִּים כִּי־תִשְׁפֹּט עַמִּים מִישֹׁר וּלְאֻמִּים בָּאָרֶץ תַּנְחֵם סֶלָה: יוֹדוּךָ עַמִּים ׀ אֱלֹהִים יוֹדוּךָ עַמִּים

People acknowledge thee as God, people acknowledge thee, — all of them.

כֻּלָּם: אֶרֶץ נָתְנָה יְבוּלָהּ

The land gives its fruit, God blesses us, — our God. God blesses us, and in fear of him are all the ends of the earth.

יְבָרְכֵנוּ אֱלֹהִים אֱלֹהֵינוּ: יְבָרְכֵנוּ אֱלֹהִים וְיִירְאוּ אוֹתוֹ כָּל־אַפְסֵי־אָרֶץ:

תפלת ערבית לחול

וְהוּא רַחוּם יְכַפֵּר עָוֹן וְלֹא יַשְׁחִית וְהִרְבָּה לְהָשִׁיב אַפּוֹ וְלֹא יָעִיר כָּל חֲמָתוֹ: יְיָ הוֹשִׁיעָה הַמֶּלֶךְ יַעֲנֵנוּ בְיוֹם קָרְאֵנוּ:

בָּרְכוּ אֶת־יְיָ הַמְבֹרָךְ:

בָּרוּךְ יְיָ הַמְבֹרָךְ לְעוֹלָם וָעֶד:

2. בָּרוּךְ אַתָּה יְיָ אֱלֹהֵינוּ מֶלֶךְ הָעוֹלָם. אֲשֶׁר בִּדְבָרוֹ מַעֲרִיב עֲרָבִים. בְּחָכְמָה פּוֹתֵחַ שְׁעָרִים. וּבִתְבוּנָה מְשַׁנֶּה עִתִּים. וּמַחֲלִיף אֶת־הַזְּמַנִּים. וּמְסַדֵּר אֶת־הַכּוֹכָבִים בְּמִשְׁמְרוֹתֵיהֶם בָּרָקִיעַ כִּרְצוֹנוֹ. בּוֹרֵא יוֹם וָלָיְלָה. גּוֹלֵל אוֹר מִפְּנֵי־חשֶׁךְ וְחשֶׁךְ מִפְּנֵי־אוֹר. וּמַעֲבִיר יוֹם וּמֵבִיא לָיְלָה. וּמַבְדִּיל בֵּין יוֹם וּבֵין לָיְלָה. יְיָ צְבָאוֹת שְׁמוֹ. אֵל חַי וְקַיָּם תָּמִיד יִמְלוֹךְ עָלֵינוּ לְעוֹלָם וָעֶד. בָּרוּךְ אַתָּה יְיָ הַמַּעֲרִיב עֲרָבִים:

3 אַהֲבַת עוֹלָם בֵּית יִשְׂרָאֵל עַמְּךָ אָהָבְתָּ. תּוֹרָה וּמִצְוֹת חֻקִּים וּמִשְׁפָּטִים אוֹתָנוּ לִמַּדְתָּ. עַל־כֵּן יְיָ אֱלֹהֵינוּ בְּשָׁכְבֵנוּ וּבְקוּמֵנוּ נָשִׂיחַ בְּחֻקֶּיךָ. וְנִשְׂמַח בְּדִבְרֵי תוֹרָתֶךָ וּבְמִצְוֹתֶיךָ לְעוֹלָם וָעֶד. כִּי הֵם חַיֵּינוּ וְאֹרֶךְ יָמֵינוּ וּבָהֶם נֶהְגֶּה יוֹמָם וָלָיְלָה. וְאַהֲבָתְךָ אַל־תָּסִיר מִמֶּנּוּ לְעוֹלָמִים. בָּרוּךְ אַתָּה יְיָ אוֹהֵב עַמּוֹ יִשְׂרָאֵל:

Service for the Evening of Week Days.

Trustfully do we look up to thee, All-merciful God. We rely on thy kindness, that thou wilt bear with our frailties, and release us from the consequences of our sins. O Lord, grant us salvation! O King, answer us, when we raise our voice to thee.

Praise ye the Lord, unto whom all praise belongeth.

Praised be the Lord, unto whom all praise belongeth, now and for evermore.

2. Yea, praises unto thee, our God, Ruler of the universe, at whose command the shades of night are advancing, and from heaven's dark portals the shining stars appear and shed their glorious lustre. Thou hast assigned to them a station in the firmament, so that they may fulfill thy will, according to laws wise and unvaried. Thou biddest darkness vanish before light, and causest day and night to return with matchless regularity. When the toil of day has passed, thou usherest in the calm of evening, that it may invite us to praise thee, the Master of the heavenly hosts. Praised be thou, O Lord, who causest the evening to advance. Amen.

3. In like manner as the heavens make known thy glory, so is thy infinite love manifested through thy people Israel, unto whom thou didst impart the light of thy laws and statutes, even when the dark night of heathenism covered the earth. Therefore do we proclaim thy truth when we lie down and when we rise up. Yea, we rejoice in the mission assigned to us, by means of thy law, to make known thy existence and thy unity. It is this which has sustained us, and preserved our existence among all nations, and day and night will we be mindful thereof. But O, never withhold from us thy love, and unto thee be praises, O Lord, who hast in affection chosen Israel to be thy people. Amen!

קריאת שמע

4.

שְׁמַע יִשְׂרָאֵל יְהֹוָה אֱלֹהֵינוּ יְהֹוָה אֶחָד:

בָּרוּךְ שֵׁם כְּבוֹד מַלְכוּתוֹ לְעוֹלָם וָעֶד:

(דברים ו' ד' י״א י״ג במדבר ט״ו ל״ז)

וְאָהַבְתָּ אֵת יְיָ אֱלֹהֶיךָ בְּכָל־לְבָבְךָ וּבְכָל־נַפְשְׁךָ וּבְכָל־מְאֹדֶךָ: וְהָיוּ הַדְּבָרִים הָאֵלֶּה אֲשֶׁר אָנֹכִי מְצַוְּךָ הַיּוֹם עַל־לְבָבֶךָ: וְשִׁנַּנְתָּם לְבָנֶיךָ וְדִבַּרְתָּ בָּם בְּשִׁבְתְּךָ בְּבֵיתֶךָ וּבְלֶכְתְּךָ בַדֶּרֶךְ וּבְשָׁכְבְּךָ וּבְקוּמֶךָ: וּקְשַׁרְתָּם לְאוֹת עַל־יָדֶךָ וְהָיוּ לְטֹטָפֹת בֵּין עֵינֶיךָ: וּכְתַבְתָּם עַל־מְזֻזוֹת בֵּיתֶךָ וּבִשְׁעָרֶיךָ:

וְהָיָה אִם־שָׁמֹעַ תִּשְׁמְעוּ אֶל־מִצְוֹתַי אֲשֶׁר אָנֹכִי מְצַוֶּה אֶתְכֶם הַיּוֹם לְאַהֲבָה אֶת־יְיָ אֱלֹהֵיכֶם וּלְעָבְדוֹ בְּכָל־לְבַבְכֶם וּבְכָל־נַפְשְׁכֶם: וְנָתַתִּי מְטַר־אַרְצְכֶם בְּעִתּוֹ יוֹרֶה וּמַלְקוֹשׁ וְאָסַפְתָּ דְגָנֶךָ וְתִירֹשְׁךָ וְיִצְהָרֶךָ: וְנָתַתִּי עֵשֶׂב בְּשָׂדְךָ לִבְהֶמְתֶּךָ וְאָכַלְתָּ וְשָׂבָעְתָּ: הִשָּׁמְרוּ לָכֶם פֶּן־יִפְתֶּה לְבַבְכֶם וְסַרְתֶּם וַעֲבַדְתֶּם אֱלֹהִים אֲחֵרִים וְהִשְׁתַּחֲוִיתֶם לָהֶם: וְחָרָה אַף־יְיָ בָּכֶם וְעָצַר אֶת־

4. THE CONFESSION OF FAITH.

Hear, O Israel! The Lord is our God; the Lord is One!

Blessed be the name of his glorious kingdom for evermore.

(Deut. vi. 4–9, xi. 13–21 ; Numb. xv. 37–41.)

And thou shalt love the Lord thy God with all thy heart, and with all thy soul, and with all thy might. And these words, which I command thee this day, shall be in thy heart. And thou shalt teach them diligently unto thy children, and shalt speak of them when thou sittest in thy house, and when thou walkest by the way; when thou liest down, and when thou risest up. And thou shalt bind them for a sign upon thy hand, and they shall be as frontlets between thy eyes. And thou shalt write them upon the door-posts of thy house, and upon thy gates.

And it shall come to pass, that if ye will hearken diligently unto my commandments which I command you this day, to love the Lord your God, and to serve him with all your heart and all your soul, then will I send rain for your land in its due season, the first rain and the latter rain, that thou mayest gather in thy corn, thy wine, and thy oil. And I will give grass in thy field for thy cattle, and thou shalt eat and be satisfied. Take heed of yourselves, lest your heart be deceived, and ye turn aside, and serve other gods, and worship them. For then the Lord's wrath will be kindled

הַשָּׁמַיִם וְלֹא-יִהְיֶה מָטָר וְהָאֲדָמָה לֹא תִתֵּן אֶת-יְבוּלָהּ וַאֲבַדְתֶּם מְהֵרָה מֵעַל הָאָרֶץ הַטֹּבָה אֲשֶׁר יְיָ נֹתֵן לָכֶם: וְשַׂמְתֶּם אֶת-דְּבָרַי אֵלֶּה עַל-לְבַבְכֶם וְעַל-נַפְשְׁכֶם וּקְשַׁרְתֶּם אֹתָם לְאוֹת עַל-יֶדְכֶם וְהָיוּ לְטוֹטָפֹת בֵּין עֵינֵיכֶם: וְלִמַּדְתֶּם אֹתָם אֶת-בְּנֵיכֶם לְדַבֵּר בָּם בְּשִׁבְתְּךָ בְּבֵיתֶךָ וּבְלֶכְתְּךָ בַדֶּרֶךְ וּבְשָׁכְבְּךָ וּבְקוּמֶךָ: וּכְתַבְתָּם עַל-מְזוּזוֹת בֵּיתֶךָ וּבִשְׁעָרֶיךָ: לְמַעַן יִרְבּוּ יְמֵיכֶם וִימֵי בְנֵיכֶם עַל הָאֲדָמָה אֲשֶׁר נִשְׁבַּע יְיָ לַאֲבֹתֵיכֶם לָתֵת לָהֶם כִּימֵי הַשָּׁמַיִם עַל-הָאָרֶץ:

וַיֹּאמֶר יְיָ אֶל-מֹשֶׁה לֵּאמֹר: דַּבֵּר אֶל-בְּנֵי יִשְׂרָאֵל וְאָמַרְתָּ אֲלֵהֶם וְעָשׂוּ לָהֶם צִיצִת עַל-כַּנְפֵי בִגְדֵיהֶם לְדֹרֹתָם וְנָתְנוּ עַל-צִיצִת הַכָּנָף פְּתִיל תְּכֵלֶת: וְהָיָה לָכֶם לְצִיצִת וּרְאִיתֶם אֹתוֹ וּזְכַרְתֶּם אֶת-כָּל-מִצְוֹת יְיָ וַעֲשִׂיתֶם אֹתָם וְלֹא תָתוּרוּ אַחֲרֵי לְבַבְכֶם וְאַחֲרֵי עֵינֵיכֶם אֲשֶׁר אַתֶּם זֹנִים אַחֲרֵיהֶם: לְמַעַן תִּזְכְּרוּ וַעֲשִׂיתֶם אֶת-כָּל-מִצְוֹתָי וִהְיִיתֶם קְדֹשִׁים לֵאלֹהֵיכֶם: אֲנִי יְיָ אֱלֹהֵיכֶם אֲשֶׁר הוֹצֵאתִי אֶתְכֶם מֵאֶרֶץ מִצְרַיִם לִהְיוֹת לָכֶם לֵאלֹהִים אֲנִי יְיָ אֱלֹהֵיכֶם:

יְיָ אֱלֹהֵיכֶם אֱמֶת:

against you, and he will shut up the heavens, that there be no rain, and the land will not yield her fruit, and ye shall perish quickly from off the goodly land which the Lord giveth you. Therefore shall ye lay up these my words in your heart and in your soul, and bind them for a sign upon your hand, and they shall be as frontlets between your eyes. And ye shall teach them to your children, speaking of them when thou sittest in thy house, and when thou walkest by the way; when thou liest down, and when thou risest up. And thou shalt write them upon the door-posts of thy house, and upon thy gates. That your days may be multiplied, and the days of your children, in the land which the Lord swore unto your fathers to give them, as the days of heaven over the earth.

And the Lord spoke unto Moses, saying, Speak unto the children of Israel, and bid them to make themselves fringes in the borders of their garments, throughout their generations, and that they put upon the fringes of the borders a thread of blue. And it shall be unto you for a fringe, that ye may look upon it, and remember all the commandments of the Lord, and do them; and that ye seek not after the inclinations of your own heart and the delight of your eyes, in pursuit of which ye have been led astray. That ye may remember, and do all my commandments, and be holy unto your God. I am the Lord your God, who brought you out of the land of Egypt, to be your God: I am the Lord your God.

The Lord your God is ever true and faithful!

תפלת ערבית לחול

5. אֱמֶת וֶאֱמוּנָה כָּל־זֹאת וְקַיָּם עָלֵינוּ. כִּי הוּא יְיָ אֱלֹהֵינוּ וְאֵין זוּלָתוֹ וַאֲנַחְנוּ יִשְׂרָאֵל עַמּוֹ: הַפּוֹדֵנוּ מִיַּד־מְלָכִים. מַלְכֵּנוּ הַגּוֹאֲלֵנוּ מִכַּף כָּל־הֶעָרִיצִים: הָעֹשֶׂה גְדוֹלוֹת עַד־אֵין חֵקֶר. וְנִפְלָאוֹת עַד־אֵין מִסְפָּר: הַשָּׂם נַפְשֵׁנוּ בַּחַיִּים. וְלֹא־נָתַן לַמּוֹט רַגְלֵנוּ: הָעֹשֶׂה־לָּנוּ נִסִּים בְּפַרְעֹה. אוֹתוֹת וּמוֹפְתִים בְּאַדְמַת בְּנֵי־חָם. וַיּוֹצֵא אֶת־עַמּוֹ יִשְׂרָאֵל מִתּוֹכָם לְחֵרוּת עוֹלָם: הַמַּעֲבִיר בָּנָיו בֵּין גִּזְרֵי יַם־סוּף. וְהֶרְאָה לָהֶם גְּבוּרָתוֹ: שִׁבְּחוּ וְהוֹדוּ לִשְׁמוֹ. וּמַלְכוּתוֹ בְּרָצוֹן קִבְּלוּ עֲלֵיהֶם: משֶׁה וּבְנֵי יִשְׂרָאֵל לְךָ עָנוּ שִׁירָה בְּשִׂמְחָה רַבָּה וְאָמְרוּ כֻלָּם:

מִי־כָמֹכָה בָּאֵלִם יְיָ. מִי כָּמֹכָה נֶאְדָּר בַּקֹּדֶשׁ. נוֹרָא תְהִלֹּת. עֹשֵׂה פֶלֶא:

מַלְכוּתְךָ רָאוּ בָנֶיךָ. בּוֹקֵעַ יָם לִפְנֵי משֶׁה. זֶה אֵלִי עָנוּ וְאָמְרוּ:

יְיָ׳ יִמְלֹךְ לְעֹלָם וָעֶד:

וְנֶאֱמַר כִּי־פָדָה יְיָ אֶת־יַעֲקֹב. וּגְאָלוֹ מִיַּד חָזָק מִמֶּנּוּ. בָּרוּךְ אַתָּה יְיָ גָּאַל יִשְׂרָאֵל:

6. הַשְׁכִּיבֵנוּ יְיָ אֱלֹהֵינוּ לְשָׁלוֹם. וְהַעֲמִידֵנוּ מַלְכֵּנוּ לְחַיִּים. וּפְרוֹשׂ עָלֵינוּ סֻכַּת שְׁלוֹמֶךָ. וְתַקְּנֵנוּ בְּעֵצָה טוֹבָה מִלְּפָנֶיךָ. וְהוֹשִׁיעֵנוּ לְמַעַן שְׁמֶךָ. וְהָגֵן בַּעֲדֵנוּ. וְהָסֵר

5. True and unfailing is it unto us, that thou art the Lord our God, and that there is none else besides thee, while we, the children of Israel, are thy people. Thou hast delivered us from many a tyrannical power, and hast redeemed us from the hand of oppression. Without number are thy wonderful deeds, beyond mortal knowledge the miracles thou hast wrought for our sake. When hope had fled from our hearts, thou didst instill new life within us; when on the brink of destruction, thou didst interpose and save us. Even thou didst perform signs and wonders on our behalf, both when leading us from Egyptian slavery to everlasting freedom, and when paving a road through the sea, so that thy children might pass. Thus was thy marvelous power made known to them; and in acknowledging thy majesty, Moses and the children of Israel with one accord chanted the anthem of praise:

WHO AMONG THE MIGHTY IS LIKE UNTO THEE, O LORD? WHO IS LIKE UNTO THEE, GLORIFIED IN HOLINESS, FEARFUL IN PRAISED DEEDS, PERFORMING WONDERS?

Thy children beheld thy omnipotence, when the foaming billows of the sea were divided for their rescue. "This is my God," did they shout; and closing their song, they exclaimed:

THE LORD REIGNETH FOREVER AND EVER.

And thus art thou proclaimed in the words of inspiration: "The Lord is the redeemer of Jacob, his deliverer from the hand too powerful for him." Praised be thou, O Lord, who redeemest Israel. Amen!

6. O Lord our God! vouchsafe unto us thy protection, that we may lie down this night in peace, and awake in the morning to refreshed existence. Spread over us thy pavilion of peace, guide us with good

תפלת ערבית לחול

מֵעָלֵינוּ אוֹיֵב דֶּבֶר וְחֶרֶב וְרָעָב וְיָגוֹן. וְהָסֵר שָׂטָן מִלְּפָנֵינוּ וּמֵאַחֲרֵינוּ. וּבְצֵל כְּנָפֶיךָ תַּסְתִּירֵנוּ. כִּי אֵל שׁוֹמְרֵנוּ וּמַצִּילֵנוּ אָתָּה. וּשְׁמוֹר צֵאתֵנוּ וּבוֹאֵנוּ לְחַיִּים וּלְשָׁלוֹם מֵעַתָּה וְעַד עוֹלָם. בָּרוּךְ אַתָּה יְיָ שׁוֹמֵר עַמּוֹ יִשְׂרָאֵל לָעַד:

בָּרוּךְ יְיָ בַּיּוֹם. בָּרוּךְ יְיָ בַּלָּיְלָה. בָּרוּךְ יְיָ בְּשָׁכְבֵנוּ. בָּרוּךְ יְיָ בְּקוּמֵנוּ: כִּי בְיָדְךָ נַפְשׁוֹת הַחַיִּים וְהַמֵּתִים אֲשֶׁר בְּיָדוֹ נֶפֶשׁ כָּל־חָי וְרוּחַ כָּל־בְּשַׂר אִישׁ: בְּיָדְךָ אַפְקִיד רוּחִי פָּדִיתָה אוֹתִי יְיָ אֵל אֱמֶת: אֱלֹהֵינוּ שֶׁבַּשָּׁמַיִם יַחֵד שִׁמְךָ וְקַיֵּם מַלְכוּתְךָ תָּמִיד וּמְלוֹךְ עָלֵינוּ לְעוֹלָם וָעֶד:

יִרְאוּ עֵינֵינוּ וְיִשְׂמַח לִבֵּנוּ וְתָגֵל נַפְשֵׁנוּ בִּישׁוּעָתְךָ בֶּאֱמֶת בֶּאֱמֹר לְצִיּוֹן מָלַךְ אֱלֹהָיִךְ יְיָ מֶלֶךְ יְיָ מָלָךְ יְיָ יִמְלֹךְ לְעֹלָם וָעֶד. כִּי הַמַּלְכוּת שֶׁלְּךָ הִיא וּלְעוֹלְמֵי עַד תִּמְלוֹךְ בְּכָבוֹד כִּי אֵין לָנוּ מֶלֶךְ אֶלָּא אָתָּה: בָּרוּךְ אַתָּה יְיָ הַמֶּלֶךְ בִּכְבוֹדוֹ תָּמִיד יִמְלוֹךְ עָלֵינוּ לְעוֹלָם וָעֶד וְעַל כָּל מַעֲשָׂיו:

(Here follows the Benediction, p. 546, No. 11, after which say Kol Yisroël and Kaddish, p. 562, No. 13.)

PRAYER FOR THE DEPARTED.
(In the house of mourning the following is said before Kaddish.)

׳׳ אָנָּא יְיָ מֶלֶךְ מָלֵא רַחֲמִים. אֲשֶׁר בְּיָדְךָ נֶפֶשׁ כָּל חָי. וְרוּחַ כָּל בְּשַׂר אִישׁ. קַבֵּל בְּרַחֲמִים וּבְרָצוֹן אֶת תְּפִלָּתֵנוּ בַּעֲבוּר נִשְׁמַת (פ״ב״פ). גְּמָל נָא עִמָּהּ בְּחַסְדְּךָ הַגָּדוֹל. לִפְתּוֹחַ לָהּ שַׁעֲרֵי רַחֲמִים וָחֶסֶד.

counsels, and send us assistance for the sake of thy Holy Name. Be thou, at all times, our shield and protector from harm, our guardian from danger, our savior from all manner of trouble and distress. Keep far from us anxiety and sorrow, and shelter us under the shadow of thy wings; for it is in thee only, O God, that we put our trust. Guard then our going out and our coming in, that we may lead a life of happiness and contentment. Praised be thou, O Lord, who guardest thy people Israel for ever. Amen!

We bless thee, O Lord, when night invites us to rest; we bless thee, O Lord, when day awakens us for our daily toil. For in thy hand, O God, are the souls of the living and the dead; it is thou who breathest the living spirit into all flesh. Into thy hand I will then resign my life, for thou art my Redeemer, O God of truth.—O our heavenly Father! may thy unity be acknowledged, and thy kingdom be established among us for evermore.

O that we may live to behold and rejoice in the victory of truth, when all mankind shall say unto Zion, "Truly, the God thou proclaimest is King; he is, he was, and he will be King for all eternity." For thine is the kingdom, and thy glory shall never cease, and we have no king besides thee. Blessed be thou, O King, who in imperishable glory reignest over all thy creatures. Amen.

(Here follows the Benediction, p. 546, No. 11, after which say Kol Yisroël and Kaddish, p. 562, No. 13.)

PRAYER FOR THE DEPARTED.

(In the house of mourning the following is said before Kaddish.)

O Lord our God, King of mercy, who dispensest life and death according to thy inscrutable wisdom, we beseech thee to accept our prayer on behalf of our brother (sister) —— who has departed this life. Open to his (her) soul the gates of compassion that she may

תפלת ערבית לחול

וְלִצְרוֹר אוֹתָהּ בִּצְרוֹר הַחַיִּים. עִם נִשְׁמוֹת כָּל הַיְשָׁרִים וְהַיְשָׁרוֹת. וְהַגּוּף יָנוּחַ בַּקֶּבֶר בִּמְנוּחָה נְכוֹנָה. וְעַל מִשְׁכָּבוֹ יִהְיֶה שָׁלוֹם:

סְלַח וּמְחַל לוֹ (לָהּ) עַל כָּל פְּשָׁעָיו (פְּשָׁעֶיהָ) כִּי אָדָם אֵין צַדִּיק בָּאָרֶץ. אֲשֶׁר יַעֲשֶׂה טוֹב וְלֹא יֶחֱטָא. וּזְכוֹר לוֹ (לָהּ) זְכִיּוֹתָיו (זְכִיּוֹתֶיהָ). וְצִדְקוֹתָיו (וְצִדְקוֹתֶיהָ) אֲשֶׁר עָשָׂה (עָשְׂתָה) פֹּה בָאָרֶץ:

הַשְׁפִּיעַ לְנִשְׁמָתוֹ (לְנִשְׁמָתָהּ) מֵרֹב טוּבְךָ. אֲשֶׁר צָפַנְתָּ לִירֵאֶיךָ. לַחֲזוֹת בְּנֹעֲמֶךָ. וּלְהִתְעַדֵּן בְּאוֹר פָּנֶיךָ. אָמֵן כֵּן יְהִי רָצוֹן:

---

enjoy everlasting life, united with the souls of all righteous men and women who have walked on this earth. Vouchsafe also that his (her) mortal remains which we have conveyed to their resting-place may repose in undisturbed peace.

And as there is no man on earth so righteous that never fails in good, we pray thee, O Lord, forgive our deceased brother (sister) any wrongs which he (she) may have committed, and remember all the deeds of virtue which he (she) has performed while among us.

Bestow upon his (her) soul the abundance of thy goodness, which thou reservest for those who fear thee, that she may behold thy glory, and find beatitude in the light of thy countenance. Amen.

(Kaddish, p. 564, No. 14.)

APPENDIX.

CONTENTS OF THE APPENDIX.

		PAGE
I.	Hoshanoth	581
II.	For Chanuckah	584
III.	For Purim	585
IV.	For the Ninth of Ab	587
V.	Scriptural Portions for the Cycle of three Years	591
VI.	The Annual Cycle arranged for three Years	593

I. Hoshanoth.

הוֹשַׁע נָא. הוֹשַׁע נָא. לְמַעַנְךָ אֱלֹהֵינוּ. הוֹשַׁעֲנָא.
לְמַעַנְךָ בּוֹרְאֵנוּ. הוֹשַׁעֲנָא. לְמַעַנְךָ גּוֹאֲלֵנוּ. הוֹשַׁעֲנָא.
לְמַעַנְךָ דּוֹרְשֵׁנוּ. הוֹשַׁעֲנָא: (כהושעת :On Sabbath)

תִּתְּנֵנוּ לְשֵׁם וְלִתְהִלָּה. תִּפְדֵּנוּ מִכָּל נֶגַע וּמַחֲלָה.
תְּעַטְּרֵנוּ בְּאַהֲבָה כְּלוּלָה. תְּנַהֲלֵנוּ עַל מֵי מְנוּחוֹת
סֶלָה. תְּמַלְּאֵנוּ חָכְמָה וְשִׂכְלָה. תְּיַשְּׁרֵנוּ בְּאֹרַח סְלוּלָה.
תִּטָּעֵנוּ בְּיֹשֶׁר מְסִלָּה. תְּחָנֵּנוּ בְּרַחֲמִים וּבְחֶמְלָה.
תּוֹשִׁיעֵנוּ בְּיָדְךָ הַגְּדוֹלָה. תְּאַמְּצֵנוּ בְּרֶוַח וְהַצָּלָה.
תְּחַזְּקֵנוּ אֱלֹהֵי יַעֲקֹב סֶלָה. הוֹשַׁעֲנָא:

Save us, O save us! For thine own sake, Almighty, save us! For thine own sake, our Maker, save us! For thine own sake, our Redeemer, save us! For thine own sake, our Guardian, save us!

Save us, save us, O Lord! and exalt our name,
   Redeem us from ill, when by sorrow oppress'd;
O, crown us with joy, with honor and fame,
   And lead us beside the still waters of rest.

Let us knowledge and virtue and wisdom embrace,
   And teach us thy way, who dwellest above;
Implant Thou within us uprightness and grace,
   And grant us compassionate pity and love.

Save us, save us, O Father! and let us behold
   Thy omnipotent hand, as in days of old;
Uphold us, O Lord! to whom e'er we have pray'd;
   Give strength to Thy people, enlargement and aid.

Hoshanoth for Sukkoth.

Read. כְּהוֹשַׁעְתָּ אַבְרָהָם בְּהַר הַמּוֹרִיָּה.
Ch. & Cong. עֲנִיתוֹ מִשְׁמֵי עֲלִיָּה. כֵּן הוֹשַׁע נָא:

Read. כְּהוֹשַׁעְתָּ יִצְחָק בְּנוֹ יְחִידוֹ.
Ch. & Cong. מָנַעְתּוֹ מִשְּׁלוֹחַ לוֹ יָדוֹ. כֵּן הוֹשַׁע נָא:

Read. כְּהוֹשַׁעְתָּ יַעֲקֹב אִישׁ תְּמִימֶךָ.
Ch. & Cong. בִּשַּׂרְתּוֹ יֵשַׁע כִּמְרוֹמֶךָ. כֵּן הוֹשַׁע נָא:

Read. כְּהוֹשַׁעְתָּ אֲהוּבֶיךָ זֶרַע יְדִידִים.
Ch. & Cong. הוֹצֵאתָם מִבֵּית עֲבָדִים. כֵּן הוֹשַׁע נָא:

Read. כְּהוֹשַׁעְתָּ מֹשֶׁה בְּאֶרֶץ צִיָּה.
Ch. & Cong. הִנְחַלְתּוֹ דָּת וְתוּשִׁיָּה. כֵּן הוֹשַׁע נָא:

Read. כְּהוֹשַׁעְתָּ אַהֲרֹן מְכַהֵן בְּאֵלֶּמֶךָ.
Ch. & Cong. פֵּאַרְתּוֹ בְּאוּרֶיךָ וְתֻמֶּיךָ. כֵּן הוֹשַׁע נָא:

Read. As thou didst save thy servant Abraham,
And on Moriah's mount didst answer him,
Ch. and Cong. So save us now!
Read. As thou didst save his son, his only one,
And didst withhold the hand raised 'gainst his life,
Ch. and Cong. So save us now!
Read. As thou didst Jacob save, — the upright man, —
And cheer him with glad tidings of thy grace,
Ch. and Cong. So save us now!
Read. As thou didst save the seed of thy beloved,
Delivering them from Egypt's servile yoke,
Ch. and Cong. So save us now!
Read. As thou didst Moses save 'mid wastes untracked,
And make thy glorious law his heritage,
Ch. and Cong. So save us now!
Read. As thou didst Aaron save — thy Temple's priest,
And deck him with the shield of Light and Truth,
Ch. and Cong. So save us now!

Hoshanoth for Sukkoth.

Read. כְּהוֹשַׁעְתָּ בַּמִּדְבָּר בְּנֵי אֱמוּנֶיךָ.

Ch. & Cong. כֵּן הוֹשַׁע נָא: כִּלְכַּלְתָּם לָשׂוֹבַע בְּמַנֶּךָ.

(On the Sabbath.)

Read. כְּהוֹשַׁעְתָּ מֵאָז יְגִיעֵי כֹחַ.

Ch. & C. כֵּן הוֹשַׁע נָא: בְּשַׁבְּתוֹתֶיךָ הַמְצֵאתָם מָנוֹחַ.

הוֹשִׁיעָה אֶת עַמֶּךָ. וּבָרֵךְ אֶת נַחֲלָתֶךָ. וּרְעֵם וְנַשְּׂאֵם עַד הָעוֹלָם: וְיִהְיוּ דְבָרַי אֵלֶּה אֲשֶׁר הִתְחַנַּנְתִּי לִפְנֵי יְיָ קְרוֹבִים אֶל יְיָ אֱלֹהֵינוּ יוֹמָם וָלָיְלָה לַעֲשׂוֹת מִשְׁפַּט עַבְדּוֹ וּמִשְׁפַּט עַמּוֹ יִשְׂרָאֵל דְּבַר יוֹם בְּיוֹמוֹ: לְמַעַן דַּעַת כָּל עַמֵּי הָאָרֶץ כִּי יְיָ הוּא הָאֱלֹהִים אֵין עוֹד:

Read. As thou didst save, amidst the desert's drear,
And feed thy people with celestial food,
Ch. and Cong. So save us now!

(On the Sabbath.)

Read. As thou didst save the wearied at all times,
In offering the Sabbath's joyful rest,
Ch. and Cong. So save us now!

O, save thy people and bless thy inheritance; feed them and lift them up forever. — May these my words wherewith I have made supplication before the Lord, be nigh unto the Lord our God day and night, that he maintain the cause of his servant, and the cause of his people Israel day after day, that all the nations of the earth may know that the Lord is God, and that there is none else.

For Chanukah. 584

II.   CHANUKAH.

(Before the Evening Service the festival lights are kindled, and the following Benedictions said:)

בָּרוּךְ אַתָּה יְיָ אֱלֹהֵינוּ מֶלֶךְ הָעוֹלָם שֶׁעָשָׂה
נִסִּים לַאֲבוֹתֵינוּ בַּיָּמִים הָהֵם בַּזְּמַן הַזֶּה׃

Blessed be thou, O Lord, Sovereign of the universe, who didst perform wondrous acts on behalf of our fathers, in olden days, at this particular season.

בָּרוּךְ אַתָּה יְיָ אֱלֹהֵינוּ מֶלֶךְ הָעוֹלָם
שֶׁהֶחֱיָנוּ וְקִיְּמָנוּ וְהִגִּיעָנוּ לַזְּמַן הַזֶּה׃

Blessed be thou, O Lord, Sovereign of the universe, who hast vouchsafed to us to enjoy this festive season.

(When the lights are kindled, the Rabbi says:)

These lights remind us of the glorious events and the heroic deeds that distinguish the period of our history during the time of the Maccabees. Antiochus Epiphanes, the King of Syria, violently sought to make Israel give up their belief in the One spiritual Being, and worship heathen Gods. But the members of the priestly Maccabean family arose, and gathered the faithful and pious around them. Though few in number and unaccustomed to warfare, they with death-defying valor battled against the mighty and war-trained Syrian armies, and the Lord crowned their heroic efforts with victory and glory. With praises and thanksgivings, the victors then entered the Temple at Jerusalem, which the haughty enemy had defiled, renewed therein its sacred rites, and appointed this festival of light and consecration. Ever sacred to us are these festive days and these symbolic lights, in sight of which we praise the Lord, with hymns of thanksgiving to his never-ending mercy and love. Amen.

(An appropriate hymn is sung.)

III. PURIM.

(On Purim the Book of Esther (Megillah) is read, preceded by the following Benedictions:)

בָּרוּךְ אַתָּה יְיָ אֱלֹהֵינוּ מֶלֶךְ הָעוֹלָם שֶׁעָשָׂה נִסִּים לַאֲבוֹתֵינוּ בַּיָּמִים הָהֵם בַּזְּמַן הַזֶּה:

Blessed be thou, O Lord, Sovereign of the universe, who didst perform wondrous acts on behalf of our fathers, in olden days, at this particular season.

בָּרוּךְ אַתָּה יְיָ אֱלֹקֵינוּ מֶלֶךְ הָעוֹלָם שֶׁהֶחֱיָנוּ וְקִיְּמָנוּ וְהִגִּיעָנוּ לַזְּמַן הַזֶּה:

Blessed be thou, O Lord, Sovereign of the universe, who hast preserved us in life and health to enjoy this festive season.

(After the Reading, the Rabbi says:)

Praises and thanksgivings do we offer up unto thee, All-bountiful Father, for the paternal grace which from the remotest days and in all generations thou hast manifested on behalf of our race. At all times thou hast pleaded our cause, and given us shelter and protection from the numberless and powerful adversaries that so frequently rose against us in olden days.

If thou, O faithful Guardian of Israel, hadst not been our aid, when men stood up against us, the wicked would have destroyed us; their hatred would have swept us away like a rapid torrent. For we were but few in number against the many enemies whose wrath raged against us. We were among the nations like a lamb among rapacious wolves and roaring lions. But thou, Almighty, hast been our Rock and Refuge in all generations. Thou didst destroy the counsels of wickedness, and frustrate the devices which our enemies had in store for us, causing them to fall on their own heads, thus leading innocence and righteousness to victory.

Therefore do our hearts rejoice, and our lips give forth praises unto thy Name. Praises be unto thee, O Lord, for the innumerable wonders thou hast wrought on behalf of our ancestors, and for the protection and assistance which thou hast bestowed on us to this day. Amen.

HYMN.

From my earliest days, O Lord,
   Erring mankind grièved me;
Slander's sting and hatred's sword
   Of my rest bereaved me.
But the enemies' furious wrath
Could not rob me of my faith.

Trustful I resigned my fate
   To the Rock of ages;
Knowing that the storm of hate
   Not for ever rages.
This, my trust in darkest night,
Was my staff, my leading light.

Lord, my heart did entertain
   Hopes, no foe could banish:
Love and truth at last will reign,
   Bidding hatred vanish,
And sweet brotherhood extend
O'er the earth, from end to end.

IV. THE NINTH OF AB.

(During the Morning Service of the Ninth of Ab (Tishah-BeAb), the following prayer is said after reading the Haftarah:)

With sad emotions, Almighty Ruler of the universe, do we commemorate the return of that sorrowful day whereon thou didst twice see fit to execute severe judgment on our fathers, because they had abandoned the covenant which thou in olden days hadst made with them.

First, it was the ruthless Chaldeans that invaded the Holy Mount of Zion, and unsparingly devastated all those glorious abodes which were our pride and our ornament in the eyes of the nations. They broke down the walls of the Holy City, laid in ashes the Temple wherein thy Name was worshiped, and destroyed the Holy Altar whence the fervent offerings of Israel ascended to thee, when those of the nations around were consecrated to vain idols. The noblest and best of our people were made to leave the sweet homes to which their souls were attached with ties of elevating and glorious remembrances, and forced to wander in the gloomy land of captivity. The pious bards, wont, in heaven-ascending choruses, to attune thy praises in the Temple of Zion, sat by the rivers of Babylon and wept. Oh, the heart-rending lamentations and woful cries of those melancholy days still reverberate on our ears, touching the strings of our hearts in sadness. "Ah, how doth she sit solitary, the City of God, that was once full of people! She, the princess among the countries, how is she become a mourning widow!"

Soon, however, didst thou again turn thy compassion unto our fathers. After a short captivity, they were allowed to return to their home and again erect the abode from whence the light of thy truth was to shine forth over the earth. But, however ardently they now worshiped thy Name, their pious zeal was not powerful enough to twine around them the bonds of union. Fierce hatred divided them into parties, profaning thy Holy Name through discord. Therefore didst thou reject them from being a nation before thee, and didst deliver them into the hands of their Roman rulers. Oh, how terribly did their fury-rage in thy holy inheritance! They laid waste our country, destroyed the high-towering Temple, and gave up all our treasures as a prey to the consuming fire.

And how much more vehement was their wrath against thy people! Hundreds of thousands, men and women, age-stricken and young, were slaughtered on the highways; hundreds of thousands made captives and exiled from the sweet memories of home into all parts of the world.

Oh, bitter sadness seizes our souls, when we call to mind that period! And since then, who counts the sufferings and trials that passed over that tribe which, though few in number, thou didst choose to be the bearers of thy Name? From one end of the earth to the other, we have been pursued, and nowhere allowed to find a resting-place. The miseries which have passed over our heads since the day our exile commenced, defy all description. "We were a reproach to our neighbours, a scorn and derision to our fellow-men. We were a by-word among the nations, a shaking of the head among the people. For thy sake were we cruelly killed, and counted as sheep for the slaughter."

And yet, though moved to our inmost hearts at the memory of all the agonies we had to suffer on our long pilgrimage, we still recognize thy wondrous and gracious rulership amidst all these vicissitudes. True, we were deserving of thy chastisement, yet thy severe judgment was a means of fulfilling the sublime mission which we received at Sinai. Now that the genial sun of milder days shines over us, we are enabled better to understand what thy plans were. Thou didst not suffer us to perish because of our sins; thou didst not destroy us from the face of the earth. No, as the witnesses of thy truth, as the promulgators of thy unity, thou didst scatter us among the nations, in order that we might, in the course of centuries, serve as instruments for spreading sacred truth, as the messengers of thy kingdom on earth.

In meekness do we bow before thy holy will, knowing that it is wise and merciful.

Therefore do we not unduly lament over the Temple that is destroyed, for thou wilt henceforth rear up thy Temple in the hearts of all sons of men, so that all nations may form one brotherhood to serve thee in truth. We mourn not despairingly over the downfall of Jerusalem; for all places whither thou hast sent us, shall be consecrated unto thee through the worship of thy Name. We lament not over the degradation to which we were delivered up, for we know we suffered it for the sake of thy Holy Name.

And now, in thy great mercy, thou hast lifted from our shoulders the burden of oppression under which our ancestors once drooped; thou hast given us another home in place of that which we lost in the land of our fathers, and hast granted us a full share in the liberties of the great and free nation that has adopted us as its children. Thou, O Lord, wilt cause the kingdom of love to increase in extent and power on earth, so that all our brethren may enjoy its fruits as we do, and thou wilt grant that we work together for the fulfillment of the great mission thou hast appointed to the human race.

Wondrous, O Lord, are thy ways; unsearchable are the decrees of thy wisdom. Love has sprouted forth where the seeds of hatred were strewed; and where all things were shrouded in the gloom of night, there the light of truth and love now shines in bright radiance. Yea, the downcast can now lift up their heads as worshippers of thy Unity, as the nation chosen by thee as the standard-bearers of eternal truth before the sons of men.

Grant, O Lord, that we may constantly labor in thy service, until all the world shall acknowledge thee, and all mankind worship thee, the One and Infinite God. Amen.

Choir.

Lord, thy Temple was destroyed,
Lord, thy land laid waste and void,—
  But though scattered o'er the earth,
  Israel held thy standard forth,
As thy holy priest employed.

Suffering, they fought for thee,
Offerings they brought for thee—
  But their flag they did not hide:
  In our faith we still abide.
Lord, thou gav'st us victory.

Prophets' words have ceased to well
From the place where thou didst dwell—
  But on thousand places still,
  Scattered by thy holy will,
We exclaim, "Hear, Israel!"

V.

Scriptural Portions

FOR THE

Cycle of three years.

Sabbath after Atzereth.	In the First year.		In the Second year.		In the Third year.		Annual Cycle.
	First Book of Moses.		Second Book of Moses.		Fourth Book of Moses.		
	From	To	From	To	From	To	
1.	1. 1	2. 3	12.29	12.51	2. 1	2.34	בראשית
2.	2. 4	2.25	13. 1	13.22	3. 1	3.39	נח
3.	3. 1	3.24	14. 1	15.21	3.40	4.20	לך לך
4.	4. 1	4.26	15.22	16.36	4.21	4.49	וירא
5.	5. 1	6. 8	17. 1	18.27	5. 1	5.31	חיי שרה
6.	6. 9	7.16	19. 1	20.22	6. 1	6.27	תולדות
7.	7.17	8.22	21. 1	21.27	7. 1	7.89	ויצא
8.	9. 1	9.29	21.28	22.16	8. 1	8.26	וישלח
9.	10. 1	11. 9	22.17	23.19	9. 1	10.10	וישב
10.	11.10	12. 9	23.20	24.18	10.11	10.36	מקץ
11.	12.10	13.18	25. 1	25.40	11. 1	12.16	ויגש
12.	14. 1	14.24	26. 1	26.30	13. 1	14.10	ויחי
13.	15. 1	16.16	26.31	27.19	14.11	14.45	שמות
14.	17. 1	17.27	27.20	28.43	15. 1	15.41	וארא
15.	18. 1	18.33	29. 1	29.37	16. 1	16.35	בא
16.	19. 1	19.38	29.38	30.21	17. 1	17.26	בשלח
17.	20. 1	21.21	30.22	31.18	17.27	18.32	יתרו
18.	21.22	22.19	32. 1	32.29	19. 1	20.13	משפטים
{ 19.	22.20	23.20	32.30	33.23	20.14	21. 9	תרומה }
{ 20.	24. 1	24.67	34. 1	34.35	21.10	22. 1	תצוה }
21.	25. 1	25.34	35. 1	35.29	22. 2	22.38	כי תשא
{ 22.	26. 1	26.35	35.30	36.19	22.39	23.30	ויקהל }
{ 23.	27. 1	28. 9	36.20	37.24	24. 1	25. 9	פקודי }
24.	28.10	29.13	37.25	38.20	25.10	26.65	ויקרא
25.	29.14	30.21	38.21	39.32	27. 1	27.23	צו
26.	30.22	31.16	39.33	40.38	28. 1	30. 1	שמיני

Sabbath after Atzereth	In the First year.		In the Second year.		In the Third year.		Annual Cycle.
	First Book of Moses.		Third Book of Moses.		Fourth Book of Moses.		
	From	To	From	To	From	To	
27.	31.17	32. 3	1. 1	2. 6	30. 2	31.54	תזריע
28.	32. 4	32.33	2. 7	3.17	32. 1	32.42	מצורע
29.	33. 1	34.31	4. 1	4.35	33. 1	34.29	אחרי מות
30.	35. 1	35·29	5. 1	5.26	35. 1	36.13	קדושים
					Fifth Book of Moses.		
					From	To	
31.	36. 1	36.43	6. 1	7.10	1. 1	2. 1	אמור
32.	37. 1	37.36	7.11	7.38	2. 2	2.37	בהר
33.	38. 1	38.30	8. 1	8.36	3. 1	3.29	בחקתי
34.	39. 1	40.23	9. 1	9.21	4. 1	4.49	במדבר
35.	41. 1	41.52	9.22	10.20	5. 1	6. 3	נשא
36.	41.53	42.28	11. 1	11.47	6. 4	7.11	בהעלתך
37.	42.29	43.34	12. 1	13.28	7.12	8.20	שלח לך
38.	44. 1	45.20	13.29	13.59	9. 1	10.11	קרח
39.	45.21	46.27	14. 1	14.32	10.12	11.25	חקת
40.	46.28	47.27	14.33	14.57	11.26	12.19	בלק
41.	47.28	48.22	15. 1	15.33	12.20	13.19	פינחס
42.	49. 1	49.33	16. 1	16,34	14. 1	14.29	מטות
43.	50. 1	50.26	17. 1	18.30	15. 1	16.17	מסעי
	Second Book of Moses.						
	From	To					
44.	1. 1	1.22	19. 1	19.22	16.18	18. 8	הדברים
45.	2. 1	2.25	19.23	20.27	18. 9	19.21	ואתחנן
46.	3. 1	4.17	21. 1	21.24	20. 1	21. 9	עקב
47.	4.18	6. 1	22. 1	22.25	21.10	23. 9	ראה
48.	6. 2	7. 7	22.26	23.22	23.10	24.13	שופטים
49.	7. 8	8.11	23.23	24. 9	24.14	25.19	כי תצא
50.	8.12	9. 7	24.10	25.24	26. 1	29. 8	כי תבא
51.	9. 8	9.35	25.25	26. 2	29. 9	30.20	נצבים
52.	10. 1	11.10	26. 3	27.34	31. 1	31.30	וילך
			Fourth Book of Moses.				
			From	To			
53.	12. 1	12.28	1. 1	1.54	32. 1	32.52	האזינו

If a year counts less than 53 Sabbaths on which the regular weekly portions may be read, some or all of those above designated with braces, are combined.

VI.
The Annual Cycle
ARRANGED FOR
Three Years.

	In the First Year.		In the Second Year.		In the Third Year.		Annual Cycle.
	From	To	From	To	From	To	
Genesis or First Book of Moses.	1, 1	2, 3	2, 4	3, 21	3, 22	6, 8	בראשית
	6, 9	8, 14	8, 15	9, 17	9, 18	11, 32	נח
	12, 1	13, 18	14, 1	15, 21	16, 1	17, 27	לך לך
	18, 1	18, 33	19, 1	21, 4	21, 5	22, 24	וירא
	23, 1	24, 9	24, 10	24, 52	24, 53	25, 18	חיי שרה
	25, 19	26, 12	26, 12	26, 33	26, 34	28, 9	תולדת
	28, 10	29, 35	30, 1	30, 43	31, 1	32, 3	ויצא
	32, 4	33, 20	34, 1	35, 29	36, 1	36, 43	וישלח
	37, 1	37, 36	38, 1	39, 6	39, 7	40, 23	וישב
	41, 1	41, 52	41, 53	43, 15	43, 16	44, 17	מקץ
	44, 18	45, 15	45, 16	46, 27	46, 28	47, 27	ויגש
	47, 28	48, 22	49, 1	49, 33	50, 1	50, 26	ויחי
Exodus or Second Book of Moses.	1, 1	2, 25	3, 1	4, 17	4, 18	6, 1	שמות
	6, 2	7, 7	7, 8	8, 18	8, 16	9, 35	וארא
	10, 1	11, 10	12, 1	12, 28	12, 29	13, 16	בא
	13, 17	14, 25	14, 26	15, 26	15, 27	17, 16	בשלח
	18, 1	18, 27	19, 1	19, 25	20, 1	20, 23	יתרו
	21, 1	22, 3	22, 4	23, 19	23, 20	24, 18	משפטים
	25, 1	25, 30	25, 31	26, 14	26, 15	27, 19	{ תרומה
	27, 20	28, 43	29, 1	29, 37	29, 38	30, 10	{ תצוה
	30, 11	31, 17	31, 18	33, 11	33, 12	34, 35	כי תשא
	35, 1	36, 7	36, 8	37, 16	37, 17	38, 20	{ ויקהל
	38, 21	39, 21	39, 22	39, 43	40, 1	40, 38	{ פקודי
Leviticus	1, 1	2, 16	3, 1	4, 26	4, 27	5, 26	ויקרא
	6, 1	7, 10	7, 11	7, 38	8, 1	8, 36	צו
	9, 1	9, 24	10, 1	10, 20	11, 1	11, 47	שמיני

	In the First Year.		In the Second Year.		In the Third Year.		Annual Cycle.
	From	To	From	To	From	To	
Third Book of Moses.	12, 1	13,17	13,18	13,39	13,38	13,59	תזריע
	14, 1	14,32	14,33	14,57	15, 1	15,34	מצרע
	16, 1	16,24	16,25	17,16	18, 1	18,30	אחרי מות
	19, 1	19,22	19,23	20, 7	20, 1	20,27	קדשים
	21, 1	22,16	22,17	23,22	23,23	24,23	אמר
	25, 1	25,28	25, 1	25,28	25,29	26, 2	בהר
	26, 3	26,46	26, 3	26,46	27, 1	27,34	בחקתי
Numbers or Fourth Book of Moses.	1, 1	1,54	2, 1	3,13	3,14	4,20	במדבר
	4,21	5,31	6, 1	6,27	7, 1	7,89	נשא
	8, 1	9,14	9,15	10,36	11, 1	12,16	בהעלתך
	13, 1	14,10	14,11	14,45	15, 1	15,41	שלח לך
	16, 1	17, 5	17, 6	18, 7	18, 1	18,32	קרח
	19, 1	20, 6	20, 7	20,29	21, 1	22, 1	חקת
	22, 2	22,38	22,39	23,26	23,27	25, 9	בלק
	25,10	26,51	26,52	27,23	28, 1	30, 1	פינחס
	30, 2	31,24	31,25	31,54	32, 1	32,42	מטות
	33, 1	33,49	33,50	34,29	35, 1	36,13	מסעי
Deuteronomy or Fifth Book of Moses.	1, 1	1,46	2, 1	2,30	2,31	3,22	הדברים
	3,23	4,40	4,41	6, 3	6, 4	7,11	ואתחנן
	7,12	9, 3	9, 4	10,11	10,12	11,25	עקב
	11,26	12,28	12,29	14,29	15, 1	16,17	ראה
	16,18	17,20	18, 1	19,13	19,14	21, 9	שופטים
	21,10	22 12	22,13	24, 4	24, 5	25,19	כי תצא
	26, 1	27,10	26, 1	27,10	27,11	29, 8	כי תבא
	29, 9	30,20	29, 9	30,20	29, 9	30,20	נצבים
	31, 1	31,30	31, 1	31,30	31, 1	31,30	וילך
	32, 1	32,52	32, 1	32,52	32, 1	32,52	האזינו

An ordinary Jewish Almanac will tell each year which of the portions above designated with braces are combined.

www.ingramcontent.com/pod-product-compliance
Lightning Source LLC
Chambersburg PA
CBHW020925230426
43666CB00008B/1569